S0-AAZ-602

Children's Bible Dictionary

Children's Bible Dictionary

Written and Illustrated by Richard Guthrie

I am grateful to all my friends and family without whose help, support, and prayers this dictionary would not have been possible. This book is thus dedicated to those who share in the belief of the awesomeness of God's Word.

Copyright © 1998 by Barron's Educational Series, Inc.

All rights reserved.
No part of this book may be reproduced in any form, by photostat, microfilm, xerography, or any other means, or incorporated into any information retrieval system, electronic or mechanical, without the written permission of the copyright owner.

All inquiries should be addressed to:
Barron's Educational Series, Inc.
250 Wireless Boulevard
Hauppauge, New York 11788

International Standard Book No. 0-8120-6577-8

Library of Congress Catalog Card No. 96-15008

Library of Congress Cataloging-in-Publication Data

Guthrie, Richard L.
   Children's Bible dictionary / written and illustrated by Richard L. Guthrie.
      p.   cm.
   Summary: Defines approximately 1300 terms, including the names of people and places, with reference to where they appear in the Old and New Testaments.
   ISBN 0-8120-6577-8
   1. Bible—Dictionaries, Juvenile [1. Bible—Dictionaries.] I. Barron's Educational Series, Inc.   II. Title
BS440.G85   1996
220.3—dc20   96-15008
                                                          CIP
                                                          AC

PRINTED IN HONG KONG/CHINA
987654321

A Note to Parents and Teachers

Barron's Children's Bible Dictionary is meant to help children make sense of the Bible by listing many of the important words, people, and events that appear in the *King James' Version* of the Bible. Each term has a definition, a guide to pronunciation, and reference to the actual scriptural verse in which it appears. Cross references to other entries are given where appropriate.

Delightful color illustrations are included for many of the entries in order to help young children relate to the people, places, and events that are listed in the Bible. These illustrations will encourage young children to browse through the book on their own. While younger children may need an adult to read the definitions to them, older children will be able to read the book on their own.

Barron's Children's Bible Dictionary offers opportunities for the whole family to learn about the Bible.

A

Aaron *(AIR-un)*

was the brother of Moses. Aaron and Moses were born to the tribe of Levi. Aaron was the first High Priest for the Israelites. He usually did what God wanted him to do. The Israelites could not wait for the return of Moses from the mount. They had Aaron make them a golden calf to worship. This was a sin. God did not allow Aaron to enter the Promised Land.

[Aaron and the golden calf are found in Exodus 32:1–35.]

Aaron helps build a golden calf.

Aaron's rod *(AIR-uns ROD)*

was a straight piece of wood. It was a symbol of power for the High Priest. God had Aaron perform miracles with his rod. Once, when the people rebelled, twelve rods were placed in the Tabernacle. The next day, Aaron's rod had buds, blossoms, and almonds on it. His rod was placed in the Ark of the Covenant as a testimony.

[The budding rod of Aaron is recorded in Numbers 17:1–11.]

Aaron's rod budded overnight!

abased *(uh-BASTE)*

is the same as being humble.

*[See **humble**.]*

abated *(uh-BATE-ud)*

means to go away. The waters of the Flood abated. This left the ark resting on top of a mountain.

[The story of the Flood is found in Genesis, Chapters 6 to 8.]

The Flood waters abated from Noah's ark.

Abba *(AB-uh)*

means father in Aramaic. It is a word that shows love. Today, you would say, "Daddy." This is what Jesus called God the Father. We are to follow

Abba means "Daddy!"

Abednego

Abel was a shepherd.

Jesus. As sons and daughters of God, we can call God, "Abba."

[Paul tells us how we become children of God in Romans 8:14–17.]

Abednego (ab-ED-nee-go)

was a young man and a friend of Daniel. He was taken as a slave when Babylon conquered Israel. Shadrach, Meshach, and Abednego refused to worship the statue of King Nebuchadnezzar. This broke the law. The king threw them into a fiery furnace. The Lord was with the three men. The flames did not harm these young men.

[The story of the fiery furnace is found in Daniel, Chapter 3.]

Abel (AY-bel)

was the second son of Adam and Eve. Abel was a shepherd and a righteous man. Cain was his older brother. He was jealous of Abel. Cain killed Abel.

[The story of Cain and Abel is found in Genesis, Chapter 4.]

People are to abhor sin.

abhor (uh-BOR)

means to hate something. God abhors evil and wicked things. We are to abhor sin.

[David wrote a song about this in Psalm 5. Paul told us to abhor sin in Romans 12:9.]

Abiathar (uh-BYE-uh-thar)

was one of the priests for the Israelites. King Saul killed all the priests of Nob. Abiathar was the only one to get away. He was a close friend of David.

[The story of Abiathar's escape from King Saul is found in I Samuel, Chapters 22 and 23.]

abide (uh-BIDE)

means to dwell or live with. If we follow Jesus, we are to abide in Him. Jesus sent the Holy Spirit to abide in us.

[John wrote of God's abiding in I John 2:24–28.]

Abigail (AB-uh-gale)

was the wife of Nabal. Nabal was a shepherd. He was very rich. David and his men asked for food,

Abiathar escaped from King Saul.

but Nabal did not help. David was going to kill Nabal. Abigail brought David and his men some food. The Lord killed Nabal because of his evil deed. Abigail became David's third wife.

[The story of Abigail may be found in I Samuel, Chapter 25.]

Abigail fed David and his men.

Abihu *(uh-BYE-hoo)*

was a son of Aaron. Abihu had a brother, Nadab. They were priests of Israel. Abihu did not obey God. Abihu and Nadab used the wrong fire in their incense burners before the Lord. A fire from God destroyed both of them.

[God's judgment of Abihu may be found in Leviticus 10:1–7.]

Abihu offered strange fire to God.

Abimelech *(uh-BIM-uh-lek)*

was a popular name for kings. The Philistines had a King Abimelech who tried to take Abraham's wife, Sarah [*Genesis, Chapter 20*]. Another Philistine king named Abimelech started to take Isaac's wife [*Genesis, Chapter 26*]. Gideon's son was named Abimelech. He killed his brothers and became King of Shechem [*Judges, Chapter 9*]. Finally, there was a priest named Abimelech who was the son of Abiathar [*I Chronicles 18:16*].

King Abimelech tried to take Sarah from Abraham.

Abinadab *(uh-BIN-uh-dab)*

lived on a hill. The city he lived in was called Kirjath-Jearim. Many people died because they looked inside the Ark of God. They were afraid of the Ark of God. The ark was left at Abinadab's house. He was keeper of the Ark of God for twenty years. Then David took the ark to Jerusalem.

[The story of the Ark and Abinadab is found in I Samuel 6:19–7:2 and in II Samuel 6:1–15.]

The Ark of God was left in Abinadab's house.

Abner *(AB-ner)*

was King Saul's cousin. King Saul made him the leader of Israel's army. Abner protected King Saul. Joab thought Abner was a spy and killed

Abner was the leader of Israel's army.

Abraham moved to Canaan.

Absalom's hair was caught in a tree.

him. David was sad when he heard of Abner's death. David said Abner was a prince and a great man.

[Abner's death is recorded in II Samuel, Chapter 3.]

abomination *(uh-bom-uh-NA-shun)*

is something very bad. Sin is an abomination to God. Sins done inside the Temple are abominations. Jesus said one specific abomination will be a sign of His return. This is called the abomination of desolation. The abomination of desolation is probably when something bad is done to God's Temple.

[This final abomination is found in Daniel 11:28–31 and in Matthew, Chapter 24.]

abound *(uh-BOUND)*

means to have a lot of something or to be rich. God's love and grace abounds for His children.

[Paul writes of God's abounding grace in Romans 5:18–21.]

Abraham *(AY-bruh-ham)*

was the father of the Hebrew nation through his son, Isaac. Abraham lived in Ur. God told him to move to Canaan. Abraham was to have many children and grandchildren. Abraham was one hundred years old when he had the son God promised him. Sarah gave birth to Isaac. God changed his name from Abram to Abraham. God made many other promises to Abraham. The Messiah was to come from his children. All nations would be blessed by the nation of Israel. God has fulfilled many of these promises. God will keep the rest of the promises.

[The life of Abraham (Abram) is found in Genesis, Chapters 12 to 25.]

Abraham's bosom *(AY-bruh-ham's BU-zum)*

was a place like heaven. It was a place of comfort. The poor man Lazarus went to Abraham's bosom when he died. Jesus opened the way to heaven. Today, heaven is where Christians go when they die.

[The story of the rich man and Lazarus is found in Luke 16:19–31.]

Abram *(AY-brum)*

obeyed God. God changed his name to Abraham.

*[See **Abraham**.]*

Fasting is abstaining from food.

Absalom *(AB-suh-lom)*

was King David's third son. Absalom rebelled against his father. He made himself king in Hebron. This started a war. When Absalom was riding a mule, his hair got tangled in a tree. King David's men found and killed him. King David was sad and tore his clothes.

[Absalom's death is recorded in II Samuel, Chapter 18.]

abstain *(uhb-STAIN)*

is to stay away from something. Fasting is abstaining from food. Christians are to abstain from sin.

[Paul tells us to abstain from evil in I Thessalonians 5:22.]

Abundant is to have a lot of something.

abundant *(uh-BUN-dunt)*

is to have a lot of an item. It means the same as abound. Christ came to give abundant life.

[Jesus tells about the abundant life in John 10:7–10.]

acacia wood *(uh-KAY-shuh WOOD)*

was the type of wood used to build the Ark of God. It was also used a lot in making things for the Tabernacle. It was usually covered with gold or brass.

*[See **shittim**.]*

The Ark of God was made of acacia wood.

accord *(uh-CORD)*

means to agree upon something. The disciples were of one accord in their purpose. They agreed to follow Jesus and His teachings. Peter and the apostles met at Pentecost in one accord.

[The Book of Acts shows how the early Christians were of one accord.]

The apostles were of one accord.

Satan accuses us before God.

Achan hid gold in his tent.

An acre is an amount of land.

accursed (uh-KERST)

means doomed or hated. It is the opposite of blessed. Obeying God's commandments results in being blessed. Disobeying God results in being cursed.

*[See **curse**.]*

accuse (uh-KYOOZ)

means to charge someone of a crime. Satan accuses us of sin before God. Jesus is a Christian's defender when we are accused of sin.

[Our accuser is described in Revelation 12:10.]

Achan (ACK-un)

was a soldier for Israel. The walls of Jericho fell and God gave the Israelites the victory. They were not to take gold or clothing from the people they defeated. Achan hid clothing, gold, and silver in his tent. This sin caused the Israelites to lose their next battle at Ai. Achan and his family were put to death for this sin.

[The story of Achan is found in Joshua, Chapter 7.]

Achish (ACK-ish)

was one of the kings of the Philistines. David went into his city to hide from Saul. Achish's men did not trust David. David had to pretend to be crazy in order to escape.

[David's first meeting with Achish is found in I Samuel 21:10–22:1.]

acre (AY-ker)

is an amount of land. The Hebrew word means a team of oxen. It refers to the amount of land an oxen team can plow in one day.

[Acre is recorded in I Samuel 14:14 and Isaiah 5:10.]

Acts of the Apostles (ACTS of the uh-POSS-uls)

is the fifth book in the New Testament. It was probably written by Luke. It tells the history of the early Christian church. Acts is the story of how Jesus went out to the world. Paul met Jesus on the Damascus Road. This event is recorded in the Book of Acts. Paul preached the good news of Jesus to most of the Roman Empire.

[Paul meets Jesus in Acts, Chapter 9.]

Adam names the animals.

Adam (ADD-um)

was the name of the first human being God created. Adam named each of the animals that God created. He lived in the Garden of Eden until he sinned. This sin was eating fruit from the Tree of Knowledge of Good and Evil. Adam and his wife, Eve, were thrown out of the Garden.

[The story of Adam is found in Genesis, Chapters 2 and 3.]

Adar (AH-dar)

is the name of a Jewish month. It is the sixth month of their civil calendar and the twelfth month of their sacred calendar. It includes part of February and part of March.

[Adar is mentioned a lot in the Book of Esther.]

Adar is a Jewish month.

adder (ADD-er)

is a type of deadly snake.

*[See **asp**.]*

admonish (add-MAH-nish)

is to encourage someone. Parents are supposed to raise their children in the nurture and admonition of the Lord.

[Paul explains admonition in Ephesians, Chapter 6.]

Adonijah (ad-uh-NYE-juh)

was the fourth son of King David. Adonijah wanted to be king. When Solomon was selected to be the next King of Israel, Adonijah led a rebellion. Solomon had Adonijah killed.

[This story is recorded in I Kings, Chapters 1 and 2.]

Adonijah led a rebellion.

Paul's ship sank in the Adria.

Jesus' birth was the first advent.

A roaring lion is an adversary.

Adversity is when bad things happen to us.

adoption (uh-DOP-shun)

is to accept a person as part of your family. You become a son or daughter of God when you follow Christ. God adopts you into His family.

[Paul explains adoption in Galatians, Chapter 4.]

Adria (AH-dree-uh)

is part of the Mediterranean Sea. It is located between the island of Crete and the island of Sicily. Paul's ship sank on his trip to Rome in this part of the sea.

[Paul's story is recorded in Acts 27:27–28:1.]

adultery (uh-DUL-ter-ee)

is a sin of being unfaithful to one's wife or husband. You shall not commit adultery is one of the Ten Commandments. God referred to Israel as an adulterer when the people worshipped false gods.

[The Ten Commandments are found in Exodus, Chapter 20.]

advent (ADD-vent)

is the arrival of something special. Jesus was born in a stable. This was His First Advent. Jesus will come again to set up His Kingdom. This will be His Second Advent. When Jesus went up to heaven, an angel told his followers that He would return.

[Jesus foretold of His return in Matthew, Chapter 24.]

adversary (ADD-ver-sair-ee)

is another word for enemy. Satan is our adversary. He goes around this earth as a roaring lion. He seeks those that he can destroy. Jesus can protect us from our enemy.

[Peter speaks of our adversary in I Peter 5:8–10.]

adversity (ad-VERSE-uh-tee)

is something that causes problems in our lives. We are to pray for other Christians who have adversities.

[Paul tells Christians to remember those with adversities in Hebrews 13:3.]

advocate (ADD-vuh-cut)

is a defender. Satan accuses us of sin before God. Jesus is the advocate for the believer.

[John explains this in I John, Chapter 2.]

Agabus (AG-uh-bus)

was a New Testament prophet. He told of a famine that would come upon Antioch. Agabus warned Paul not to go into Jerusalem.

[This is recorded in Acts 11:27–30.]

Jesus is our advocate before God.

agape (uh-GAH-pay)

is a Greek word for love. It is a very special kind of love. The early church members had agape love for each other. This is the kind of love we are to have for other believers of Christ.

[God's love is detailed in I Corinthians, Chapter 13.]

$$\alpha\gamma\alpha\pi\eta$$

Agape is written like this in Greek.

Agrippa (uh-GRIP-uh)

was the last name for a couple of kings of Israel.

*[See **Herod**.]*

Ahab (AY-hab)

was the king of the northern kingdom of Israel. He married Jezebel. They were evil. Ahab led the Israelites away from God. He built idols and killed God's prophets. His prophets of Baal challenged Elijah and the true God. Elijah soaked his offering with barrels of water. God sent fire down from heaven and burned Elijah's offering. This was a sign of God's power.

[The story of Ahab is found in I Kings, Chapters 18 to 22.]

King Ahab led the prophets of Baal.

Ahasuerus (a-HASS-you-AIR-us)

is the Hebrew spelling for Xerxes.

*[See **Xerxes I**.]*

Ahijah (uh-HYE-juh)

was the name for a lot of people. One of these men was a prophet from Shiloh. He was blind. This Ahijah tore his clothes in twelve pieces. He gave

Ahijah gave ten pieces of cloth to the king.

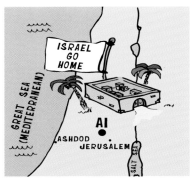

Ai defeated Israel.

Aileth is to be sick.

A woman breaks an alabaster jar of ointment at Jesus' feet.

Alas can mean "Oh, no!"

ten pieces to King Jeroboam. This was God's message that the kingdom was to be divided.

[This story is found in I Kings 11:29–40.]

Ahithophel *(uh-HITH-uh-fell)*

was David's guide. Absalom started a war against his father, King David. Ahithophel joined with Absalom. Ahithophel gave good advice about the war. Absalom decided not to follow his advice. Ahithophel killed himself.

[The sad story of Ahithophel is recorded in II Samuel 17:15–23.]

Ai *(AY-eye)*

is a city near Bethel. Israel disobeyed God. They were not to take certain things when they defeated Jericho. Achan was the one who sinned. Israel could not defeat Ai. Israel turned back to God. God gave them the victory over Ai.

[The defeat of Israel by Ai is found in Joshua 7:1–8.]

aileth *(AIL-eth)*

is to suffer or be sick. An angel asked Hagar, Abraham's wife, what aileth her.

[Hagar's prayer is answered in Genesis 21:16–21.]

alabaster *(AL-uh-bass-ter)*

is a smooth, creamy colored stone. It was used to make jars. A woman brought an alabaster box of ointment to Jesus. The woman washed His feet with her tears and her hair. Then she broke the box and covered His feet with the ointment.

[This special gift to the Lord is made in Matthew 26:7.]

alas *(uh-LASS)*

is an old word that is used to show regret, sorrow, or fear. Today, we might say, "Oh, no!" It is used a lot when describing the judgments.

[Alas is sounded several times in Revelation 18:10–19.]

alleluia *(al-uh-LOO-yuh)*

means praise the Lord. It is another word for hallelujah. In heaven, it is a word used to praise God.

*[These praises are listed in Revelation 19:1–6. See **hallelujah**.]*

Almighty *(all-MYE-tee)*

is having more power than anyone. God is the Almighty One. No one has more power than God.

[Almighty God is worshipped in Revelation 4:8.]

alms *(ALMS)*

are small gifts given to the poor. It was part of the Jewish custom to help the widows, the sick, and the poor. One way was to give alms to them. It is much like someone today giving pocket change to help someone in need. A lame man sat in front of the Temple begging alms. Peter and John healed this man.

[The story of this lame man is found in Acts, Chapter 3.]

Alpha and Omega *(AL-fuh and oh-MAY-guh)*

are the first and last letters of the Greek alphabet. In English, we would say *A* and *Z*. This was used to tell us about God. God is the beginning and the end of all things.

[God includes this title in the last chapter of the Bible in Revelation 22:13.]

altar *(ALL-ter)*

is a place where sacrifices or offerings are made. Altars were usually made of stone or brass. The Temple had two important altars. The altar for sacrifices was shittim wood covered with brass. The altar of incense was shittim wood covered with gold.

[The plans for building these altars is given in Exodus, Chapters 27 and 30.]

Amalekites *(uh-MAL-uh-kites)*

were a wandering tribe. They first attacked the Israelites after their exodus. They were

Alms are gifts to the poor.

Alpha and Omega are Greek letters.

Sacrifices were made on an altar.

The Amalekites were the first people to attack the Israelites.

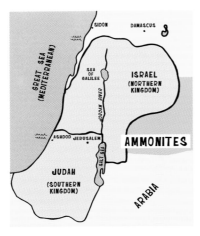

Ammonites was a nation that hated Israel.

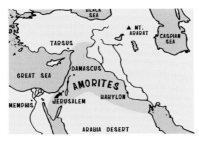

Amorites lived along the Jordan River.

Amos was a shepherd before he was a prophet.

descendants of Esau. They were a wicked people. God told Saul to destroy the Amalekites. Saul did not obey. The Amalekites gave Israel a lot of problems.

[The first battle is recorded in Exodus 17:8–16.]

amen (AY-MEN)

means "may it be so." Amen is said at the end of prayers. Many books in the New Testament end with amen.

[Amen is used to show that Jesus fulfills all of God's promises in II Corinthians 1:20.]

amethyst (AM-uh-thist)

is a purple stone. It was used on the breastplate of the High Priest.

[The twelve stones of the breastplate are described in Exodus 39:8–14.]

Ammon (AM-mun)

was a son of Lot. Ammonites are from the family of Ammon. They did not worship God. They were a wicked people. The Ammonites were enemies of Israel.

[One of these battles is recorded in Judges 11:4–33.]

Amorites (AM-uh-rites)

were the people who lived along the Jordan River. They lived in the Promised Land. The Israelites fought with the Amorites. Sometimes Israel worshipped the Amorite idols. This was to disobey God.

[Israel's victory over the Ammorites is found in Numbers 21:21–32.]

Amos (AY-mus)

was a prophet of Judah. He was a shepherd. Amos cared very much for God's people and preached against sin. Amos told of the coming of God's judgment against the nations surrounding Israel. He wrote a small book in the Old Testament. That is why Amos is called a "minor prophet."

[The story of how Amos became a prophet is found in Amos 7:14–15.]

Amos, Book of (AY-mus, Book of)

was written by Amos. It is a short book. Amos preached against sin. He told of God's judgment against many enemies of Israel. He also revealed God's love for Israel. Amos wanted the Hebrews to follow God.

[The details of these judgments are found in Amos 1:3–2:3.]

Ananias (an-uh-NYE-us)

was the name of three people.

1. Ananias was the husband of Sapphira. They lied to Peter about the sale of their property. They said they had given it all to God. God struck both of them dead for this sin [*Acts 4:32–5:10*].
2. Ananias was a disciple of Christ. He lived in Damascus. He healed Saul (later called Paul) of his blindness. Ananias baptized Saul [*Acts 9:10–17*].
3. Another Ananias was a High Priest. He was a Sadducee. Ananias was the judge for Paul's trial in Jerusalem [*Acts 23:1–9*].

Ananias healed Paul of blindness.

Andrew (ANN-droo)

was a follower of John the Baptist and his teachings. Jesus chose Andrew as one of the first disciples. Andrew led his brother Simon Peter to Jesus. Andrew and Peter were fishermen. They both became "fishers of men" for Christ.

[The story of Andrew's first meeting with Jesus is in John 1:35–44.]

Andrew led Peter to Jesus.

angel (AIN-jul)

is a created being that lives in heaven. We do not know when angels were created. Some angels deliver messages to people. Some angels guard God's throne. Most of the angels worship and honor God. The angels that don't worship God are called demons.

[Angels praise God in Revelation 5:11.]

Some angels deliver God's messages.

Annas was the High Priest who questioned Jesus.

Gabriel made an annunciation to Mary.

Samuel anointed David as king.

anger *(ANG-ger)*

is when some one gets mad.

*[See **wrath**.]*

Anna *(AN-uh)*

was an old prophetess. She was at the Temple when Jesus was brought to be circumcised. She recognized Jesus as the Messiah. She gave thanks to God for His arrival.

[Anna is mentioned in Luke 2:36–38.]

Annas *(AN-uhs)*

was a High Priest of Israel. Annas was one of the priests that questioned Jesus. After Christ rose from the dead, Annas questioned Peter about his teachings of Jesus. He did not like people believing that Jesus was the Messiah.

[The trial of Jesus is found in John 18:12–24.]

annunciation *(uh-nuhn-see-AY-shun)*

is the name for the first message given to Mary. A chief angel delivered this important message. The angel Gabriel said that Mary would have a son. His name would be Jesus.

[This story is recorded in Luke 1:26–38.]

anoint *(uh-NOINT)*

means to pour oil over something. Sick people were anointed with healing oils. Kings and priests were anointed with oil when they took office. Anointing was usually given with a blessing.

[Anointing for the sick is found in James 5:14. King David's anointing is found in I Samuel 16:1–13.]

antichrist *(ANN-tee-cryste)*

is anyone who tries to take the place of Jesus. There is going to be a very evil person in the last days. He will be known as the antichrist. He will make peace with Israel. He will then attack the Jews. He will be an enemy of God.

[The antichrist is shown in I John 2:18–22.]

Antioch *(ANN-tee-ock)*

was a large city. It was north of Israel. Many Jews lived there. Antioch had many followers of Christ. Believers were first called Christians in Antioch.

[The early church at Antioch is recorded in Acts 11:19–26.]

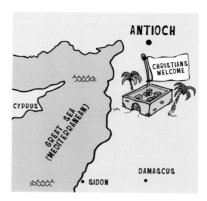

Believers were first called Christians in Antioch.

apocalypse *(uh-POCK-uh-lips)*

means to show or uncover. The apocalypse shows things about the last days. John reveals things about the end times in the Book of Revelation. Daniel was another prophet who talked about the apocalypse.

[See the Books of Daniel and Revelation.]

Apollos *(uh-POL-us)*

was a follower of Jesus Christ. He knew and worked with the apostle Paul. Some scholars think he may have written the Book of Hebrews. He was one of the people who helped spread the Gospel after Christ went back to heaven.

[Apollos' ministry is shown in I Corinthians, Chapter 3.]

Revelation describes the four horsemen of the apocalypse.

apostle *(uh-POSS-el)*

is someone who is sent out to preach the Gospel of Jesus. An apostle was a special follower of Jesus. An apostle was also someone who had seen Jesus. They had special power from God. Many of the apostles performed miracles.

[Jesus first called His followers apostles in Luke 6:13–16.]

Apostles, The Twelve *(uh-POSS-els, the Twelve)*

were men personally selected by Jesus. They are better known as the Twelve Disciples. The Twelve Disciples were known as apostles after Jesus went back to heaven.

*[See **Twelve Disciples**.]*

Jesus selected the Twelve Apostles.

appeal to Caesar *(uh-PEEL to SEE-zer)*

is to move the place of a trial to Rome. Only Roman citizens could appeal to Caesar. Paul was

Paul appealed his trial to Rome.

An apron was a cloth worn around the waist.

Aquila and Priscilla made tents.

Arabia is the land around Israel.

a Roman citizen. The Jews from Jerusalem made charges against Paul. Paul appealed to Caesar. Paul went to Rome for his trial.

[Paul made his appeal in Acts 25:11.]

appointed (uh-POINT-ud)

is to be selected for a special purpose. The writer of Hebrews tells us that Jesus was appointed heir of all things created.

[This gift is shown in Hebrews 1:2.]

approved (uh-PROOVED)

is to be accepted or find favor with somebody. Timothy wants all Christians to study and show themselves approved by God.

[Timothy's desire is shown in II Timothy 2:15.]

apron (AY-prun)

was a cloth worn around the waist. A girdle is one type of apron. A robe can be tucked into the girdle. This kept it out of the way. It was called "girding up the loins." This was done to get ready for work or battle.

*[See **girdle**.]*

Aquila and Priscilla (uh-KWIL-uh and pruh-SIL-uh)

were tent makers. They were married. They were Christians. A church met in their home in Ephesus. They helped Paul preach the Gospel.

[This couple is mentioned in Acts 18:24–26.]

Arabia (uh-RABE-ee-uh)

is the land around Israel. The name *Arab* probably means to wander. Many countries are in Arabia. Arabs are the most common people in this area. Abraham is the father of the Arab nations through his first son, Ishmael.

[Solomon traded with Arabia in I Kings 10:15.]

Aramaic (air-uh-MAY-ick)

was the language of the Arameans or early

Syrians. It is similar to Phoenician and Hebrew. Jesus spoke Aramaic. Parts of the Old Testament are written in Aramaic.

[The part of Daniel written in Aramaic is from 2:4b until the end of Chapter 7.]

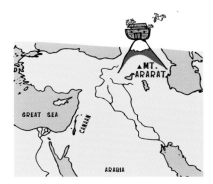

Noah's ark came to rest on Mount Ararat.

Ararat (AIR-uh-rat)

is a large area of mountains. It is north of Israel. Ararat is mentioned after the Flood. It is the place that Noah's ark came to rest.

[The final resting place of the ark is found in Genesis 8:4.]

archangel (ARK-AIN-jul)

means a chief angel. An archangel is in charge of many other angels. Michael is the only archangel mentioned in the Bible.

[Michael the archangel is called by name in Daniel 10:13, 12:1, and Jude 9.]

An archangel is a chief angel.

archer (ARCH-er)

shoots arrows from a bow. Archers hunt animals for food. They also fought in wars.

[Jacob tells that Joseph is to be a great archer in Genesis 49:22–24.]

arise (uh-RIZE)

is to get up. Abraham and his family arose and went into the land of Canaan. Peter and John told a lame man to arise and walk. Lame men arose when Jesus healed them. Jesus arose from the dead after three days.

[One story of Jesus healing the lame is found in Mark 2:3–12.]

Joseph became a great archer.

Ark of God (ARK of GOD)

is another name for ark of the covenant.

*[See **ark of the covenant**.]*

ark of the covenant (ark of the CUH-vuh-nunt)

was a chest made of shittim wood. It was covered in gold. The lid for the ark is called the mercy seat. Two gold angels were over the lid. The ark contained Aaron's rod, Moses' tablets of the Ten

The ark of God was a gold-plated chest.

Armour protected a soldier.

An armourbearer brought weapons to a soldier.

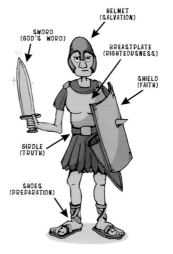

HELMET
(SALVATION)

SWORD
(GOD'S WORD)

BREASTPLATE
(RIGHTEOUSNESS)

SHIELD
(FAITH)

GIRDLE
(TRUTH)

SHOES
(PREPARATION)

Christians are to put on the armour of God.

Commandments, and a bowl of manna. The ark was kept inside the Tabernacle or Temple. It was kept in a special room. The room was called the Holy of Holies. This is where God showed Himself to His people.

[The building of the ark is found in Exodus 25:10–22.]

ark, Noah's (ARK, NO-uz)

was a large boat built by Noah.

*[See **Noah's ark**.]*

Armageddon (arm-uh-GED-un)

is the valley at the mountain of Megiddo. An old road from Egypt to Damascus went through Armageddon. There will be a big battle between good and evil here. Jesus will set up His kingdom after this fight.

[This final battle is revealed in Revelation 19:17–21.]

armour (ARM-er)

was worn to protect a soldier. A helmet protected the head. The breastplate guarded the chest. Sandals protected the feet. A shield on the arm defended against arrows and swords. Some of the armour was for attacking. Spears and swords were the most common. Paul tells us to put on the whole armour of God. This would protect every part of our life. King Saul's armour was too large for the young David.

[David tries on the king's armour in I Samuel 17:38–39.]

armourbearer (ARM-er-BARE-er)

was a servant of a soldier who brought extra weapons to the battle. The armourbearer helped the soldier get ready for battle. Some of the armour was heavy. David became King Saul's armourbearer.

[This is recorded in I Samuel 16:21.]

armour of God (ARM-er of God)

is the special spiritual armour that a Christian

should use. It starts with the helmet of salvation. It has the breastplate of righteousness. The Christian's feet are to wear shoes of preparation. His sword is to be the Word of God.

[The entire list of the armour of God is found in Ephesians 6:11–18.]

Artemis *(ART-uh-mus)*

is a Greek goddess of the moon. Artemis is also called Diana. This was a false god worshipped by the Greeks. They thought that she could help in childbirth or in hunting. Worshipping idols or other gods breaks one of the Ten Commandments.

*[See **Diana**.]*

Christ ascended through the clouds.

ascend *(uh-SEND)*

means to go up. Ascension is when someone goes to heaven. Enoch ascended into heaven. Elijah ascended into heaven in a chariot of fire.

[Elijah's ascension is told in II Kings 2:1–12.]

Ascension of Christ *(uh-SEN-shun of CRYSTE)*

was when Jesus went back to heaven. This was forty days after He arose from the dead. He ascended from the Mount of Olives. Jesus lives with God the Father. Jesus is preparing a special home for His followers.

[Christ's ascension is recorded in Acts 1:6–11.]

Adam and Eve used fig leaves because they were ashamed.

ashamed *(uh-SHAMED)*

is to feel regret and sorrow for doing wrong. Adam and Eve were ashamed when they sinned. As Christians, we are not to be ashamed of the Gospel of Christ.

[Paul speaks of this in Romans 9:33.]

Ashdod *(ASH-dodd)*

was a large city of the Philistines. Ashdod made purple cloth. This cloth was worn by royalty. The Philistines captured the ark of the covenant at Ashdod.

[This story is told in I Samuel 5:1–7:2.]

Ashdod made purple cloth.

19

Men sat in ashes when they were sad.

An asp is a poisonous snake.

Kings rode on asses.

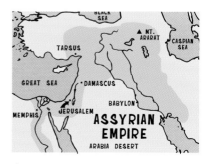

Assyria was a country north of Israel.

Asherah (ASH-uh-ruh)

was a goddess. She was the mother of Baal. A wooden object was the idol used to worship her. The idol was put in the middle of a grove of trees. The Israelites were told to cut down these places. They were not to plant trees as an Asherah.

[These groves are mentioned in Exodus 34:13 and Deuteronomy 12:3.]

ashes (ASH-es)

are the powder remains from burning wood. People showed sadness by putting ashes on their heads. An unhappy person would also tear the clothes he was wearing. He wore coarse clothes. He would stop eating. Sometimes he would shave his head. It was easy to see if someone was sad.

[Job sat in ashes as recorded in Job 2:8.]

ask (ASK)

is to make a request or state a question. We are promised that God hears us when we ask anything according to His will.

[John reminds us of this promise in I John 5:14–15.]

asp (ASP)

is a deadly snake. There are other snakes that are deadly. These are vipers, adders, and serpents.

[Paul was bitten by a viper in Acts 28:1–6.]

ass (ASS)

is a word for donkey. The Hebrews used an ass to carry things. Kings rode on asses as a sign of power. Jesus entered Jerusalem riding on a young ass. This showed that Jesus was the King of the Jews and the Messiah.

[Jesus' final entry into Jerusalem is recorded in Matthew 21:1–9.]

Assyria (uh-SEER-ee-uh)

was a country that was north of Israel. It was an enemy of Israel and Judah. They paid the Assyrians money to keep them from attacking.

This sometimes did not work. The Assyrians tried to capture Jerusalem. An angel killed thousands of their soldiers during the night.

[This battle is found in II Kings 19:35–37.]

The priests were astonished at the teachings of Christ.

astonish *(uh-STON-ish)*

is to amaze or surprise. When Jesus was a young boy, He visited the Temple. The priests were astonished at Jesus' understanding of the Bible.

[A young Jesus visited the Temple in Luke 2:41–47.]

astray *(uh-STRAY)*

means to go the wrong way or to get lost. The Bible tells us that all have gone astray just like sheep. Jesus is the Way to keep from going astray. That is why He is called the Good Shepherd.

[Peter reminds us of this in I Peter 2:25.]

Sheep can easily go astray.

astrologers *(uh-STROL-uh-jers)*

are people who look at and study the stars. They try to predict the future from what the stars do. Babylon had a lot of astrologers. The King of Babylon asked his astrologers to interpret his dream. They could not tell him his dream. Daniel was able to interpret the king's dream correctly. God does not want us to listen to astrologers. He wants us to trust Him and His Word.

[The king's dream is recorded in Daniel, Chapter 2.]

Astrologers study the stars.

asunder *(uh-SUN-der)*

means to break into pieces. Marriage is sacred to God. Marriages are not to be put asunder.

[Jesus said that marriages were not to be put asunder in Matthew 19:6.]

at hand *(at HAND)*

means within reach. When it is used to describe the time something will happen, it means soon. Jesus used this phrase to let us know when He will be returning. When we see certain things occur, His coming is at hand.

[Jesus' return is announced in Matthew, Chapter 24.]

Something in reach is at hand.

Athens is a city in Greece.

The High Priest released one goat for Israel on the Day of Atonement.

Augustus Caesar ruled Rome.

Athaliah *(ath-uh-LYE-uh)*

was the wife of a king. Ahaziah was their son. He died in battle. Athaliah killed all the heirs to the throne and ruled Judah for six years. She taught Judah to worship Baal. She was wicked. She did not follow God's teachings.

[The story of Athaliah is found in II Chronicles, Chapters 22 and 23.]

Athens *(ATH-uns)*

is a large city. It is located in Greece. Paul preached the Gospel in Athens. He taught at the Temple of the unknown god. Paul told them that the unknown god they sought was Jesus.

[Paul's visit to Athens is recorded in Acts 17:15–34.]

atonement *(uh-TONE-ment)*

means to make things right. God is holy. People are sinful. A blood sacrifice was made to bring God and people together. This was done on the Day of Atonement. Today, Jesus' death, burial, and resurrection is our atonement for sin.

[Sacrifices for atonement of sin are listed in Leviticus 16:15–22. Christ as our atonement is shown in Romans 5:11.]

Atonement, Day of *(uh-TONE-ment, Day of)*

is a day of fasting. It is also called Yom Kippur by the Jews. This was the day that the High Priest went into the Holy of Holies. He made a sin offering for himself and for his family. He made a sin offering for the nation of Israel. Two goats were used. One was killed. The sins of the nation were laid on the other. It was released into the wild.

[The sacrifices required are listed in Leviticus, Chapter 16.]

Augustus *(uh-GUS-tus)*

means honored. It was the title given to a ruler of the Roman Empire.

*[See **Augustus Caesar.**]*

Augustus Caesar *(uh-GUS-tus SEE-zer)*

was a ruler of Rome. He was the adopted son of

Julius Caesar. Augustus defeated Israel and Egypt. Augustus ruled Rome when Jesus was born and appointed Herod the Great to rule over the Jews. The Roman Senate declared him a god when he died. Augustus decided to tax all the world. His new tax brought Joseph and Mary into Bethlehem.

[This tax is mentioned in Luke 2:1.]

The Authorized Version is an English translation of the Bible.

Authorized Version (AWTH-uh-rized verz-yun)

is the translation of the Bible that was funded by King James of England. This was finished in the year 1611. The Authorized Version is sometimes called the King James Version.

[Some of the King James Version Bibles give a brief history of the translation in the opening pages.]

availeth (uh-VAIL-eth)

is to be useful or to provide help. James says that the prayers of a righteous man availeth much. This means that God hears the prayer of those who obey Him.

[James talks more about prayer in James 5:16.]

The prayer of a righteous man availeth much.

awe (AW)

is to show honor, fear, and respect. God is an awesome God.

[David wrote a prayer about this in Psalm 4.]

axe head (AX-HED)

is a heavy iron object that is sharp on one end. It is used to cut down trees. Metal was a precious item in the Old Testament days. The woodsman who dropped a borrowed axe head almost lost a costly item. Elisha threw a stick into the river and this caused the axe head to float.

[The story of the floating axe head is found in II Kings 6:1–7.]

Elisha makes the axe head float.

Baal

Baal is a false god.

The magi gave the babe Jesus gifts.

The city of Babylon was known for its Hanging Gardens.

Baal *(BAY-el)*

was the chief god of the Canaanites. Baal was a god of the sun. Offerings to Baal required a human sacrifice. God commanded Israel to destroy all the temples of Baal, but they did not. The Israelites began to worship Baal. God judged them for the sin of idolatry.

[The Israelites worship Baal in Judges 2:11–15.]

babe *(BABE)*

is a word for baby. As a babe, John the Baptist jumped in his mother's womb for joy. The wise men found Jesus as a babe wrapped in swaddling clothes. New followers of Jesus are called babes in Christ.

[Jesus' birth is found in Luke, Chapter 2:1–20.]

Babel *(BAY-bel)*

was a city of ancient Babylon. Babel usually refers to the tower built by Nimrod.

*[See **Babylon** or **Tower of Babel**.]*

Babylon *(BAB-uh-lon)*

was a large city in Babylonia. It was built by Nimrod. Some scholars believe that the Tower of Babel was built there. Babylon was known for its Hanging Gardens. It was the greatest and strongest city in the world. It was a very wicked city. God refers to wicked nations as Babylon.

[The final defeat of Babylon is predicted in Revelation, Chapter 18.]

backsliding *(BACK-SLIDE-ing)*

is going back to the old way of doing things. Backsliders do not obey God. Israel kept backsliding into worshipping false gods. God wants us to be faithful. He does not want us to backslide into sin. God can heal our backsliding.

[Jeremiah tells Israel they can return to God in Jeremiah 3:21–23.]

Balaam *(BAIL-um)*

was a Midianite prophet. King Balak of Moab wanted Balaam to curse Israel. He offered Balaam a lot of money. Balaam was going to put a curse on Israel. He met an angel. The angel changed his mind. Balaam gave Israel three blessings instead. Israel defeated Moab.

*[Balaam's sin is described in Numbers, Chapters 22 to 24. See **Balaam's donkey**.]*

An angel kept Balaam from cursing Israel.

Balaam's donkey *(BAIL-um's donkey)*

was the animal Balaam rode. Balaam was on his way to curse Israel. Balaam's donkey saw an angel of the Lord. The donkey tried to turn away from the angel three times. Balaam struck the donkey three times. Balaam's donkey then spoke to Balaam. The Lord allowed Balaam to see the angel. The angel told Balaam to speak God's words. Balaam blessed Israel three times.

*[The story of the talking donkey is found in Numbers 22:22–35. See **Balaam**.]*

Young men made fun of the bald head of Elisha.

baldness *(BALD-ness)*

was rare in Israel. A man might shave his head if he was very sad. Elisha is the only bald person mentioned in the Bible. Some young people made fun of his bald head. This was a sin. Two bears destroyed these young people.

[Elisha and these young people are found in II Kings 2:23–24.]

balm *(BALM)*

is a type of sap or gum that comes from plants. Some balms were used as a perfume. Other balms were used to heal wounds. The balm of Gilead is one of the healing balms.

[Jeremiah mentions the balm of Gilead in Jeremiah 8:22.]

The balm of Gilead was used for perfumes and medicines.

Banners were used in battle.

A banquet is a big meal.

To immerse in water is to baptize.

Barabbas was set free instead of Jesus.

banner (BANN-er)

is a flag or a carved figure. Each tribe of Israel had its own banner. It let the people know where to gather. Banners were used to locate armies during a battle. A bronze banner in the shape of a serpent was used to heal the Israelites. They had to look at the banner if they were bitten by a serpent.

[The banner of the brass serpent is found in Numbers 21:4–9.]

banquet (BANG-kwet)

is a big meal or feast. The Hebrews ate this meal lying on bedlike seats. There were many tables at a banquet. It was an honor to sit at the upper tables. Banquets were given to honor friends, rejoice in victories, and celebrate weddings. There will be a large banquet for believers when Jesus returns. It is called the marriage supper of the Lamb.

[Invitations to the marriage supper of the Lamb are given in Revelation 19:1–9.]

baptist (BAP-tist)

is one who baptizes. This usually refers to John the Baptist.

[See John the Baptist.]

baptize (BAP-tize)

is to immerse a believer in water. It is a testimony of the believer. Baptism is a Christian sign of the death, burial, and resurrection of Jesus Christ. It also shows that the Christian is to be dead to sin and to live for Jesus. This is how baptism is a picture of the Gospel and the way of salvation.

[Jesus' command to go and baptize is given in Matthew 28:18–20.]

Barabbas (buh-RAB-us)

was a murderer. Jesus was condemned to be crucified. Barabbas was also condemned to death. Pilate let the crowd choose which one to free. The crowd chose Barabbas. Barabbas was set free. Jesus died on the cross.

[Barabbas is freed in Matthew 27:15–26.]

Barak *(BARE-uk)*

was the military leader for Israel against the Canaanites. He was afraid of fighting this battle. Deborah was a judge for Israel. Deborah convinced Barak to lead the army. They battled near Mount Tabor. God gave Barak and the Israelites the victory. Deborah and Barak sang praises unto the Lord.

[Barak's battle is described in Judges 4:4–5:1.]

Deborah convinced Barak to lead the army.

barley *(BAR-lee)*

is a grain. Barley was used to feed horses, mules, and donkeys. Only poor people ate barley bread. This was the type of bread Jesus used to feed thousands of people.

[Barley bread was fed to the multitude in John 6:1–13.]

Barley was a grain used by the poor.

Barnabas *(BARN-uh-bus)*

was a Levite. John Mark was Barnabas' cousin. Barnabas lived on the island of Cyprus. His original name was Joseph. Paul and Barnabas were leaders in the early church. Barnabas went on missionary journeys with Paul. They preached the Gospel to most of the Roman Empire.

[One of Barnabas' trips is listed in Acts, Chapter 15.]

Paul and Barnabas were leaders in the early church.

barren *(BARE-un)*

means bare or dead. It is used to describe a woman who can't have any children. People felt that a barren woman was cursed from God. God showed grace to many barren women in the Bible. Sarah, Rebekah, and Rachel were barren. Each of them received a blessing from God by having children.

[Sarah gives birth to Isaac in Genesis 21:1–8.]

Bartholomew *(barth-AH-lum-yoo)*

was one of the Twelve Disciples. Not much is known about him. Many scholars think Nathanael was another name for Bartholomew.

[Bartholomew is listed with the other apostles in Matthew 10:2–4.]

Barren is bare or dead.

Bartimaeus

Bartimaeus was blind until he met Jesus.

Bartimaeus *(bar-tuh-MAY-us)*

was blind and very poor. He sat next to the road and begged for alms. Bartimaeus asked Jesus to have mercy on him. Jesus healed him. Bartimaeus followed Jesus.

[Bartimaeus's meeting with Jesus is recorded in Mark 10:46–52.]

Baruch *(BAR-ook)*

was a scribe and a friend to Jeremiah. Baruch wrote down Jeremiah's preaching. He then read it to King Jehoiakim. The king burned the letter. Baruch also helped Jeremiah buy a field. This field was a symbol of hope for Israel.

[Baruch delivers a letter to the king in Jeremiah, Chapter 36.]

Baruch gave a letter to the king from Jeremiah.

Bathsheba *(bath-SHEE-buh)*

was the beautiful wife of Uriah. King David committed adultery with Bathsheba. Bathsheba became pregnant. David arranged to have Uriah killed in battle. David married Bathsheba. God judged this sin, and their first son died. God forgave David of his sin. Bathsheba became the mother of King Solomon.

[David first sees Bathsheba in II Samuel 11:2–27.]

Beatitudes *(bee-AT-uh-tudes)*

are blessings spoken by Jesus at the beginning of the Sermon on the Mount. There are eight Beatitudes. Each Beatitude carries a promise from God. The eight Beatitudes states that God blesses

1. the poor in spirit,
2. those who mourn,
3. the meek,
4. those who hunger and thirst after righteousness,
5. the merciful,
6. the pure in heart,
7. the peacemakers, and
8. those who are persecuted.

*[The Beatitudes are listed in Matthew 5:3-12. See **Sermon on the Mount.**]*

Jesus gave the Beatitudes during the Sermon on the Mount.

Beelzebub *(bee-EL-zuh-bub)*

is one of the names for Satan or the Devil. It is based on the Hebrew word *Baalzebub*. It means "lord of the flies."

*[See **Satan**.]*

Beelzebub means "lord of the flies."

Beersheba *(ba-AIR-she-BAH)*

was a city in south Judah. Abraham and King Abimelech made an agreement at Beersheba. This gave Abraham water for his flocks and herds. Beersheba was on one of the main roads going to Egypt. Jacob had a dream near Beersheba. Jacob dreamed of a ladder going up to heaven.

[Abraham names Beersheba in Genesis 21:22–32.]

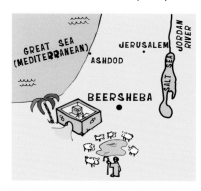

Abraham watered his flock of sheep at Beersheba.

beget *(be-GET)*

means to become a father. The Bible uses *begat* to list relatives. Jesus was a relative of Abraham and King David. The Gospels of Matthew and Luke have different lists of Jesus' relatives. Matthew lists His relatives through His step-father, Joseph. Luke lists His relatives through His mother, Mary. Jesus is the only begotten Son of God.

[The lists of Jesus' relatives can be found in Matthew 1:2–16 and Luke 3:23–38. God is listed as the Father of Jesus in John 3:16.]

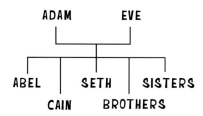

The Bible uses the word "begat" to list relatives.

beginning and the end *(bee-GIN-ing and the END)*

is one of the many titles for God.

*[See **Alpha and Omega**.]*

behold (bee-HOLD)

means to look and see. This word is used every time something is important. It is one way of having us pay close attention to what is being said. John the Baptist saw Jesus and said, "Behold the Lamb of God, which taketh away the sin of the world."

[John baptizes Jesus in John 1:29–34.]

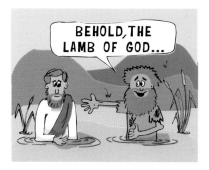

John the Baptist told his followers to behold Jesus.

believe *(be-LEEV)*

is to have faith and trust in something. God

beloved

Belteshazzar was a name given to Daniel.

Benjamin was the youngest son of Jacob.

The Jews chased Paul out of Berea.

To beseech is to search.

promises eternal life to those who believe Jesus is the Son of God.

*[Jesus told Nicodemus to believe in the Son of God in John 3:16–18. See **faith**.]*

beloved *(bee-LOVE-ed)*

is one who is loved. John baptized Jesus in the Jordan River. God called Jesus His beloved Son. Followers of Christ are beloved of God.

[God tells us Jesus is His beloved Son in Matthew 3:13–17.]

Belteshazzar *(belt-SHA-zer)*

was the Babylonian name given to Daniel. The name Daniel means "judgment of God." Daniel was given a new name to replace the reference to God with Baal. Belteshazzar means "favored of Baal."

[Daniel's name was changed in Daniel 1:7.]

Benjamin *(BEN-juh-mun)*

was the youngest son of Jacob. His mother, Rachel, died when Benjamin was born. Jacob loved Benjamin as much as he had loved Rachel. The children of Benjamin became one of the Twelve Tribes of Israel.

[The story of Benjamin's birth is found in Genesis 35:16–20.]

Berea *(buh-REE-uh)*

was a city in Macedonia. Paul preached the Gospel to the Jews of Berea. Many of the Jews became believers. The Jews from Thessalonica chased Paul out of town. Paul continued on his second missionary journey.

[Paul is chased out of Berea in Acts 17:10–14.]

beseech *(bee-SEECH)*

is to search or beg for something. Paul beseeches Christians to live godly lives.

[Paul talks to every Christian in Romans 12:1–2.]

bestow *(be-STOWE)*

means to give. God bestows love to all followers of Christ.

[God bestows His love to believers in I John 3:1–3.]

Bestow means to give.

Bethany *(BETH-uh-nee)*

was a small town located on the eastern slope of the Mount of Olives. Bethany was the home of Mary, Martha, and Lazarus. Jesus stayed at their home when He visited Jerusalem. Bethany is where Jesus raised Lazarus from the dead.

[The miracle of Lazarus is found in John 11:1–46.]

Lazarus was raised from the dead in Bethany.

Bethel *(BETH-el)*

was a small village named by Jacob. It was built at the site where Abraham entered Canaan and built an altar. Bethel was where Jacob had his dream about the ladder going up into heaven. The Ark of the Covenant stayed in Bethel until the Temple was built.

[Jacob's amazing dream is recorded in Genesis 28:10–19.]

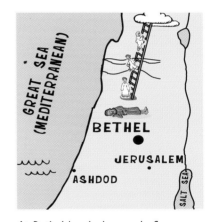

At Bethel Jacob dreamed of a ladder reaching into heaven.

Bethesda *(buth-EZ-duh)*

was the name of a pool.

*[See **Pool of Bethesda.**]*

Bethlehem *(BETH-luh-hem)*

is a small town. It is five miles southwest of Jerusalem. Bethlehem was the home of King David. The Messiah was to be born in Bethlehem. Mary and Joseph traveled from Nazareth to Bethlehem in order to pay taxes. Jesus was born in a stable in Bethlehem.

[Bethlehem was promised to be the birthplace of the Messiah in Micah 5:2.]

Bethsaida *(beth-SAY-uh-duh)*

was a fishing village on the northwest side of the Sea of Galilee. Andrew, Peter, and Philip lived there. It was near Bethsaida that Jesus fed the

Bethlehem was the birthplace of Jesus.

betray

Judas Iscariot betrayed Jesus.

Jesus and Mary were betrothed.

The Bible is God's Word to us.

Esau sold his birthright for a bowl of stew.

five thousand. Jesus cursed Bethsaida because of their unbelief.

[The miracle of feeding five thousand is told in Luke 9:10–17.]

betray *(be-TRAY)*

is to turn someone over to an enemy. Judas Iscariot betrayed Jesus. He turned Him over to the Pharisees.

[Judas's betrayal of Jesus is found in Matthew, Chapter 26:14–56.]

betroth *(be-TROTH)*

was the act of engagement for marriage. In Bible times, a betrothal was as binding as marriage. Mary and Joseph were betrothed. Joseph and Mary did not live together before marriage. God gave Mary a child. It was a miracle. An angel told Joseph not to divorce Mary. Paul tells us that the church is betrothed to Christ.

[The early betrothal of Joseph and Mary is described in Matthew 1:18–25.]

Bible *(BYE-bul)*

is a collection of books. These books are divided into the Old Testament and the New Testament. There are thirty-nine books in the Old Testament. There are twenty-seven books in the New Testament. God is the real author of all the books of the Bible. God used the talents of many men to write these books. All the books reveal the salvation offered by the Gospel of Jesus.

[God's inspiration of the Bible is shown in II Timothy 3:16.]

birthright *(BERTH-RITE)*

was a special blessing given to the oldest son. This included a double portion of inheritance. The oldest son had to take care of the family if anything happened to the father. Esau sold his birthright to Jacob. The price was a bowl of stew and a piece of bread.

[Esau sold his birthright to Jacob in Genesis 25:21–34.]

Bishop *(BISH-up)*

is one of the assigned offices of the church. A bishop is to watch over and help the members of the church. He also teaches and helps the church to grow spiritually. A bishop is sometimes called an elder or a pastor.

[The things a bishop does are listed in I Timothy 3:1–7.]

Bishops teach in the church.

blaspheme *(BLASS-feem)*

is to speak with disrespect against God. One of the Ten Commandments tells us not to take the Lord's name in vain. The penalty of blasphemy was death. Many people will be judged for their sins in the last days. A lot of these people blaspheme God.

[Blasphemes of these people are found in Revelation, Chapter 16.]

To blaspheme is to curse God.

blemish *(BLEM-ish)*

is a defect. Animals brought to be sacrificed were to be free of blemishes. This is to show that only a perfect animal is a worthy offering to God. Blemish is also used to represent sin. Jesus Christ lived a life without blemish. Christ was the perfect sacrifice for our sin. The life of the believer is to be lived without blemish.

[Jesus is the lamb without blemish as shown in I Peter 1:14–23.]

Lamb offerings were not to have any blemishes.

blessed hope *(BLESS-ed HOPE)*

means the second coming of Christ. It is called the blessed hope because Jesus will return as King. There will be peace throughout the world.

*[The blessed hope is described in Titus 2:13. See **Second Coming of Christ.**]*

blessing *(BLESS-ing)*

is a promise of good things. A father gave blessings to his sons. Isaac blessed his sons Jacob and Esau. The priests of Israel blessed the people. Jesus blesses His followers. He has given them forgiveness, peace, and everlasting life.

[Isaac's blessings are recorded in Genesis, Chapter 27.]

Isaac gave Jacob a blessing.

33

A blood sacrifice is required by God.

Boaz let Ruth glean in his field.

The church is the body of Christ.

Job had many boils.

blood (BLUDD)

is important for life. Israelites were not to eat blood. God requires a blood sacrifice for sin. The first sacrifice was the animals whose skins God gave to Adam and Eve. The Mosaic Law lists those animals that are acceptable for sacrifices. Jesus shed His blood on the cross for our sin. We remember Christ's shed blood when we have the Lord's Supper.

[The work of Jesus' blood is described in Ephesians 1:5–12.]

Boaz (BOE-az)

was a rich man. Boaz lived in Bethlehem. He was a relative of Naomi and Ruth. Boaz bought Naomi's land and returned it to her. Boaz married Ruth. Ruth became a relative of Jesus.

[The romantic story of Boaz and Ruth is found in the Book of Ruth.]

body of Christ (BOD-ee of CRYSTE)

is used by Paul to describe the Christian church. Christ is the head of the church. Every believer is a member of the body of Christ. Each one has different abilities just as eyes, hands, and feet do different things. All members of the body of Christ are important. The body of Christ also refers to the earthly body of Jesus. The sacrifice of the body of Christ is remembered by the church. This is when the church celebrates the Lord's Supper. The bread of the Lord's Supper is a symbol of the broken body of Jesus.

[Paul describes the church as the body of Christ in Romans 12:4–8.]

boil (BOIL)

is a swelling type of sore on the skin. Boils were the sixth plague on Egypt. Hezekiah and Job are men who had painful boils. Job's boils hurt so much he sat in ashes. Satan was the one who gave boils to Job to test his faith in God.

[The story of Job and his problems are found in the Book of Job.]

bold *(BOLD)*

is to be without fear. Faith in Christ gives us boldness. Our love of Jesus gives us boldness to stand before God. Christians do not have to fear God's judgment.

[Paul explains the Christian's boldness in Ephesians 3:9–12.]

bondage *(BOND-uj)*

is slavery. The Israelites were in bondage to the Pharaoh. Moses led them to freedom. We are in bondage to sin without Christ. Faith in Jesus will set us free.

[The story of Moses leading the Israelites out of bondage is found in Exodus 13:3–10.]

Bondage is being a slave.

bones *(BONES)*

were in a vision given to Ezekiel. Ezekiel saw a bunch of scattered bones. These dried bones came together and took on flesh. Then they came to life. These bones were a symbol of Israel. They were to be scattered as a nation. They would come back together. Everyone thought that Israel was destroyed. God will keep His promise of blessing Abraham's children.

[Ezekiel sees the dry bones in Ezekiel 37:1–14.]

book *(BOOK)*

of the Bible is a group of songs or writings. The Bible has sixty-six books. Each of the writers were guided by the Holy Spirit. Christians have their names written in a special book. It is the book of life.

[The Lamb's book of life is described in Philippians 4:3 and Revelation 21:27.]

Ezekiel saw bones that became an army.

born again *(BORN uh-GEN)*

means that a person is born in the spirit. Jesus told Nicodemus that he must be born again. Being born again is the only way to get to see the Kingdom of God. This is done by becoming a follower of Christ.

[Jesus talks about being born again in John 3:1–16.]

A book is a group of writings.

A mother holds her baby to her bosom.

Bowing shows honor to a king.

The church is a branch grafted into Israel.

A brasen altar was a place of sacrifice.

bosom *(BUZ-um)*

means chest. It is a place of comfort. A mother holds her children to her bosom. Abraham's bosom was a place of comfort for Jews when they died.

[Abraham's bosom is described in Luke 16:19–22.]

bow *(BOW—rhymes with cow)*

is to bend your head toward the ground. One or both knees are usually put on the ground. This was a way to show honor to a king. Bowing is a sign of worship. God is worthy of worship. Paul tells us that every knee shall bow before Christ.

[Paul tells us why Jesus is worthy of worship in Philippians 2:5–11.]

bowels *(BOW-els)*

are the center of a person's feelings. Today, we would say, "I love you from the bottom of my heart."

*[See **heart**.]*

bramble *(BRAM-bul)*

is a type of thorn.

*[See **thorns**.]*

branch *(BRANCH)*

is a name given for the Messiah. Jeremiah and Zechariah gave Him this title. The Messiah was to be a branch from the family of King David. The church is also referred to as a branch. It is grafted into an olive tree. The olive tree means Israel. The church has access to some of God's promises for Israel.

[Paul tells us how the church is grafted into the olive tree in Romans 11:11–25.]

brasen altar *(BRAY-zen ALT-er)*

was the place where sacrifices were made. It was located in the Tabernacle. It was made of shittim wood and covered with brass. The brasen altar had a horn on each corner. This was where offerings were made.

[The brasen altar is described in Exodus 38:1–7.]

brasen laver (BRAY-zen LAY-ver)

was a large brass bowl that stood in the Tabernacle. It was made from the brass mirrors of the Israelite women. The brasen laver was used for washing before sacrifices were made. It was replaced by the brazen sea when the Temple was built.

[The donation of the women's mirror's is mentioned in Exodus 38:8.]

A brasen laver was a large bowl in the Tabernacle.

brasen sea (BRAY-zen SEE)

was the name for a large brass bowl that stood in the Temple. The brasen sea was used for washing before sacrifices were made. It was supported by twelve brasen bulls.

[The brasen sea was made by King Solomon as shown in Jeremiah 52:20.]

The brasen sea was a large brass bowl in the Temple.

brasen serpent (BRAY-zen SER-pent)

was made of polished brass. It was put on top of a banner pole. The brasen serpent was placed in the middle of the Israelite camp. The Israelites spoke against God and Moses. God sent fiery serpents. People were dying because they were being bitten. They had to look up at the brasen serpent to be healed. This showed faith and trust in God.

[Moses makes the brasen serpent in Numbers 21:4–9.]

The brasen serpent could heal the Israelites.

brass (BRASS)

was used for solid copper or copper and tin. Brass was used for many things in the Temple. The laver and the altar were two of the items made of brass. Moses made a brass serpent. Brass means the same as brasen.

[The brass armour worn by Goliath is listed in I Samuel 17:5–7. See **brasen altar, brasen laver, brasen sea,** *and* **brasen serpent.**]*

Bread of Life (BRED of LIFE)

is one name for Jesus. Jesus reminded Israel of the manna God provided. Jesus told us that He was the living bread. The breaking of bread is part of communion. It shows that Jesus' body was

Jesus is the Bread of Life.

A bride and bridegroom are the people getting married.

God destroyed Sodom with fire and brimstone.

A wide path is broad.

Jesus had four half brothers.

broken for us. Jesus tells us that He is the bread that brings eternal life.

[Jesus offers us the bread of life in John 6:47–51.]

bride (BRIDE)

is the woman in a marriage. She is called the wife after they are married. The church is to become the bride of Christ. There will be a big meal for this occasion. It is called the marriage supper of the Lamb. The church is to be without spot or blemish.

[An invitation to this great feast is given in Revelation 19:1–9.]

bridegroom (BRIDE-GROOM)

is the man in a marriage. He is called the husband after the marriage. Jesus is the bridegroom to the church.

[The Lamb gets ready for his bride in Revelation 21:1–9.]

brimstone (BRIM-STONE)

is an old term for sulfur. Brimstone burns easily. It has a terrible odor when burned. Sodom and Gomorrah were very wicked. God sent two angels to remove Lot and his family from these cities. God destroyed Sodom and Gomorrah with fire and brimstone.

[The destruction of Sodom and Gomorrah is detailed in Genesis 18:20–19:29.]

broad (BROAD)

means wide. Jesus said that the way to destruction was broad. He also said that the way to salvation was narrow. This was part of Jesus' Sermon on the Mount. Jesus was saying that most people do not follow God. Few people will find eternal life through Jesus Christ.

[Jesus' Sermon on the Mount is given in Matthew, Chapters 5 to 7. See **Sermon on the Mount**.]

Brothers of our Lord (BRO-thers of our LORD)

are listed as James, Joses, Judas, and Simon. They had the same mother. Joseph was their father. These are Jesus' half brothers. The Books of James and Jude were probably written by Jesus' brothers. Nothing is known about Joses and Simon. Jesus also had half sisters but nothing else is written about them.

[Jesus preached in His hometown in Mark 6:1–6.]

buckler *(BUCK-ler)*

is a small shield. A buckler was used to protect the soldier's arm and chest. He used this shield when he fought at close range. God is our buckler against evil.

[Samuel talks of the help God gives us in II Samuel 22:25–41.]

A buckler is a small shield used in battle.

bullock *(BULL-uk)*

is a young bull. This animal was considered a clean animal. Israelites were allowed to eat clean animals. A bullock was one of the animals used for sacrifices. This was an offering for sin. God's acceptance of a bullock offering covered the sin of the family for the past year. Jesus is our perfect sin offering. His shed blood covers our sin forever.

[The sin offering is listed in Leviticus, Chapter 16.]

A bullock is a young bull.

bulrush *(BULL-RUSH)*

is a kind of reed. It is also called papyrus. Bulrushes or papyruses grow to heights of fifteen feet. Papyrus was used for making paper. Papyrus was also used to make boats. Moses was saved by hiding him in the bulrushes. Pharaoh's daughter found baby Moses in an ark made of bulrushes.

[The story of baby Moses is found in Exodus 1:22–2:10.]

Bulrushes are reeds that grow in the water.

burden *(BURD-en)*

is the load an animal or a person carries. Paul tells Christians to bear each other's burdens. Jesus says that His burden is light. Jesus gives His followers strength and rest.

[Jesus' offer to carry our burden is found in Matthew 11:28–30.]

A burden is a load an animal can carry.

A burial place is a place for someone who dies.

God spoke to Moses from a burning bush.

Burnt offerings are one type of sacrifice.

burial *(BARE-ee-ul)*

is the act of placing a dead person in a grave or tomb. The grave clothes were the clothes that the dead usually wore. The body was wrapped with linen bandages and anointed with myrrh and aloes. Jesus' body was placed in a rich man's tomb. Herod had a large stone rolled in front of the tomb. The tomb was sealed. Guards were placed at Jesus' tomb. Herod did not want anyone to steal the body of Jesus.

[The empty tomb of Jesus is shown in Luke 23:50–24:9.]

burning bush *(BURN-ing BUSH)*

was a shrub seen by Moses in the desert. Moses was looking after his father-in-law's flock. Moses saw a burning bush that kept on burning. God spoke to Moses from the burning bush. Moses took off his shoes. He was standing on holy ground. God told Moses to lead His people out of Egypt.

[Moses and the burning bush story is presented in Exodus 3:1–4:17.]

burnt offering *(BURNT OFF-er-ing)*

was a special sacrifice. The entire offering was burned in the fire. Everything went up in smoke. The burnt offering was used to dedicate a person or a nation to serve God.

*[Burnt offerings are described in Exodus 29:38–42 and Numbers 28:9–31. See **sacrifice**.]*

Caesar was the title for the Roman ruler.

Caesar (SEE-zer)

was the title of the ruler of Rome. It was the same as being a king. The Pharisees asked Jesus about paying taxes to Caesar. Jesus said to give those things to Caesar that belonged to Caesar. He also told the crowd that they should give to God what belonged to God.

[Jesus talks of taxes in Matthew 22:15–22.]

Paul was thrown in jail in Caesarea.

Caesarea (sez-uh-REE-uh)

was a city located on the Mediterranean Sea. Philip talked about Jesus to the Ethiopian eunuch at Caesarea. Caesarea was where Cornelius became a Christian. Paul was thrown in jail in Caesarea. It was here that Paul appealed to Caesar.

[Cornelius met Peter in Acts 10:1–24.]

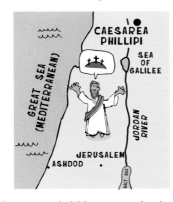

Jesus revealed His coming death at Caesarea Philippi.

Caesarea Philippi (sez-uh-REE-uh FILL-uh-pye)

is a city located at the beginning of the Jordan River. This city guards a large plain. Mount Hermon is located at Caesarea Philippi. It was here that Jesus told of His coming arrest, death, and resurrection.

[The disciples call Jesus the Christ in Matthew 16:13–23.]

Caiaphas was the high priest who sentenced Jesus to death.

Caiaphas (KYE-uh-fus)

was the High Priest at the time of Jesus' death. He was son-in-law to Annas. Annas was the leader in the plot to kill Jesus. Caiaphas asked Jesus if He was the Son of God. Caiaphas said that Jesus blasphemed God. Caiaphas sentenced Jesus to death.

[The first trial of Jesus was held in Matthew 26:57–68.]

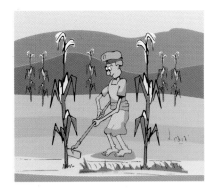

Cain was a farmer.

Caleb was one of the twelve spies sent into Canaan.

HERE AM I, LORD

Samuel was called by God.

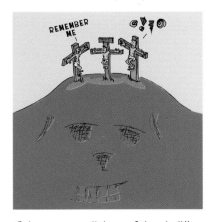

REMEMBER ME

Calvary means "place of the skull."

Cain (CANE)

was a farmer. His younger brother Abel was a shepherd. These two men each brought an offering to the Lord. God accepted Abel's offering. It was a sacrificed lamb. God did not accept Cain's offering. Cain offered fruits and vegetables. Cain got mad at Abel and killed him. God gave Cain a mark. Cain spent the rest of his life wandering.

[Abel is killed in Genesis 4:3–15.]

Caleb (KAY-leb)

was a spy. Moses sent twelve spies into the land of Canaan. Caleb and Joshua were the only spies who gave a good report. They wanted to enter into the Promised Land. Moses trusted the other spies. God made Israel wander in the wilderness for forty years. God allowed Caleb and Joshua to enter into the Promised Land.

[The adventure of the spies is found in Numbers 13:2–31.]

call (CALL)

is used in the Bible to summon. Moses and Samuel were called into God's service. Christians are those whom God has called. Believers are called to salvation, holiness, and faith. They are also called to an eternal life in heaven.

[Samuel was called by God in I Samuel, Chapter 3.]

Calvary (CAL-vuh-ree)

is the place Jesus was killed. Another name for this place is Golgotha. Golgotha means "place of the skull." Most scholars think it was called Golgotha because of its shape. The hill may have looked like a human skull.

[Jesus was led to Calvary in Luke 23:32–33.]

camp (CAMP)

is a temporary place to live. Israel wandered in the desert for forty years. They lived in camps. Each tribe had its own camp. The Israelites camped around the Tabernacle. Sin offerings were burned outside of the camp.

[Details of the Israelite camp are in Numbers, Chapters 2 and 3.]

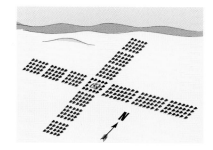

Israelites formed their camp in the shape of a cross.

Cana *(CAY-nuh)*

was located in Galilee. This is the town where Jesus performed His first miracle. Jesus was at a wedding in Cana. The host ran out of wine. Jesus turned water into wine.

[Jesus turned water into wine in John 2:1–11.]

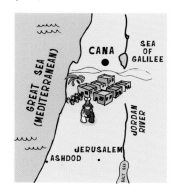

Jesus turned the water into wine at the wedding in Cana.

Canaan *(CAY-nun)*

is the land between the Mediterranean Sea and the Jordan River. God promised this land to Abraham. Baal was the chief god of this land. God told Israel to destroy the Canaanites, but they did not. They kept falling into sin by worshipping Baal.

[God makes a promise to Abraham in Genesis 13:14–17.]

Canaanites *(CAY-nuh-nites)*

were the people who lived in Canaan. They were the enemies of Israel.

*[See **Canaan**.]*

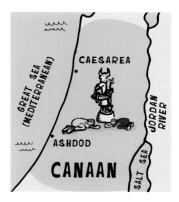

The Canaanites worshiped Baal.

Candace *(CAN-duh-see)*

was the name for the queen of Ethiopia. Philip told Candace's servant about Jesus. The servant became a believer in Christ. Philip baptized the servant.

[Philip met the Ethiopian in Acts 8:26–40.]

Capernaum *(cuh-PER-nay-um)*

was on the north shore of the Sea of Galilee. Fishing and farming were important to this city. Jesus centered His ministry in Capernaum. Jesus healed a boy who lived in Capernaum. This was his second miracle.

[This miracle is recorded in John 4:46–54.]

Candace was an Ethiopian Queen.

Prisoners of war are captives.

The Good Samaritan cared for the traveler.

Carpenters work with wood.

Satan was cast out of Heaven.

captive *(CAP-tiv)*

is a prisoner of war. Assyria defeated Israel and Judah. They were made slaves. Many of the people were marched to Babylon. This was God's punishment for sin.

[Israel went into captivity in II Kings 15:29; Judah went into captivity in II Kings 24:10–16.]

care *(CARE)*

is to look after someone. God cares for the church. Christians are to care for each other. The Good Samaritan cared for a wounded man.

[The Good Samaritan cared for the wounded traveler in Luke 10:25–37.]

Carmel *(CAR-mul)*

is the name of a mountain. It is located in Palestine on the Mediterranean coast.

*[See **Mount Carmel**.]*

carnal *(CAR-nul)*

has to do with the body. Carnal is used to describe earthly needs and desires. The opposite is to be spiritual. God does not want us to be carnal.

[Paul tells us not to be carnal in Romans 8:1–10.]

carpenter *(CAR-pen-ter)*

works and carves wood. Carpenters helped to build the Temple. They also crafted the Ark of God. Joseph, husband to the Virgin Mary, was a carpenter. Jesus was also a carpenter.

[Jesus' first job is listed in Mark 6:1–6.]

cast *(CAST)*

means to throw. Satan was cast out of heaven. Daniel was cast into the lion's den. Shadrach, Meshach, and Abednego were cast into a fiery furnace.

[The three men are cast into the fiery furnace in Daniel, Chapter 3.]

cedar *(SEE-der)*

is a tree grown in Lebanon. It was a valuable wood for building. Kings used cedar for palaces. Cedar showed royal power and wealth.

[King Solomon used cedars to build the Temple in I Kings 5:1–6.]

Cedar is a type of evergreen tree.

census *(SEN-sus)*

is the numbering of the people. This was done for taxes. A census was made to find the strength of the army. Moses took a census of Israel at Mount Sinai. He decided to tax each man over twenty to support the Tabernacle. Rome made a decree that all the world should be taxed. Joseph and Mary had to travel from Nazareth to Bethlehem to be taxed. This allowed Jesus to be born in Bethlehem.

[Joseph went to Bethlehem to pay taxes in Luke 2:1–7.]

A census is a counting of the people.

centurion *(sen-TOO-ree-un)*

is a Roman soldier who was in charge of one hundred men. A centurion who lived at Capernaum came to Jesus. He wanted his servant healed. A centurion who witnessed the crucifixion said Jesus was the Son of God.

[A centurion saw Jesus die in Matthew 27:50–54.]

A centurion was a Roman soldier in charge of one hundred men.

Cephas *(SEE-fus)*

was one of the names of Peter.

*[See **Peter, the apostle**.]*

chaff *(CHAFF)*

is the husk separated from the kernel of grain. The grain was beaten by threshing. The wind blew away the chaff. Chaff had no value to the farmer. John the Baptist said Jesus would keep the wheat and burn the chaff. This means that those who obey God will be rewarded. Those who disobey God will be punished.

[John the Baptist talks of chaff in Matthew 3:1–12.]

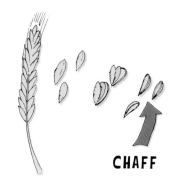

Chaff is the husk that is separated from the grain.

A chariot is a two-wheeled cart.

chariots (CHAIR-ee-uts)

are two-wheeled carts. They were pulled by horses. Egyptian chariots were the first to be mentioned in the Bible. The Philistines had chariots made of iron. Elijah was taken up to heaven in a fiery chariot.

[Elijah is taken up in II Kings 2:9–12.]

charity (CHAIR-uh-tee)

is an old word that means love.

[See **agape**.]

chasten (CHASE-un)

is to punish for doing wrong. God chastens those He loves. This is like parents correcting their children. God makes promises to those who listen to His chastening.

[God promises to chasten and to bless in Revelation 3:19–21.]

To chasten is to punish.

cherub (CHAIR-ub)

is a type of angel that has wings. Cherubim are guards and attendants. They guard the entrance to the Garden of Eden. Four cherubim attend the throne of God. Images of two cherubim are on the Ark of God.

[Cherub guards are found in Genesis 3:24. See **angel**.]

Chief Priest (CHEEF PREEST)

is the same as the High Priest. The Chief Priest was in charge of all the other priests. Aaron was the first Chief Priest of Israel. Only the Chief Priest could go into the Holy of Holies in the Temple.

[Aaron was selected the first Chief Priest in Exodus 30:30. See **Aaron**.]

Chosen People (CHO-zun PEE-pul)

refers to Israel. God chose Israel as a nation. Israel was chosen to be an example to all other nations. They were to follow and obey God. The New Testament refers to Christians as the called. Christians are also chosen by God.

[God told Moses why Israel was chosen in Deuteronomy 7:6–11.]

A cherub is a type of angel with wings.

Christ (CRYSTE)

means the anointed one. It has the same meaning as Messiah. Jesus was the anointed one. Christ is a title given to Jesus of Nazareth.

*[Jesus is called the Christ in Matthew 1:16. See **God the Son**.]*

Christians (CRIST-yuns)

are followers of Jesus Christ. Believers were first called Christians in Antioch. They were called Christians because they behaved, acted, and spoke like Christ. Not everyone who hears the Gospel becomes a Christian. Paul told Agrippa about Jesus. Agrippa said, "Almost thou persuadest me to be a Christian."

[Paul tells Agrippa about Jesus in Acts 26:24–29.]

Chronicles, I and II (CRON-uh-kuls, I and 2)

are two books that tell part of the history of Israel. These books record the reign of King David and King Solomon. They tell how King Solomon built the Temple. These books tell how to worship God at the Temple.

[King Solomon builds the Temple in II Chronicles 2:1–10.]

church (CHURCH)

is a group of Christians who meet together to worship and serve God. The first church was at Jerusalem. The early Christians met on the first day of the week. They met in households. The church can also mean all the believers in the world. The Church is the bride of Christ.

[A church met in Priscilla and Aquilas' house in I Corinthians 16:19.]

circumcision (SIR-cum-SIZ-yun)

removes the foreskin of a male. A baby boy was circumcised on his eighth day. Circumcision was a sign of God's promises to Abraham. It shows obedience to God's leadership. Circumcision was an outward sign of obeying God.

[God told Abraham to be circumcised in Genesis 17:9–14.]

Jesus is also called Christ.

Paul almost persuaded Agrippa to be a Christian.

The first church met in homes.

47

Paul was a citizen of Rome.

Jerusalem and Bethlehem are each called the City of David.

Jesus sent the healed leper to the Temple to be cleansed.

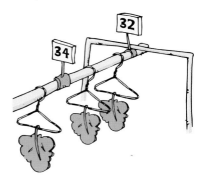

The first clothing was fig leaves.

citizenship (SIT-uh-zen-ship)

refers to where you live. Being a citizen allows you to do many things. A citizen can own property. Christians have their citizenship in heaven. Paul used his Roman citizenship when he appealed to Rome. Paul's Roman citizenship allowed him to take the Gospel to Rome.

[Paul appeals to Rome in Acts 25:8–12.]

City of David (SIT-ee of DAY-vud)

may refer to Jerusalem. This was where King David ruled. Bethlehem was also called the City of David. It was the birthplace of King David.

[Jesus is born in the City of David in Luke 2:1–12.]

city of refuge (SIT-ee of REF-yuje)

is one of six cities that was a place of escape or refuge. A person who killed another would be sentenced to die. That person could go to one of these cities without fear of punishment if the killing was an accident. Three of the cities of refuge were put on each side of the Jordan River.

[Six cities of refuge were set aside in Numbers 35:15.]

clean (CLEEN)

is being pure. Being clean was obeying God's law. Israelites were to be clean in their thoughts, in their actions, and in what they ate. Certain illnesses were unclean. Christ obeyed the Law on cleanness. He sent the healed leper to the priest for cleansing. The blood of Jesus cleanses us from all sin.

[Jesus sends the healed leper to the priest in Matthew 8:2–4.]

clothing (CLOE-thing)

is what people wear on their bodies. The first clothes were fig leaves. God gave Adam and Eve hides of animals to wear. The clothes of the priests were colored indigo, purple, and scarlet. Men and women wore tunics made of linen or wool. The tunics hung from the neck to the knees or ankles. The cloak was an outer garment.

Women wore a headcloth and a veil. Festive clothing was made of costly white material.

[The first clothes are listed in Genesis 3:7 and 3:21.]

cloud (CLOUD)

showed the presence of God. Israel wandered in the wilderness. God guided them by using a pillar of smoke that went in front of the nation. God appeared to Moses in a dark cloud on Mount Sinai. Jesus went to heaven in a cloud. Jesus will return in the last days in a cloud.

[The pillar of smoke is described in Exodus 13:21–22.]

A cloud showed the presence of God.

cock (COCK)

is a rooster. Jesus said Peter would deny Him three times before the cock crow. Peter denied Jesus three times. The cock crowed. Peter wept bitterly because of his sin.

[Peter denies Christ in Matthew 26:74–75.]

A cock is a rooster.

Colossians, Epistle to the (cuh-LOSS-ee-uns, uh-PIS-ul to the)

was written to the church at Colosse. This church was teaching wrong things. Paul wrote this book to correct those teachings. Paul reminds us that Jesus is the head of the church.

[Paul shows the church the importance of Christ in Colossians 1:15–29.]

comfort (CUMM-fert)

is to help someone or ease sorrow. Jesus was going to leave His disciples. Jesus knew that they would be sad. He promised to give them a Comforter. This Comforter is the Holy Spirit. He is our Comforter, too.

[Jesus promised that the Comforter will be with us in John 14:16–26.]

commandment (cuh-MAND-ment)

is a rule or a law. Moses gave the Ten Commandments to Israel. Jesus said that the great commandment is to love God. The second com-

To comfort is to help someone or ease sorrow.

Communion is an act of sharing.

mandment is to love your neighbor. All of the other commandments are made from these two rules. Those who love Jesus keep His commandments.

*[Jesus tells us of the great commandment in Matthew 22:36–40. See **Ten Commandments**.]*

communion (*cum-YUNE-yun*)

is an act of sharing. Communion is also a word for the Lord's Supper. The Lord's Supper is a sharing with other Christians of the life and death of Jesus. Communion is an outward sign of the Christian faith.

[The church celebrates communion in I Corinthians 11:23–26.]

compass (*CUMM-pus*)

is to surround or to march around. Israel compassed the city of Jericho. They compassed Jericho six days in a row. They compassed the city seven times on the seventh day. They blew trumpets. The walls of Jericho tumbled to the ground.

[The Israelites compassed Jericho in Joshua 6:1–20.]

Israel compassed Jericho.

compassion (*cum-PAS-shun*)

is feeling the pain or sorrow of another person. Pharaoh's daughter had compassion on baby Moses. God gave Nehemiah compassion for Israel. God is full of compassion. His compassion has provided salvation and forgiveness.

[Jesus showed compassion to Lazarus in John 11:34–38.]

concubine (*CONK-you-bine*)

is a secondary wife. Concubines were common in the Old Testament. Abraham and Nahor had concubines. King Solomon had three hundred concubines and seven hundred wives. His concubines led him away from God.

[King Solomon loved his concubines more than God in I Kings 11:2–4.]

condemn (*cun-DEM*)

is to declare someone guilty. Sin condemns people.

Pharaoh's daughter had compassion for Moses.

Being condemned keeps people apart from God. God did not send His Son to condemn the world. Jesus came to save people from sin.

[Jesus offers to save us in John 3:16–17.]

confess (cun-FESS)

is to admit faith in something. Christians confess that Jesus is Lord. They also believe that God raised Him from the dead. This is Jesus' plan to save people.

[Paul tells us about confession in Romans 10:9–10.]

conscience (CON-shunse)

is being aware of right and wrong. Our conscience is how we think and speak. Christians are to have a good conscience. A good conscience allows us to follow God.

[Peter wishes us to have a good conscience in I Peter 3:15–17.]

conversion (cun-VERZ-yun)

is turning to God. Conversion makes a person new to God. Conversion is the same as being "born again."

*[See **Born Again.**]*

Corinth (COR-inth)

is a city located in southern Greece. Corinth had one of the first churches. Paul taught and preached at the church of Corinth.

[Paul visited Corinth in Acts 18:1.]

Corinthians, Epistle to the, I and II (cu-RINTH-ee-uns, up-PIS-ul to the, I and 2)

are two letters written to the church at Corinth. Paul told the Corinthians to avoid sin. He told the church to not do the same things as the world. The church is to follow Jesus.

[Paul gives instructions to the church in I Corinthians 16:1–24.]

Cornelius (cor-NEE-lee-us)

was a Roman centurion. He was a gentile. Peter

To have a conscience is to be aware of right and wrong.

An early church was located in Corinth.

Cornelius and his whole household became Christians.

A cornerstone is an important part of a building.

To be corrupt is to be polluted.

A covenant is a special kind of promise.

To covet something is to desire something that belongs to another.

told him about Jesus. Cornelius became a follower of Jesus. His whole household also became Christians.

[Cornelius finds Jesus in Acts, Chapter 10.]

cornerstone (KOR-ner-stone)

is a large stone at the corner of two walls. This makes the building strong. Jesus Christ is the cornerstone of our faith.

[The plans for building the church are in I Peter 2:5–7.]

corrupt (cu-RUPT)

is to be polluted. God wants everything to be holy and pure. People corrupted the entire world. They did not follow God. God sent the Flood to destroy this corruption. God saved only Noah and his family.

[Corruption of the earth is found in Genesis 6:11–13.]

counsel (COUN-sul)

is to give advice. God's counsel lasts forever.

[Counsellor is one of the names listed for the Messiah in Isaiah 9:6–7.]

covenant (CUV-uh-nant)

is an agreement between two people. It is a special kind of promise. Testament is another word for covenant. Noah received God's first covenant. This was a promise not to destroy the earth with another flood. God made His second covenant with Abraham. God promised to give the land of Canaan to Abraham's descendants.

[The rainbow is a sign of God's first covenant and is first shown in Genesis 9:9–17.]

covet (CUV-et)

is to desire something that belongs to another. The Tenth Commandment forbids us to covet. Achan coveted treasure. He hid some in his tent. This made Israel lose their next battle at Ai.

[Achan confesses to coveting treasure in Joshua 7:20–21.]

creation (cree-AY-shun)

is the act of making something new. Creation is how everything began. God created everything in six days. The creation described in Genesis was the beginning of the world.

[Creation of all things is briefly described in Genesis, Chapters 1 and 2.]

Crete is an island in the Great Sea.

Crete (CREET)

is a long island south of Greece. People from Crete were present in Jerusalem on the day of Pentecost. Paul left Titus in Crete to pastor a church.

[Paul leaves Titus in Crete in Titus 1:5.]

cross (CROSS)

was special structure used to execute convicted people. They would hang on the cross until they died. The Romans used the cross to crucify Jesus. These crosses were put in public places outside the city. It was the Roman way of controlling crime.

[See Crucifixion.]

Jesus was crucified on a cross.

crown (CROWN)

was a special headdress worn by royalty. Both the king and the High Priest of Israel wore crowns. James tells us that we can have the crown of life. This crown is promised to those who love Jesus.

[James tells us of this special crown in James 1:12.]

Kings wore different kinds of crowns.

crown of thorns (CROWN of THORNS)

was a special headdress made by the Roman soldiers to make fun of Jesus. They put the crown of thorns on His head and called Jesus the "King of the Jews."

[Jesus is crowned by the Romans in Matthew 27:27–29.]

crucifixion (croo-suh-FIX-shun)

was how the Romans killed Jesus Christ. They first beat Jesus with a whip. Then Jesus was forced to carry the cross to Calvary. He was

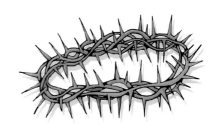

The Romans made a crown out of thorns.

Jesus died by crucifixion.

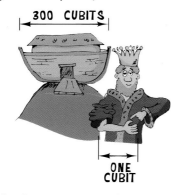

A cubit is a measure of length.

Cyprus is a large island in the Great Sea.

King Cyrus gave back the treasures of the Temple.

nailed to the cross. Jesus died after being on the cross for six hours.

[Jesus is nailed to the cross in Mark, Chapter 15.]

cubit *(CUBE-it)*

is a unit of measure. It was one of the measuring sticks used in the Old Testament. A cubit was the distance from a person's elbow to the tip of the middle finger. This was about eighteen inches.

[The size of the ark is listed in Genesis 6:14–16.]

cupbearer *(CUP-bare-er)*

was an important person to the king. He served wine at the king's table. The cupbearer tasted the wine before the king drank. This was to protect the king from poisoning. Nehemiah was the cup-bearer for Artaxerxes.

[The king sends Nehemiah to Jerusalem in Nehemiah 1:11–2:6.]

curse *(CURSE)*

is to promise bad things. A curse is the opposite of a blessing. Adam's sin is called the curse. Death began because of sin. Jesus has power over the curse.

*[The first curse is given by God in Genesis 3:14–19. See **blessing**.]*

Cyprus *(SY-prus)*

is a large island in the Mediterranean Sea. Paul visited Cyprus on his first missionary trip.

[Paul first goes to Cyprus in Acts 13.]

Cyrene *(sy-REE-nuh)*

is located in northern Africa. Cyrene was the home of Simon. Simon of Cyrene carried the cross for Jesus.

*[See **Simon**.]*

Cyrus *(SY-rus)*

was a king of Persia. Cyrus was the ruler of the world. He rebuilt the Temple in Jerusalem. Cyrus gave back treasures of the Temple. Cyrus was kind to the Jews and worshipped God.

[Cyrus frees the Jews in Ezra 1:1–4.]

The Dagon idol was broken.

Dagon (DAY-gon)

was one of the gods of the Philistines. They praised Dagon for defeating Samson. The Philistines put the Ark of God next to a statue of Dagon. The statue was knocked down the next day. They again put Dagon next to the Ark of God. The following day it was knocked over and broken. One of the Ten Commandments says that we are to worship only the one true God.

[The Philistines put the Ark of God next to Dagon in I Samuel 5:1–7.]

Damascus (duh-MASK-us)

is the capital of Syria. Saul went to Damascus. Saul was killing all the Christians he found. Saul met Jesus on the Damascus Road. Saul became a follower of Jesus. But Saul was blinded for three days. Saul had his sight restored in Damascus. Saul's name was changed to Paul. Paul was hated by other Christians. He had to escape from Damascus in a basket lowered over the city wall.

[Damascus is where Paul begins his work as an apostle as shown in II Corinthians 11:32.]

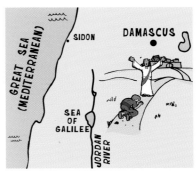

Paul met Jesus on the road to Damascus.

damn (DAM)

is to be separated from God. God wants us to be holy and pure. Sin keeps people away from God. Jesus came to save the world. Followers of Jesus are promised a heavenly home. Those who reject Jesus are separated from God. They are damned.

[Jesus taught that the wicked are to be separated from God in Matthew 23:14–33.]

Dan (DAN)

was the first son born to Jacob by Rachel's maid

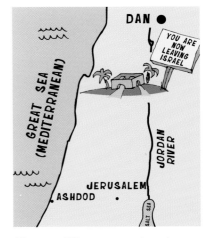

The city of Dan was used to show the borders of Israel.

Daniel

Daniel told Nebuchadnezzar about his dream.

Darius threw Daniel into a den of lions.

David killed Goliath.

Bilhah. Dan was the beginning of the Tribe of Dan. They settled on the western coast of Canaan. Samson was of the tribe of Dan. He fought the Philistines. The city of Dan was used to show the borders of Israel. "From Dan to Beersheba" is a saying that meant the whole nation of Israel.

[The birth of Dan is recorded in Genesis 30:1–6.]

Daniel (DAN-yul)

was a young man captured by Nebuchadnezzar, king of Babylon. Nebuchadnezzar had a troubling dream. Daniel told the king about his dream. The king gave Daniel an important job. Daniel remained an important person with the new king, Darius. Darius made a new law. This law said it was illegal to pray to God. Daniel kept praying to God. Daniel was thrown into a den of lions. God kept the mouths of the hungry lions closed.

[God protected Daniel from the lions in Daniel, Chapter 6.]

Daniel, Book of (DAN-yul, Book of)

was written by the prophet Daniel. This book shows that God is more powerful than false gods. Daniel interpreted the king's dream and the handwriting on the wall. God protected His people from the flames of a fiery furnace. God saved Daniel from being lunch for a bunch of hungry lions.

[The handwriting on the wall is recorded in Daniel, Chapter 5.]

Darius (duh-RYE-us)

was the name of some of the kings of Persia. One Darius threw Daniel into a den of lions. Another Darius looked at the records of King Cyrus. He found that the Jews were allowed to go home and rebuild. This Darius gave money to the Jews to help rebuild the Temple.

[Darius gives supplies for the rebuilding of the Temple in Ezra 6:8–9.]

David (DAY-vud)

was born in Bethlehem. He was the son of Jesse. The prophet Samuel anointed David as the new king of Israel. The giant Goliath challenged the Israelites. David accepted this challenge. He used only his sling for a weapon. Goliath was killed by young David. David was known as a man after God's own heart.

[David fights Goliath in I Samuel, Chapter 17.]

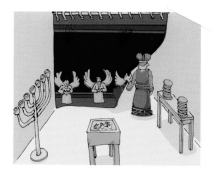

The High Priest went into the Holy of Holies on the Day of Atonement.

Day of Atonement (DAY of uh-TONE-ment)

was the day sacrifices were made for the nation of Israel. This is the only day the High Priest entered the Holy of Holies of the Temple. A young bull was the sin offering for the priest and his family. Then the priest chose between two goats. One was offered as a sin offering for the nation. The other was presented alive as a scapegoat. The High Priest confessed the sin of the people over its head. It was released into the wilderness. The people did not eat on the Day of Atonement. Today, Jews call this day Yom Kippur.

[The Day of Atonement is described in Leviticus, Chapter 16.]

day's journey (DAY'S JER-nee)

was the distance a person could travel in one day on foot. Joseph and Mary went to Jerusalem to celebrate the passover. After the feast, they traveled one day's journey. Joseph and Mary found that young Jesus was missing.

[Young Jesus visited Jerusalem in Luke 2:41–49.]

A day's journey was the distance a person could travel in one day on foot.

deacon (DEE-cun)

means servant. A deacon is a servant for the church. The deacons were selected to serve the needs of the poor. A deacon was to be wise, honest, and full of the Holy Spirit.

[The first deacons were selected in Acts 6:1–6.]

Dead Sea (DED SEE)

is a large lake on the eastern border of Canaan. The Jordan River flows into the Dead Sea. It has no outlets for water that runs into it. It is very

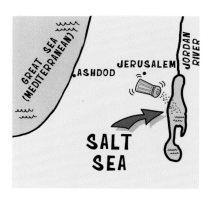

The Dead Sea is also called the Salt Sea.

death

Death began when Adam and Eve sinned.

The Death of Christ is also called the crucifixion.

Deborah was a judge.

salty. The Dead Sea is also called the Salt Sea, the Sea of the Plain, and the Eastern Sea. Sodom and Gomorrah were located on the south coast of the Dead Sea.

[These cities were located on the Dead Sea as shown in Genesis 14:2–3.]

death *(DETH)*

occurs when the body quits working. Death began because Adam and Eve sinned. Jesus had power over death when He rose from the dead on the third day. Jesus wants all of us to have the same power over death. This happens when we hear His word and believe in Him.

[Jesus gave us power over death in John 5:24–27.]

Death of Christ *(DETH of CRYSTE)*

is called the crucifixion. The Israelites killed a lamb as a sin offering. Jesus died for our sins. This is why He was called the Lamb of God. Jesus came back to life on the third day. This is called the Resurrection of Christ.

[The crucifixion of Jesus is described in Mark 15:16–38.]

death, second *(DETH, SEC-und)*

is the final separation from God. The second death is the spiritual death of a person. The first death is a physical death or when the body dies. The second death comes only to unbelievers. The second death has no power over those whose names are written in the book of life.

[The second death is mentioned in Revelation 20:6–14.]

Deborah *(DEB-uh-ruh)*

was a leader and prophetess of Israel. Deborah served as a judge for the nation. Deborah summoned Barak and the army of Israel. She gave him instructions on how to defeat the Canaanite army. Deborah and Barak sang a victory song after the battle.

[The story of Deborah and her song is recorded in Judges 4:4–5:31.]

deceive (de-SEEVE)

is to make one believe something that is not true. Satan is the great deceiver. Satan will try to deceive all the nations of the world.

[The last time Satan deceives people is shown in Revelation 20:1–10.]

declare (de-CLAIR)

is to reveal or make clearly known. The power and glory of God has been declared through miracles. The apostles declared that Jesus was the Messiah.

[Paul declares Jesus to be the Son of God in Romans 1:1–6.]

decree (de-CREE)

is a command given by a king. King Cyrus made a decree to rebuild the Temple. The celebration of Purim began with the decree from Queen Esther. Caesar Augustus decreed that all the world was to be taxed. This allowed Jesus to be born in Bethlehem.

[The decree of Caesar is recorded in Luke 2:1–3.]

dedicate (ded-uh-KAYT)

is to be set apart to God. Israel is a nation that was set apart for God. All of the items in the Temple were dedicated to God. The church is set apart to God. Each believer is dedicated to God by Jesus Christ.

[Paul says that the believer is to be dedicated to God in Romans 12:1–2.]

deed (DEED)

is something done. Deeds can be good or evil. Christians are to do all deeds in the name of Jesus. This means that everything we do needs to be good and bring honor to God.

[Deeds to be done in Jesus' name are listed in Colossians 3:17.]

delight (de-LITE)

is to find great joy in something. God delights in those who obey Him. Following God's commandments delighted David and the prophets.

[A song of praise and delight is Psalm 119.]

To deceive is to make one believe something that is not true.

Caesar Augustus decreed that all the world should be taxed.

A deed is something that is done.

Delight is to find great joy in something.

Delilah deceived Samson.

Daniel spent the night in a den of lions.

Peter denied Jesus three times.

Delilah (de-LYE-luh)

was a Philistine. Samson liked Delilah very much. Delilah wanted Samson to tell her how he got his great strength. The fourth time she asked, Samson told her the truth. He was strong because he obeyed God and never cut his hair. Delilah told the Philistines his secret. They shaved his head, blinded him, and put him in chains.

*[Delilah tempts Samson in Judges, Chapter 16. See **Samson**.]*

deliver (de-LIV-er)

is to save someone from danger. Shadrach, Meshach, and Abednego were delivered out of a fiery furnace. The Hebrews were delivered from the hand of Pharaoh. Jesus can deliver us from evil.

[Paul said Jesus delivers us from evil in Galatians 1:3–5.]

demons (DEE-muns)

are angels that have not obeyed God. They are beings created by God. One third of the angels rebelled against God. God threw them out of heaven. Their leader is Satan. Demons do not have bodies. They look for people they can control. Mary Magdalene had seven demons. Jesus healed Mary.

[A story of how Jesus sent demons into two thousand pigs is found in Mark 5:1–17.]

den of lions (DEN of LYE-uns)

is a place where kings kept lions. The Assyrian kings used lions for sport. Daniel spent one night in a den of hungry lions. God kept the mouths of the lions shut. This was a miracle.

[Daniel spent a night in a den of lions in Daniel, Chapter 6.]

deny (dee-NYE)

is to claim something is untrue. Jesus predicted that Peter would deny Him three times. Jesus was arrested in the middle of the night. Peter had claimed that he did not know Jesus three different times. Peter wept when the rooster crowed.

He remembered what Jesus had said.

[Peter denies Jesus three times in Matthew 26:34 and 69–75.]

depart *(de-PART)*

means to leave. The Israelites departed from Egypt. Christians are to depart from evil and to do good. The wicked are commanded to depart from God.

[Jesus the King tells the wicked to depart from Him in Matthew 25:31–41.]

Depart means to leave.

Derbe *(DER-beh)*

was a city in the province of Galatia. Paul visited Derbe on two of his missionary journeys. Paul and Barnabas preached the Gospel in Derbe.

[Paul and Barnabas first visited Derbe in Acts 14:6–7.]

Paul and Barnabas preached in Derbe.

desert *(DEZ-ert)*

is the same as wilderness. It is a bare and open place without water.

*[See **wilderness**.]*

despise *(de-SPIZE)*

means to hate. The wicked despise God and His Word. Jesus said that those who despise His followers despise Him. Paul tells us not to despise other people.

[Paul tells Christians not to despise in I Thessalonians 4:1–9.]

Desert is the same as wilderness.

Deuteronomy *(doo-ter-AH-nuh-mee)*

is one of the books of the Old Testament. It means the second law. The Israelites were getting ready to enter into the Promised Land. All of the Israelites who had listened to the ten spies had died. The remaining people were new to the Law. Deuteronomy explained the law to these Israelites.

[Moses repeats God's great commandment in Deuteronomy, Chapter 6.]

devil *(DEV-ul)*

is another word for demon. The Devil can also mean Satan.

*[See **Satan** or **demons**.]*

To devour is to eat fast.

Simeon was a devout man.

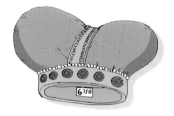

A diadem was a head covering for kings and queens.

Diana was the Roman goddess of the moon.

devour (de-VOUR)

is to eat very hungrily. Satan goes about the earth like a roaring lion. He looks for those whom he can devour. Faith in Jesus is the best protection from Satan.

[Christians are made aware of Satan in I Peter 5:8–10.]

devout (de-VOUT)

is to be godly and to obey God. Simeon was a righteous and devout man. He was looking for the Messiah. God promised him that he would live to see the Messiah. Simeon saw baby Jesus when He was eight days old. Simeon took Jesus into his arms. He blessed God for letting him see the Messiah.

[Jesus made His first visit to the Temple in Luke 2:21–35.]

diadem (DYE-uh-dem)

is a head covering for kings, queens, and priests. It was a sign of power and honor. A diadem was made from silk. Some had pearls and gold on them. The diadem of a priest was called a mitre.

[God puts the royal diadem on those He chooses as shown in Ezekiel 21:25–27.]

Diana (dye-ANN-uh)

is the Roman goddess of the moon. Diana is also called Artemis. This was a false god worshipped by the Romans. They thought that she could help in childbirth or in hunting. Worshipping idols or other gods breaks one of the Ten Commandments.

[The Ephesians worshipped Diana in Acts 19:21–41.]

diligence (DILL-uh-junse)

is to do a work or task with care. King Herod diligently asked the wise men when the bright star appeared. He told the wise men to search diligently for Jesus. The wise men did not return to Herod. King Herod tried to kill Jesus. Joseph, Mary, and Jesus escaped to Egypt.

[The wise men visit King Herod in Matthew 2:1–12.]

disciple (di-SIPE-ul)

is a student or a follower of Jesus Christ. Jesus selected twelve disciples. Seventy disciples were sent out to cities by twos. They performed miracles in the name of Jesus. Disciples are also those who have heard and believed the Gospel.

[The Jerusalem church added a lot of disciples in Acts 6:1–7.]

A disciple is a student of Jesus.

displease (dis-PLEEZ)

is to cause someone to be unhappy with something. The Chief Priests saw Jesus doing miracles and wonderful things. Jesus threw the merchants and the moneychangers out of the Temple. They were displeased with Jesus.

[Jesus made the priests unhappy in Matthew 21:10–17.]

divide (di-VIDE)

is to separate into parts. God divided the light from the darkness to make day and night. Moses divided the waters of the Red Sea. The Israelites could then walk across on dry land. Christians are to rightly divide the Word of God. This study helps Christians learn more about God.

[Timothy tells Christians to study God's Word in II Timothy 2:15.]

Moses divided the waters of the Red Sea.

divine inspiration (de-VINE in-sper-AY-shun)

is when God tells a prophet what to say or write. This is how God wrote the books of the Bible. God used different men to write these books. These men wrote with their own style and feelings.

[John tells us about divine inspiration in Revelation 1:1–3.]

divorce (di-VORSE)

is the ending of a marriage. Jesus said that Moses allowed divorce for only one reason. It was because the Jews had hardened their hearts. They lost their first love and became selfish. Joseph found out that Mary was pregnant. He was ready to divorce Mary. Joseph had a dream sent by God to keep Mary as his wife.

[Joseph is told not to divorce Mary in Matthew 1:18–25.]

Divine inspiration is when God speaks through prophets.

63

Satan has dominion over the world.

Peter raised Dorcas from the dead.

A dove brought Noah an olive branch.

Dreams are images made during sleep.

doctrine (DOCK-trun)

is the basic teachings of Christ and the Bible. God has spoken to us. God and His Word remain consistent and unchanging.

[All Scripture is good for doctrine as shown in II Timothy 3:15–17.]

dominion (duh-MIN-yun)

is to have power or control over others. God gave Adam and Eve dominion over His creation. Satan has dominion over the world until Christ returns. Sin has control over our bodies and actions. Jesus has dominion over death and sin.

[We have dominion over sin through Jesus in Romans 6:9–14.]

Dorcas (DOR-cus)

was a Christian woman. She lived in Joppa. Dorcas did many good things, but she became sick and died. Her friends sent for Peter. Peter raised Dorcas from the dead. This was the first miracle performed by the apostles after Jesus went to heaven.

[Peter visits Joppa in Acts 9:36–42.]

dove (DOVE—rhymes with love)

is a clean bird. This meant that it could be used for food and sacrifices. Jesus was baptized in the Jordan River. The Holy Spirit came from heaven and rested on Jesus like a dove. Noah sent a dove out of the ark three times. The dove returned with an olive branch the second time. The dove did not return the third time. Noah knew it was then safe to leave the ark.

[Noah releases birds in Genesis 8:6–12.]

dreams (DREEMZ)

are the images made during sleep. Dreams often have hidden meanings. They have sometimes revealed the future. Joseph and Daniel could give the correct meaning for dreams. King Nebuchadnezzar had a dream of a great image.

Daniel told him that the image was of the great kingdoms that were to come.

[Daniel describes King Nebuchadnezzar's first dream in Daniel, Chapter 2.]

The dung gate is where the garbage was taken out of the city.

drunk *(DRUNK)*

is to be dizzy from drinking wine. Noah sinned after the Flood. He became drunk from the wine he made. Christians are not to be drunk. They are to be filled with the Holy Spirit.

[Christians are not to be drunk in Ephesians 5:18–20.]

dung *(DUNG)*

is the personal waste made by man or beast. Dung was used for fertilizer. One of the gates into Jerusalem was called the dung gate. It was used to get rid of trash, garbage, and dung.

[The dung gate gets repaired in Nehemiah 3:13–14.]

A dungeon is a jail or prison.

dungeon *(DUNN-jun)*

is the same as a jail or prison. It is a place where people who broke the law were kept. Joseph was sold by his brothers. He was made a slave. Joseph was put in charge of Potiphar's house. He was accused of doing wrong. He was thrown into a dungeon. God was still with Joseph.

[God protected Joseph from evil in Genesis, Chapters 39 to 41.]

dwell *(DWELL)*

is to live. God dwells in heaven. God the Son became flesh and dwelt among people. Jesus became a man and lived among the Jews. Jesus tells us that He is preparing a mansion for us. Christians will dwell in heaven with Jesus.

[Jesus promises us a new home in John 14:1–4.]

Christians will dwell in heaven.

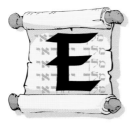

Peter cut off the ear of the High Priest's servant.

ear (EER)

is an organ used to hear with. Peter tried to protect Jesus in the Garden of Gethsemane. He used a sword and cut off the ear of the High Priest's servant. Jesus healed the ear.

[An ear is cut off in John 18:10 and in Luke 22:50–51.]

Ecclesiastes (uh-clee-zee-ASS-teez)

means preacher. King Solomon used this as one of his titles.

[Solomon calls himself preacher in Ecclesiastes 1:1.]

Ecclesiastes, Book of (uh-clee-zee-ASS-teez, Book of)

is a book about life. The book talks about only seeking pleasures and wealth. Ecclesiastes searches for the meaning of life. Serving and obeying God is the duty of man.

[The duty of man is defined in Ecclesiastes 12:8–14.]

Ecclesiastes means preacher.

Eden, garden of (EED-un, GARD-un of)

was the first home for Adam and Eve.

[See **garden of Eden.**]

edict (EE-dikt)

is a decree.

[See **Decree.**]

edify (ED-uh-fye)

means to build up. Christians are to edify each other. This is done by helping and encouraging others. God gives us spiritual gifts. These are given to edify the church.

[Christians are to edify each other in I Thessalonians 5:9–11.]

Edom *(EE-dum)*

means red. Esau was called Edom. He had sold his birthright for a bowl of red stew. Edom was also the land south of the Dead Sea. Edomites were related to Esau. Esau was the brother of Jacob. The Israelites are related to Jacob. King Saul and King David fought with the Edomites.

*[Edom buys a bowl of red stew in Genesis 25:29–34. See **Esau**.]*

The garden of Eden was Adam and Eve's first home.

Egypt *(EE-jipt)*

is a country in northern Africa. The Nile River flows through Egypt. The ruler of Egypt was called a Pharaoh. Joseph was sold to Egypt as a slave. Moses led the Israelites out of Egypt. A young Jesus went to Egypt to escape from Herod.

[Jesus went to Egypt in Matthew 2:13–15.]

Egypt is a country in northern Africa.

elder *(EL-der)*

is the spiritual leader in the church. Bishop is another word for elder. Paul and Barnabas selected elders for the churches they started. Paul said elders served as shepherds of the church. Elders are to guide, be a teacher, and be Spirit filled.

[Things needed to be an elder are found in I Timothy 3:1–7.]

elect *(ee-LECT)*

is to choose something. God has chosen the nation of Israel for Himself. He elected one small nation to honor Him. They were to be an example to all other nations of the world. God elects those who follow Jesus. People still have a free will to accept or reject Jesus as their Savior. But God knows the past, the present, and the future. That is why it can be said that God has elected Christians.

[Peter says he was an elect of God in I Peter 1:1–2.]

To elect is to choose something.

Eli *(EE-lye)*

was the High Priest at Shiloh. Hannah kept her promise to the Lord. She gave her son Samuel to the sanctuary at Shiloh. Eli became the teacher for Samuel. God spoke to Samuel. He thought it

Eli was given the baby Samuel.

Eli, Eli, lama, sabachthani?

"Eli, Eli, lama, sabachthani?" cried Jesus on the cross.

was Eli calling him. Eli told him what to say to the Lord.

[Eli tells Samuel what to say in I Samuel 3:9–10.]

Eli, Eli, lama, sabachthani? (AY-lee, AY-lee, LAM-uh, suh-back-TAH-nee)

was the cry of Jesus on the cross. This means, "My God, my God, why hast thou forsaken me?" It is taken from a Hebrew song. The song is a prophecy of the Messiah.

*[The song Jesus quotes begins in Psalm 22:1. See **seven sayings from the cross**.]*

Elijah (ee-LYE-juh)

was a prophet of God. Elijah was the teacher for Elisha. Elijah never died. God took Elijah to heaven in a whirlwind.

[Elijah goes to heaven in II Kings 2:11.]

God took Elijah to heaven in a chariot of fire and Elisha picked up the mantle of Elijah.

Elimelech (uh-LIM-uh-lek)

was the husband of Naomi. There was a famine in Israel. Elimelech led his family from Bethlehem to Moab. Elimelech died in Moab. Ruth married one of his sons.

[Elimelech leads his family to Moab in Ruth 1:1–2.]

Elisabeth (uh-LIZ-uh-beth)

was the mother of John the Baptist. She was a cousin of Mary, the mother of Jesus. Elisabeth felt baby John jump when Mary came near. Baby John knew that Mary was the mother of the Messiah.

[Mary visits Elisabeth in Luke 1:39–45.]

Elisha (ee-LYE-shuh)

was a prophet of God. Elisha followed Elijah on the day God took him to heaven. He prayed for a double portion of God's blessing. Elisha picked up the mantle of Elijah. The Bible records twice as many miracles performed by Elisha.

[Elisha parts the waters of the Jordan River in II Kings 2:14.]

Elisabeth was the mother of John the Baptist.

Elkanah (el-KAH-nuh)

was the father of Samuel. One of his wives was Hannah. God gave them a son. Elkanah and Hannah gave their son Samuel to the Lord. God blessed Elkanah and Hannah with more children.

[Elkanah and Hannah are blessed in I Samuel 2:20–21.]

Paul cursed Elymas with blindness.

Elymas (ELL-uh-mus)

was a false prophet. Paul and Barnabas went to Paphos. They were preaching the Gospel. Elymas tried to keep them from preaching. Paul cursed Elymas with blindness.

[Elymas is blinded in Acts 13:4–12.]

Emmanuel (uh-MAN-you-el)

is a name that means "God with us." It is one of the names given to Jesus. Jesus was God. He lived on earth among the Jews as a man. Jesus can truly be called Emmanuel.

[The angel of the Lord told Joseph that Jesus would be called Emmanuel in Matthew 1:20–25.]

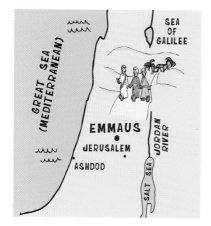

Two disciples talk to Jesus on the road to Emmaus.

Emmaus (uh-MAY-us)

is a small village outside of Jerusalem. Jesus had been in the grave for three days. Two disciples were going to Emmaus. They met a stranger on the road to Emmaus. This person asked them a lot of questions about Jesus. The disciples later found out that they had been talking with Jesus. He had risen from the grave.

[The two disciples talk with Jesus on the Emmaus road in Luke 24:13–35.]

Endor (EN-dor)

was the home of a witch. King Saul visited the witch of Endor.

*[See **witch**.]*

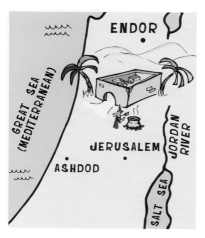

King Saul talked with a witch at Endor.

endure (en-DURE)

means to bear pain. Endure is the same as long-suffering.

*[See **long-suffering**.]*

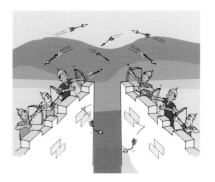

An enemy is one who hates another.

There is enmity between women and serpents.

Enoch walked with God.

Ephah was a dry weight used for grain.

enemy (EN-uh-mee)

is one who dislikes or hates another. An enemy seeks to harm another. The enemies of Israel are the enemies of God. An ungodly person is an enemy of God. Satan is also an enemy. He seeks to turn people away from God.

[The enemies of Israel are the enemies of God is shown in Exodus 23:22.]

enmity (EN-muh-tee)

is hate and a lack of trust. God put enmity between women and serpents. This was a curse on the serpent for its part in the sin of Adam and Eve.

[Enmity is given in Genesis 3:15.]

Enoch (EE-nok)

was the father of Methuselah. Enoch walked with God. Enoch never died. God took him to heaven.

[Enoch went to heaven as shown in both Genesis 5:24 and Hebrews 11:5.]

envy (EN-vee)

is to dislike and be jealous of another person. Christians are to avoid envy. Ungodly lives are shown by envy, divisions, and strife. Envy is a part of evil works.

[Envy is part of evil works is shown in James 3:14–16.]

Epaphroditus (uh-PAFF-ruh-dye-tus)

was a friend of the apostle Paul. He delivered a gift from the church at Philippi to Paul. Epaphroditus became very sick. He was sent to minister at Philippi when he healed.

[Paul sent Epaphroditus to the city of Philippi in Philippians 2:25.]

Ephah (EE-fah)

was a dry weight used for grain. It is about the same as a half bushel. Israel was to use honest weights to measure ephahs.

[Israel was told to use honest ephahs in Leviticus 19:35–37.]

Ephesians, Epistle to the *(uh-FEEZ-yunz, uh-PIS-ul to the)*

was written by Paul to a divided church. The Jews wanted to keep their old traditions. This meant that the Jews were to be separated from Gentiles. There were a lot of gentile believers in the Ephesus church. Paul told them that all are saved by the same Christ.

[Paul said that the Ephesians were of one Spirit in Ephesians 2:13–22.]

Ephesus *(EFF-uh-sus)*

was a large city in Asia Minor. Paul began a church in Ephesus. Priscilla and Aquila ministered at this church. Ephesus is one of the seven churches in Revelation.

*[Priscilla and Aquila minister to the church of Ephesus in Acts 18:18–19. See **seven churches**.]*

One of the early churches was at Ephesus.

ephod *(EE-fodd)*

was a simple linen garment much like an apron. The colors of the ephod include gold, blue, purple, and scarlet. The ephod was worn by priests over the robe. The ephod was held in place with a girdle.

[The colors of the ephod are listed in Exodus 28:4–8.]

Ephraim *(EF-ruh-im)*

was the second son of Joseph. Ephraim was adopted by Jacob. He began the line of the half tribe of Ephraim. Joshua and Samuel were Ephraimites.

[Ephraim is adopted in Genesis 48:3–5.]

Ephod was a simple linen garment.

epistle *(uh-PIS-ul)*

is a letter or message. Some of the books in the New Testament are epistles. These include letters written by Paul, James, Peter, John, and Jude. These personal letters are inspired by God and are part of the Scriptures.

[God's word is given by teaching through epistles as shown in II Thessalonians 2:15.]

Epistle is a letter or message.

Esau was a great hunter.

Esther was a Jewish girl who married King Ahasuerus.

Ethiopia is a nation located south of Egypt.

Esau *(EE-saw)*

was the older son of Isaac and Rebekah. His twin brother was Jacob. Esau was redheaded and hairy from birth. Jacob held on to his foot at birth. Esau was a great hunter. Esau sold his birthright for a bowl of red stew. Jacob tricked Isaac into giving him the blessing meant for Esau.

*[Esau lost his blessing in Genesis 27:18–29. See **Edom**.]*

Esther *(ESS-ter)*

was a Jewish girl who married King Ahasuerus. Mordecai was her uncle. Haman hated Mordecai. Haman plotted to kill Mordecai and all the Jews. Queen Esther found out the plot. Haman was killed and the Jews were saved.

[Queen Esther tells the king of the plot to kill the Jews in Esther 7:1–6.]

Esther, Book of *(ESS-ter, Book of)*

is an Old Testament book that shows how God protects His people. God put Esther into a position where she could save the Jews. Queen Esther began the Feast of Purim to celebrate God's deliverance from evil.

[Esther is chosen to be queen in Esther 2:16–17.]

eternal life *(ee-TERN-ul LIFE)*

means living forever. Eternal life is a promise made by Jesus. He promises to give His followers eternal life. This means that we can go to heaven.

*[Jesus tells us how to get eternal life in John 3:15–18. See **everlasting life**.]*

Ethiopia *(ee-thee-OH-pee-uh)*

is a nation located south of Egypt. Philip met a eunuch from Ethiopia. The eunuch was the minister of Candace who was queen of the Ethiopians. The eunuch became a Christian and was baptized.

[Philip met an Ethiopian in Acts 8:26–39.]

eunuch (YOU-nuk)

is a male without sexual organs. Physical defects prevented a person from being a priest in Israel. Eunuchs were not allowed to be priests. Kings used eunuchs to guard harems. The Ethiopian eunuch was a minister for the queen.

[Eunuchs killed wicked Queen Jezebel in II Kings 9:32–33.]

Kings used eunuchs to guard harems.

Euphrates (you-FRAY-teez)

is a large river in Asia. Nineveh and Babylon were located on the Euphrates River. The Euphrates River was one of the rivers that flowed out of the Garden of Eden.

[Euphrates flows out of the garden in Genesis 2:10–14.]

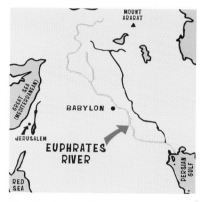

The Euphrates River runs past Babylon.

evangelism (uh-VAN-jul-iz-um)

means bringing the Gospel or good news. Evangelism is presenting God's Word and His grace to those who have never heard it. Jonah was an evangelist to the city of Nineveh. Jesus brought good news to Israel. The early church evangelized Europe, Asia, and Africa.

[One of the gifts that Christ gives is evangelism as shown in Ephesians 4:7–12.]

Jonah was an evangelist to the city of Nineveh.

Eve (EVE)

was the first woman created. She was formed from the rib of Adam. Eve was the first to be tempted by the serpent. She ate from the Tree of Knowledge of Good and Evil. She gave some of the fruit to Adam, and he ate it also. God sent them out of the Garden of Eden for this sin. Eve was the mother of Cain, Abel, and Seth.

[Eve talks to the serpent in Genesis 3:1–7.]

everlasting life (EV-er-LAST-ing LIFE)

means living forever. This is a promise given by Jesus for every believer. Jesus says that anyone who believes that He is the Messiah will have everlasting life.

*[Jesus tells Nicodemus about everlasting life in John 3:16-18. See **eternal life.**]*

Eve was the first to be tempted by the serpent.

Evil began with Lucifer.

Jesus will be exalted.

Jonah was exceedingly glad for the shade of a gourd.

To be exiled is to be sent out of your own country.

everlasting punishment (*EV-er-LAST-ing PUNN-ish-ment*)

is God's judgment for those who do not obey Him. It is the same as being damned.

*[See **damn**.]*

evil (*EE-vul*)

is anything that opposes God. Evil began with Lucifer. Lucifer is also known as Satan or the Devil. Satan wanted to be like God. This was the first sin. Evil began with the first sin.

[Evil begins in Isaiah 14:12–14.]

exalt (*egg-ZALT*)

is to lift up. Exalt also means to give praise and honor. God is to be exalted above all things. Jesus has been exalted by God. Jesus has been given a name above all other names. Everything shall bow before Jesus.

[Jesus has been exalted in Philippians 2:9–11.]

exceeding (*ex-SEED-ing*)

means to a great amount. Jonah was exceedingly glad for the gourd plant. It gave him shade from the hot sun. God is able to exceedingly provide for all that we need.

[God is exceeding in answering our prayers in Ephesians 3:20.]

exhort (*egg-ZORT*)

is to give advice or warn. Christians are exhorted to live godly lives. Believers are to help and exhort each other. Paul reminds Timothy to read the Scriptures, study doctrine, and exhort others.

[Exhortation is a gift from God as shown in Romans 12:6–8.]

exile (*EGG-zile*)

is to be sent out of your own country. Israel and Judah were conquered by Assyria. They were taken into captivity. They were exiled from the Promised Land. God sent these nations into exile because of their sin.

[Judah went into exile in II Kings 25:21.]

exodus (EKS-uh-dus)

is the journey out of Egypt. The Hebrews were slaves to Pharaoh. The exodus began when Moses led the Hebrews out of Egypt. The Egyptian army began to chase them. God drowned the entire army. The Israelites spent forty years in the wilderness. God gave them the Ten Commandments, the Tabernacle, and manna during this time. The exodus ended when Joshua took the Hebrews into the Promised Land.

[The Hebrews begin their exodus in Exodus 12:31–33.]

Exodus was the journey out of Egypt.

Exodus, Book of (EX-uh-dus, Book of)

is an Old Testament book showing how God saves His people. Moses led the Hebrews out of Egypt. Moses went to the Pharaoh ten times and asked him to let them go. Each time the Pharaoh said no. God sent a plague each time. The Pharaoh finally let the Hebrews leave. Exodus records the trip out of Egypt.

[The plague of the frogs was sent in Exodus 8:1–15.]

eye of the needle (EYE of the NEED-ul)

was the name of one of the gates into Jerusalem. This gate is a small gate. A camel with a full load had to crawl very slowly through this gate. It was very difficult.

[Jesus talks of the eye of the needle in Matthew 19:23–26.]

A camel with a load had to crawl through the eye of the needle gate.

Ezekiel (eh-ZEE-kee-ul)

was a priest and prophet. He was carried to Babylon as a slave and warned Israel of God's judgment. God sent Judah into captivity because of sin. Ezekiel told of God's promise to restore the nation.

[Ezekiel is told to warn Israel in Ezekiel 3:4–11.]

Ezekiel, Book of (eh-ZEE-kee-ul, Book of)

is an Old Testament book that tells how God judges sin. Ezekiel tells how God will send His people into captivity. Ezekiel had a vision of dried

Ezekiel was taken as a slave to Babylon.

Ezra

bones coming together. These bones took on flesh and became alive. This was God's promise to restore Israel.

[The vision of the dried bones is recorded in Ezekiel 37:1–14.]

Ezra (EZZ-ruh)

was a Hebrew priest and scribe who was in exile. The Israelites were allowed to go back to Jerusalem. Ezra studied the law of Moses. He read and taught God's word to Israel. Ezra had the people rebuild the Temple. The Hebrews began to worship God again.

[Ezra is told to teach the Israelites in Ezra 7:25.]

Ezra, Book of (EZZ-ruh, Book of)

is an Old Testament book that shows the power of God. The trip from Assyria was long and dangerous. God was able to protect the treasures of the Temple. God was able to protect His people while they worked. The people rebuilt the Temple. The people began to obey and worship God in the Promised Land.

[The Temple is finished in Ezra 6:14–15.]

Ezra helped build the Temple.

fable (FAY-bul)

is a make-believe story used to teach a lesson. Fables are rarely found in the Bible. One fable is that of the trees of the forest selecting a king. This fable warns Israel of the dangers in selecting a bad king. Another fable is that of a thistle. The thistle thinks that it is equal to the giant cedars of Lebanon. The thistle gets trampled by a wild beast of the forest. This story was about the pride of King Amaziah.

[The fable of the trees is found in Judges 9:8–15. The fable of the thistle is found in II Kings 14:8–10.]

One fable is about the thistle that is trampled by a beast.

faith (FAITH)

is the hope of things to come and not yet seen. Faith in God has always been the way of salvation. Faith is shown in the lives of Noah, Abraham, Jacob, and many others. Jesus wants us to increase our faith. Faith the size of a mustard seed can move mountains.

[A list of men and women with faith is located in Hebrews, Chapter 11.]

Faith the size of a mustard seed can move mountains.

fall (FALL)

refers to the first sin. Adam and Eve were without sin. They disobeyed God by eating the forbidden fruit. This sin caused them to be thrown out of the Garden of Eden. This was the fall from God's grace. The fall allowed sin and death to enter into the world.

[The fall occurred in Genesis, Chapter 3.]

fallen angels (FALL-un AIN-juls)

refers to demons. Demons were angels at one time. Lucifer rebelled against God. One third of the angels followed Lucifer. The angels that sinned

The first sin is called the fall.

The widow made Elijah some cakes.

Father is the male parent.

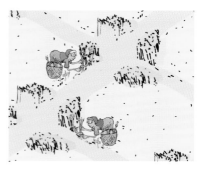

The corners of the field were left for the widows and the fatherless.

were thrown out of heaven. They are called fallen angels.

[God judges the fallen angels in II Peter 2:4.]

famine (FAMM-un)

is the lack of food to eat. This can be caused by a lack of rain. Joseph interpreted Pharaoh's dream, which told of a famine that was coming to Egypt. Naomi went to the country of Moab because of a famine in Israel. Elijah stopped the rain. This caused a famine in Samaria for three and a half years. Elijah met a widow who was running out of food. God had a miracle for the widow. He did not let her grain bin or bottle of oil run out until the famine was over.

[Elijah causes a famine in I Kings 17:1 and 18:2.]

fast (FAST)

is to not eat. Fasting separates a person from the things of the world. This is done to get closer to God. Fasting is also done to show sorrow when something bad happens. Fasting is usually done with prayer. Jesus said that fasting should be a private thing.

[Jesus tells us how to fast in Matthew 6:16–18.]

father (FA-ther)

is the male parent. Honor thy father and thy mother is one of the Ten Commandments. God the Father cares for His people.

[Honor your father and mother is listed in Exodus 20:12.]

fatherless (FA-ther-less)

refers to children whose fathers have died. The fatherless and widows were to be taken care of under the Mosaic Law. This was done by the rules for gleaning crops. The harvest was to leave a portion of each crop for the fatherless to glean.

[The fatherless were allowed to glean in Deuteronomy 24:17–21.]

fault (*FAULT*)

means blame or guilt. Jesus stood trial in Pilate's court. Pilate said he found no fault in Jesus. Pilate sentenced Jesus to death anyway.

[Pilate finds no fault in Jesus in John 18:38–19:6.]

favour (*FAY-ver*)

is to be pleased with. Esther found favour in the sight of the king. The king made her his queen. Mary found favour with God. She gave birth to the Messiah.

[Mary found favour with God in Luke 1:28–31.]

Esther found favour in the eyes of the king.

fear (*FEER*)

is to be scared. Jonah fled from God by leaving on a boat. A big storm came up. The men became fearful. They threw Jonah over the side. Jesus walked on the water during a storm. He walked to the boat that held the disciples. The men in the boat thought He was a ghost. They were fearful.

[Jesus causes men to fear in Matthew 14:24–27.]

The tempest caused fear in Jonah and the others on the ship.

feast (*FEEST*)

is a big meal. Most of the holy days were celebrated with a feast. Weddings also had a day of feasting. It was at a wedding feast that Jesus performed His first miracle. The Last Supper was one of the feasts of the Passover.

[The disciples get ready for a feast in Matthew 26:17–19.]

A feast is a big meal.

Felix (*FEEL-icks*)

was the Roman ruler of Judea. Paul was arrested in Jerusalem and taken to Felix. Felix kept Paul in jail for two years. Felix was hoping to get money to release Paul.

[Felix wanted money to free Paul in Acts 24:26–27.]

fellowship (*FELL-oh-ship*)

is time spent with friends. Christians are to share and help other believers. Christians also have fellowship with God and Jesus.

[Fellowship is important to the believer in I John 1:3–7.]

Christians have fellowship with Christ.

Satan throws fiery darts at the believer.

A fig tree provided Adam and Eve with their first clothing.

To be filthy is to be unclean and dirty.

A firkin is about ten gallons.

Festus *(FESS-tus)*

was a Roman ruler of Judea. He replaced Felix. Paul was a Roman citizen. Paul appealed to Rome. Festus sent Paul to Caesar.

[Festus sends Paul to Rome in Acts 25:12.]

fiery *(FIRE-ee)*

refers to something that is burning. Elijah saw fiery chariots. Shadrach, Meshach, and Abednego were thrown into a fiery furnace. God judged His people with fiery serpents. Satan throws fiery darts at the believer.

[God's armor protects against fiery darts as shown in Ephesians 6:11–17.]

fiery serpents *(FIRE-ee SER-pents)*

were used to bite the Israelites. They were called fiery because of the poison in their bite. It burned and caused people to die. God sent the fiery serpents to punish the Israelites for complaining. The only cure was found in looking at the brasen serpent.

*[Fiery serpents are sent in Numbers 21:6. See **brasen serpent**.]*

fig tree *(FIG TREE)*

is a type of fruit tree. A fig tree provided Adam and Eve with their first clothes. They sewed fig leaves together.

[Fig leaves are used for the first clothes in Genesis 3:7.]

filthy *(FILTH-ee)*

refers to something that is unclean and dirty. God demands us to be perfect and holy. Sin keeps us from being perfect. Our very best is like filthy rags to God. That is how God sees our righteousness.

[The best we can present to God is like filthy rags as shown in Isaiah 64:6.]

firkin *(FER-kin)*

was a liquid amount of about ten gallons. The waterpots at the wedding of Cana held two or three firkins of water. These firkins of water became firkins of water. It was Jesus' first miracle.

[Firkins of water are filled in John 2:3–9.]

firstborn *(FIRST-BORN)*

is the first son born to a couple. The firstborn was dedicated to God. The birthright of a firstborn son included twice the amount given to other sons. The firstborn of clean animals belonged to the Lord. The last plague of Egypt before the exodus killed firstborn sons. The Lord killed the firstborn son on all doors in Egypt not marked with the blood of a lamb.

[The Lord killed the firstborn son in Exodus 12:29–30.]

firstfruit *(FIRST-FROOT)*

is the first crop harvested. Firstfruits also means the best. These were dedicated to God. Firstfruits supported the priests. The tribe of Levi had no land inheritance. They depended on the gifts from the other tribes. The giving of the firstfruits was part of these gifts.

[The giving of the firstfruits was part of the Mosaic Law as shown in Exodus 23:19.]

fish *(FISH)*

is one of the animals that lives in the sea. Jonah was thrown into the sea. He was swallowed by a big fish. Fish was also one of the foods the Israelites ate. Jesus took some small fish and fed thousands of people with them.

[Jesus does a miracle with fish in Matthew 14:17–21.]

fisherman *(FISH-er-mun)*

is someone who catches fish. Fishermen went out into the lake in boats and lowered their nets. Lifting the nets out of the water would trap any fish in the area. They emptied their nets into the boat. Jesus promised to make Peter and Andrew fishers of men.

[Jesus met two fishermen in Mark 1:16–17.]

Firstborn is the first child of a couple.

The first part of the harvest is called the firstfruits.

Jonah was swallowed by a big fish.

A fisherman is someone who catches fish.

Two cherubim guard the entrance to Eden with a flaming sword.

A flock is a group of sheep or goats.

God sent the Flood to destroy evil.

Moses struck a rock and water flowed out of it.

flaming sword (FLAME-ing SORD)

is a fiery weapon used by angels to guard the entrance to the Garden of Eden. God threw Adam and Eve out of the garden. Cherubim and a flaming sword were put at the entrance to keep Adam and Eve from going back into the garden.

[A flaming sword is found in Genesis 3:24.]

flee (FLEE)

is to run away. The Hebrews fled from Egypt. Joseph, Mary, and Jesus fled from Herod. Obeying God will cause the Devil to flee from you.

[The Devil will flee from you as shown in James 4:7.]

flesh (FLESH)

is the skin and meat of animals and people. Adam and Eve were created as fleshly human beings. Flesh also refers to the things of the world. Christians are to walk in the Spirit not the flesh.

[We are not to live in the flesh as shown in Romans 8:8–10.]

flock (FLOCK)

is a group of sheep or goats. A shepherd takes care of his flock. Peter called the church the flock of God. Jesus is called the Good Shepherd.

*[Peter says to feed the flock in I Peter 5:1–4. See **Good Shepherd**.]*

Flood (FLUDD)

was the water that covered the world. God had it rain forty days and nights. The fountains of the earth opened up. The waters of the Flood were above the highest mountain. God sent the Flood to destroy evil. Those inside the ark were the only ones saved. The Flood was on the earth for over one year.

[The Flood is recorded in Genesis 7:11–8:13.]

flow (FLOW)

is the moving of a liquid. Moses struck a rock. Water flowed out of it. The Promised Land was a land of plenty. It is said to be flowing with milk and honey.

[Water flows from a rock in Exodus 17:5–6.]

follow (FAH-low)

is to go after. Israel is to follow and obey God. God wants us to follow Christ. Jesus said to each of his disciples, "Follow me."

[Jesus tells Peter and Andrew to follow Him in Matthew 4:18–20.]

fool (FOOL)

is someone who is not wise. The fool has said in his heart there is no God. The preaching about Jesus is foolish to the world.

[Foolishness and wisdom are found in I Corinthians 1:18–25.]

foot washing (FOOT WASH-ing)

was an old custom in Jesus' time. Feet got dirty quickly for anyone who was barefoot or wore sandals. Feet were washed before entering the house. It was done by a servant or slave. Jesus washed His disciples' feet. This showed that He came as a servant.

[Jesus washes feet in John 13:4–15.]

forbid (for-BID)

means to not allow. The fruit of the Tree of Knowledge of Good and Evil was forbidden. Jesus said that children are not to be forbidden to come to Him.

[No one is forbidden to come to Christ as shown in Mark 10:13–16.]

foreknowledge (FORE-NAH-luj)

refers to knowing things before they happen. God is the only one with foreknowledge. God knew Jesus was going to be crucified.

[God's foreknowledge of the cross is told in Acts 2:21–24.]

foresee (for-SEE)

is to be able to see something before it happens. This is part of foreknowledge. God is the only one who can foresee things.

[See foreknowledge.]

To follow is to go after someone.

Only a fool says, "There is no God."

Foot washing cleaned the feet before entering the house.

Adam and Eve were forbidden to eat of the Tree of Knowledge.

To forgive is to cancel a debt.

Peter had forsaken everything to follow Jesus.

Jesus called Lazarus to come forth.

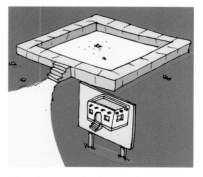

Foundation is the base of the building.

foretell *(for-TELL)*

is to tell what is to happen. This is the same as prophecy. God knows the future. He tells us things before they happen. Those things have been foretold. God foretold many things. He said the Messiah was to be born of a virgin. He told us that the Messiah was to be killed because of our sin.

[The death of the Messiah was foretold in Psalm 22.]

forgive *(for-GIVE)*

is to cancel a debt or give a pardon. Sin has a big debt. This debt is eternal separation from God. Jesus became a sacrifice for sin. Only God has the power to forgive sins. God forgave our sin because of what Jesus did on the cross. Christians are to forgive others.

[Jesus says that we are to forgive in Matthew 6:14–18.]

form *(FORM)*

is the shape of something. The world was without form and empty during the first day of creation. There was no shape to the earth until the second day of creation.

[The earth was without form in Genesis 1:1–8.]

forsake *(for-SAKE)*

is to give up or leave. God does not forsake his people. Peter forsook everything he had to follow Jesus. Jesus said he would inherit eternal life.

[Peter forsakes all to follow Jesus in Matthew 19:27–29.]

forth *(FORTH)*

is to go forward. Lazarus had been dead four days. Jesus told Lazarus to come forth. Lazarus came forth.

[Lazarus came forth from the grave in John 11:14–44.]

foundation *(foun-DAY-shun)*

is the base or bottom of a building. God built the foundation of the world. Christ's teaching is a rock-solid foundation. Jesus is the foundation of the church.

[There is only one foundation for the church as shown in I Corinthians 3:9–11.]

frankincense (FRANK-in-SENSE)

is the type of incense burned in the Holy of Holies. It was also put on the offering bread called shewbread. Frankincense comes from a tree. Frankincense was a gift to Jesus from the wise men.

[Frankincense is burned in the Holy of Holies as shown in Exodus 30:7.]

Frankincense comes from the sap of trees.

free will offering (FREE WILL OFF-er-ing)

is a gift to God. This form of giving was more than the tithe. The Tabernacle was constructed using free will offerings. Free will offerings were also given at Pentecost.

*[Free will offerings for the Tabernacle was recorded in Exodus 35:29. See **tithe**.]*

Free will offerings were given at the Temple.

friend (FREND)

is someone you like and trust. Abraham was a friend of God. A friend of the world is an enemy of God. Christians are not to make friends with the world.

[Christians are to be friends with God in James 4:4–8.]

A friend is someone you like.

fruit (FROOT)

is the product from trees. Adam and Eve were not allowed to eat the fruit from the Tree of Knowledge of Good and Evil. They could eat any other fruit in the garden.

[Adam and Eve eat fruit they were not supposed to in Genesis 3:1–7.]

fruit of the Spirit (FROOT of the SPEER-ut)

are things that result from a godly life. Some fruits of the Spirit are love, joy, and peace.

[The fruit of the Spirit is described in Galatians 5:22–23.]

Fruit comes from a tree.

To fulfill is to complete a task.

Furnaces are made of brick and stone.

fulfill (full-FILL)

is to complete a task or promise. God made a lot of promises to Israel. The promise of a Messiah was fulfilled in Jesus. Jesus will come back to set up His kingdom. This will fulfill other promises of God.

[Jesus fulfilled the prophecy of the virgin birth found in Isaiah 7:14.]

furnaces (FURN-uh-suz)

are used to hold fires. Furnaces are made of brick or stone. They were used to melt metal or make bricks and pottery. The king threw Shadrach, Meshach, and Abednego into the fiery furnace.

[The Hebrews are thrown into a fiery furnace in Daniel, Chapter 3.]

fury (FYU-ree)

is the same as wrath.

*[See **wrath**.]*

Gabriel (GABE-ree-ul)

is an angel and was God's messenger. Gabriel brought Daniel the meaning of his dream. Gabriel announced the birth of John the Baptist to Zacharias and Elisabeth. The coming birth of Jesus was announced to Mary by Gabriel.

*[Mary met Gabriel in Luke 1:26–38. See **angel**.]*

The angel Gabriel announced the coming of Christ to Mary.

Gad (GAD)

was the seventh son of Jacob. He was the Father of the tribe of Gad. His mother was Leah's maid Zilpah. The tribe of Gad settled east of the Jordan River. They owned large numbers of livestock.

[The birth of Gad is recorded in Genesis 30:9–11.]

Galatia was a province of the Roman Empire.

Galatia (guh-LAY-shuh)

was a Roman province. Galatia is located in central Asia Minor. Paul visited Galatia several times.

[Paul and Timothy visited Galatia in Acts 16:6.]

Galatians, Epistle to the (guh-LAY-shuns, uh-PIS-ul to the)

was a letter written to the Jewish church of Galatia. They were still teaching the law of Moses. Paul said that faith was the only thing needed to worship God.

[Paul shows the meaning of the law and faith in Galatians, Chapter 3.]

Galilee (GAL-uh-LEE)

was a northern province of Israel. Jesus and most of his disciples were from Galilee. Jesus spent most of His earthly ministry in Galilee.

[Jesus taught, preached, and healed in Galilee as recorded in Matthew 4:23–25.]

Galilee was a province of the Roman Empire.

Gamaliel was Paul's teacher of Jewish Law.

There was peace in the garden of Eden.

Jesus prayed in the garden of Gethsemane.

Grandfathers, fathers, and sons are from different generations.

Galilee, Sea of (GAL-uh-LEE, SEE of)

is a freshwater lake in northern Palestine. The Jordan River empties into it. Much fishing was done on the Sea of Galilee. Jesus walked on the water of this sea.

[Jesus takes an unusual walk in Matthew 14:22–33.]

Gamaliel (guh-MALE-ee-ul)

was an important teacher and doctor of Jewish law. The Pharisees and priests wanted to kill the apostles. Gamaliel said to leave them alone. He said that nothing would come of the apostles' teaching unless God was in it. Gamaliel was also Paul's teacher.

[Gamaliel gave advice to the priests in Acts 5:33–40.]

garden of Eden (GARD-un of EED-un)

was Adam and Eve's first home. The garden was an area where flowers, vegetables, and fruit trees were grown. It was pleasing to the sight. It was designed and planted by God. Adam and Eve were to take care of the garden.

[The first garden is described in Genesis 2:8–3:24.]

garden of Gethsemane (GARD-un of geth-SEM-uh-nee)

was located on the Mount of Olives. Jesus went many times to pray in this garden. Jesus was also arrested in the garden of Gethsemane.

[The arrest of Jesus is told in Mark 14:32–52.]

Gaza (GAH-zuh)

was a Philistine city on the coast of the Mediterranean Sea. Samson died in Gaza when he collapsed the Philistine temple.

[Samson pulls down the temple pillars in Judges 16:21–30.]

generation (jenn-er-AY-shun)

is the period of time one person lives. A generation is also everyone living at the same time.

Jesus called the Pharisees an evil generation. They killed Jesus.

[Jesus judges the wicked generation in Matthew 12:38–45.]

Genesis *(JEN-uh-sus)*

means beginning. It is also the name of the first book of the Bible. Genesis tells about the beginning of all things.

[God tells us how He created all things in Genesis, Chapter 1.]

gentiles *(JEN-tylez)*

are any people who are not Jewish. All the Jews did not accept Jesus as the Messiah. The Gospel was then offered to the gentiles. Paul was the preacher of the Gospel to the gentiles.

[The Gospel goes to the gentiles in Acts 13:46–48.]

Jesus and three disciples went to the Garden of Gethsemane.

Gethsemane *(geth-SEM-uh-nee)*

was a garden on the Mount of Olives. Gethsemane means olive press. Jesus went to Gethsemane after the Last Supper. Judas led the enemies of Jesus to Gethsemane. Jesus was arrested there and taken away for trial.

[Jesus was arrested at Gethsemane in Luke 22:39–53.]

Og was the tallest giant recorded in the Bible.

giant *(JYE-unt)*

is a large person. Og was the tallest giant recorded. He stood about thirteen feet tall. Giants had great strength and power. Goliath was a Philistine giant. David killed Goliath with a smooth stone.

[Goliath's last battle is found in I Samuel, Chapter 17.]

Gibeon *(GIB-ee-un)*

was a city on a hill. It was north of Jerusalem. The people of Gibeon lied to the Israelites. The Gibeonites made a treaty with Joshua. Joshua promised to protect them. Joshua discovered the truth. He made the Gibeonites water carriers and woodcutters.

[The lie of the Gibeons is listed in Joshua, Chapter 9.]

The people of Gibeon made a treaty with Joshua.

Gideon

Gideon put out a lamb skin as a test.

Gilead is an area of mountains east of the Jordan River.

To gird up one's loins is to tuck the robe up into the belt or apron.

Gideon *(GID-ee-un)*

was a judge of Israel. He was also called Jerubaal. Gideon was the son of Joash. He was of the tribe of Manasseh. Gideon was not a willing volunteer. Gideon put out a lamb's skin two times to test God's will.

[Gideon breaks pots to beat the Midianites in Judges 6:11–8:35.]

gift *(GIFT)*

is something given to someone. Christians are given a gift of eternal life. God also gives Christians spiritual gifts. Some of these are the gift of mercy and the gift of helping.

[God's greatest gift is listed in Romans 6:23.]

Gilead *(GIL-ee-add)*

is an area of mountains in north Israel. Gilead was given to the tribes of Reuben, Gad, and Manasseh. The balm of Gilead was a famous medicine. Joseph was sold as a slave to a trading caravan from Gilead.

[Joseph goes with the Gilead caravan in Genesis 37:23–28.]

gird up one's loins *(GIRD up one's LOINS)*

means to tuck the robe into the belt. Loins were girded to keep the robe out of the way. Loins were girded for running, for entering battle, or for working. Peter tells us to gird up the loins of our minds. This is to make sure our minds are always ready to follow God.

[Girding the mind is suggested in I Peter 1:13.]

girdle *(GIR-dul)*

is one of several items of clothing. It is a fancy sash worn by priests or rich people. It was a waistband for the High Priest's ephod. A girdle may also be a belt on which a sword or bow is carried.

[Jonathan gave his weapons and girdle to David in I Samuel 18:1–4.]

glad tidings *(glad TIDE-ings)*

is good news. The angels announced the birth of Jesus. This was a glad tiding. Glad tidings also refer to the Gospel. It is the good news that Jesus brought salvation. Glad tidings always brings great joy.

*[The glad tidings of the birth of Jesus was announced in Luke 2:8–11. See **Gospel**.]*

Angels announced the glad tidings of Jesus' birth to the shepherds.

gleaning *(GLEEN-ing)*

is to pick leftovers after the main harvest. Mosaic Law required leaving a portion of the harvest. The poor could have a way of earning a living by gleaning. Ruth met Boaz when she was gleaning in his field.

[Ruth gleans a barley field in Ruth, Chapter 2.]

To glean is to pick leftovers after a harvest.

glory *(GLOR-ee)*

is to give honor and praise. God has glory because He is perfect. God's glory shines like a bright light. After Moses was in the presence of God, he had to wear a veil because his face glowed with the glory of God.

[The glory of the Lord was with the angels in Luke 2:8–11.]

gnashing *(NASH-ing)*

is to grind the teeth. This was done when someone was very mad or hated someone. Extreme anger or pain is described as wailing and gnashing of teeth.

[Jesus said those who are separated from God will gnash their teeth in Matthew 13:36–43.]

Moses' face glowed with the glory of God.

God *(GOD)*

is the creator of all things. God is everywhere. He is a living God. God knows everything. God has always existed. God is eternal. God is perfect and holy. God hates sin. God is love. God gave His Son to die on the cross so we could live with Him forever.

[God gave His Son to save the world in John 3:16–18.]

Gnashing of teeth shows anger.

God the Father, God the Son, and God the Holy Spirit were present when Jesus was baptized.

The golden calf was a gold statue of a young bull.

Goliath was a giant.

God the Father (GOD the FA-ther)

is the first person of the Trinity. God the Father created all things. God the Father gave the Ten Commandments to Moses. The Father sent Jesus into the world to save it.

[God the Father sent His Son in I John 4:14–16. See **Trinity.**]

God the Holy Spirit (GOD the HO-lee SPEER-it)

is the third person of the Trinity. He is the Comforter. The Holy Spirit lives within a follower of Jesus. The Holy Spirit helps us to understand God's Word. He also guides and comforts His children.

[Jesus sent the Holy Spirit in John 14:23–26. See **Trinity.**]

God the Son (GOD the SON)

is the second person of the Trinity. God the Son is Jesus Christ. Jesus is all human and is all God. Jesus always existed. Jesus became flesh in Mary's womb. Jesus lived a perfect life. His death provided a perfect sacrifice for our sin. Jesus is the Saviour of the world. Followers need only to believe that He was God and that He died for our sins. Eternal life in heaven is the gift that God gives when you do this.

[Jesus became flesh in John 1:1–14. See **Trinity.**]

God's will (GOD's WILL)

is the desire of a perfect God. Being a follower of Jesus is part of God's will for man. God does not want any to perish. God's will is good and perfect.

[God's will is described in Romans 12:2.]

godliness (GOD-lee-ness)

is to live within God's will. Godly people obey God's commandments. Christians are to live godly lives.

[Paul reminds us to live godly lives in Titus 2:1–4.]

golden calf (GOLD-un CAFF)

was a gold statue of a young bull. This was the image of a false God. The Israelites gave Aaron their gold earrings. Aaron built the golden calf. All Israel worshipped this idol.

[The story of the golden calf is recorded in Exodus 32:1–35.]

golden rule *(GOLD-un RULE)*

was a command given by Jesus. It states that you are to do to others as you would like them to do to you. Followers of Christ obey this rule.

[The golden rule is listed in Matthew 7:12 and Luke 6:31.]

Golgotha *(GOL-guth-uh)*

is the same place as Calvary. It means the place of the skull. Golgotha is where Jesus was crucified.

[See Calvary.]

Goliath *(guh-LYE-uth)*

was a giant. He was over nine feet tall. He was a soldier for the Philistines. Goliath mocked Israel. David killed Goliath using a sling.

[Goliath's last battle is found in I Samuel, Chapter 17.]

Gomorrah *(guh-MORE-uh)*

was a wicked city. It was located on the south part of the Dead Sea. God destroyed Sodom and Gomorrah because they were evil. God rained down on these cities with fire and brimstone.

[See Sodom.]

gone astray *(gone uh-STRAY)*

means to wander and get lost. Sheep tend to go astray. A shepherd is needed to keep them together. People tend to go astray from God. But God is a Good Shepherd. He makes sure His flock is taken care of.

[Isaiah talks about going astray in Isaiah 53:6.]

Good Samaritan *(good suh-MARE-uh-tun)*

is the only person to stop and help a man who was beaten. A priest did not help the battered man. The scribe did not stop either. But the Good Samaritan made sure that the beaten man was cared for. This

God destroyed Gomorrah because it was evil.

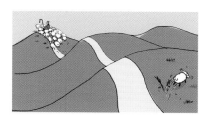

Gone astray is to become lost.

The Good Samaritan was the only person to help a man who was beaten.

good shepherd

Noah used gopher wood to build the ark.

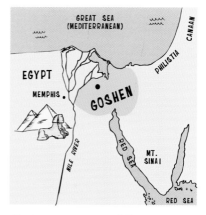

Goshen was a part of Egypt.

Gospel means good news.

was a parable given by Jesus. This story asked the question, "Who is our neighbor?" The parable says that anybody who needs help is our neighbor.

[The parable of the Good Samaritan is told in Luke 10:29–37.]

good shepherd (good SHEP-erd)

is someone who loves and tends his sheep. A bad shepherd lets his sheep get lost or eaten by wolves. The Lord is the Good Shepherd. He takes care of all our needs. He also guides and protects us.

[A song about the Good Shepherd is Psalm 23.]

gopher wood (GO-fer WOOD)

is the kind of wood that Noah's ark was built with. Nothing else is known of this wood.

[See Noah's ark.]

Goshen (GO-shun)

is part of Egypt. It is the land where the Israelites lived. Goshen is also a country where the Israelites entered into Canaan.

[Joseph gives the land of Goshen to the Hebrews in Genesis 45:10.]

Gospel (GOS-pul)

means good news. It is the story of the birth, the death, and the resurrection of Jesus. It is good news because Jesus overcame sin. It is good news because we can have everlasting life. There are four books called the Gospels. These are Matthew, Mark, Luke, and John. They are called the Gospels because they talk about the life of Christ.

[Paul was not ashamed of the Gospel as shown in Romans 1:16–17. See grace.]

grace (GRACE)

is the undeserved favor God gives to us. People are condemned by sin. God is holy. The whole world deserves to be separated from God. God accepts Christians because of the Gospel of Jesus. This is the grace of God.

[Jesus is the way to God's grace as recorded in Romans 3:23–24. See Gospel.]

grave *(GRAVE)*

is a pit or cave in which a dead body is buried. Another word for grave is tomb. Jesus was buried in the garden tomb of Joseph of Arimathea.

[Joseph puts the body of Jesus in a tomb in John 19:38–42.]

Grave is a pit or cave for keeping dead people.

grave clothes *(GRAVE CLOTHES)*

were long strips of linen cloth. These were wrapped around the body before burial. Myrrh and other ointments were also placed on the body. A square piece of cloth was sometimes placed over the face. Jesus resurrected Lazarus. He had trouble getting out of the tomb because the grave clothes were tight.

[Jesus tells the people to loose the grave clothes of Lazarus in John 11:38–44.]

Strips of linen and ointments were used for grave clothes.

graven image *(GRAY-vun IMM-uj)*

is an idol made of wood, stone, or metal. The Second Commandment tells us not to make graven images. We are to worship only the living God.

[See idol.]

Great Sea *(GRATE SEE)*

is another name for the Mediterranean Sea. It was much larger than the Sea of Galilee or the Dead Sea. The Great Sea was one border of the inheritance God promised Israel.

[The Great Sea was the western border of the Promised Land as shown in Ezekiel 47:13–21. See Mediterranean Sea.]

The picture on a coin was sometimes a graven image.

great white throne *(GRATE WITE THRONE)*

is the seat of God when He judges the nations. The great white throne is located in heaven. Those who do not accept the Gospel will stand before the great white throne. Unbelievers are separated from God forever.

[The great white throne is used for judgment in Revelation 20:11–15.]

The Mediterranean Sea was called the Great Sea.

Greek

A Greek is someone who lives in Greece.

People that grieved sometimes sat on an ash pile.

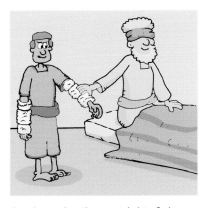

Jacob used guile to trick his father.

Greek (GREEK)

is someone who lives in Greece. It is another word used for gentile. Greek refers to anyone who is not Jewish. Paul was the Apostle to the gentiles.

*[See **gentiles**.]*

grieve (GREEVE)

is to cry and be sad when someone dies. Some people grieved by tearing their clothes and sitting in ashes. Others wore sackcloth or shaved their heads. Sometimes they poured ashes on their heads. Paul reminds Christians not to grieve the Holy Spirit. This means that we are to live godly lives and avoid sin.

*[God comforts us in grief as shown in II Corinthians 1:3–4. See **ashes**.]*

guile (GUY-ul)

is craftiness or deceitfulness. Jacob pretended to be his brother, Esau. Jacob wore Esau's clothes and put goatskins on his arms. Isaac gave Jacob the blessing intended for Esau. Jacob used guile to trick his father.

[The guile of Jacob is recorded in Genesis 27:6–29.]

Habakkuk (HAB-uh-kook)

was a prophet of God. He lived at the same time as Jeremiah. He was a priest of the tribe of Levi.

[A prayer made by Habakkuk is recorded in Habakkuk 3:1–19.]

Habakkuk, Book of (HAB-uh-kook, Book of)

is written to show that God is in control of all things. The wicked may do well for a little while. Habakkuk lets us know that God will punish evil. We will be honest and not worship idols if we love God.

[The foolishness of worshipping idols is shown in Habakkuk 2:18–20.]

Abraham sent Hagar and Ishmael into the wilderness.

Hagar (HAY-gar)

was the servant of Sarah. Hagar was a concubine of Abraham and became the mother of Ishmael. God promised Abraham a son from his wife Sarah. Abraham had a son by Hagar because he did not fully trust God. Sarah became jealous of Hagar and Ishmael. She had Abraham send them away into the wilderness.

*[Hagar talks to an angel of God in Genesis 16:7–16. See **Ishmael**.]*

Haggai (HAG-eye)

was a prophet of God. He lived at the same time as Zechariah. He is a prophet of the Temple. Haggai helped to finish building the Temple.

[Haggai saw the finished Temple in Ezra 6:14–15.]

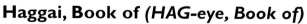

Haggai finished building the Temple.

Haggai, Book of (HAG-eye, Book of)

was written to inspire the Israelites to finish building the Temple. Doing good works is part of obeying and worshipping God.

[The Israelites obeyed God in Haggai 1:12–14.]

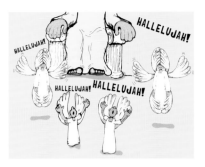

Angels in heaven sing "Hallelujah!"

Ham was Noah's second son.

Haman wanted to kill all of the Jews.

Hannah prayed for a child.

hallelujah *(hal-uh-LOO-yuh)*

means "Praise Yahweh!" or "Praise God!" It is the Old Testament version of alleluia.

*[See **alleluia**.]*

hallow *(HAL-low)*

means to set apart for holy use. It is the same as dedicating something to God. Jesus said that God's name was to be hallowed. This is found in the Lord's Prayer.

[The Lord's Prayer says that God's name is to be hallowed in Matthew 6:9–15.]

Ham *(HAM)*

was Noah's second son. Ham saw Noah naked and drunk. His brothers, Shem and Japheth, covered Noah. Noah knew what Ham had done. Noah gave a curse to Canaan the son of Ham.

[The sin of Ham is found in Genesis 9:20–27.]

Haman *(HAY-mun)*

was an important worker for King Ahasuerus. Haman hated the Jews. He wanted to kill all Jews. Queen Esther found out his evil plan. King Ahasuerus was angry when Queen Esther told him the plot. The king killed Haman instead.

[Haman's death is recorded in Esther 7:7–10.]

Hannah *(HAN-uh)*

was married to Elkanah. She did not have any children so she prayed to God. She asked God to give her a son and promised to give him back to God. She gave birth to Samuel. Hannah gave Samuel to the High Priest Eli of the Shiloh sanctuary to work for God. Hannah also gave birth to other sons and daughters.

[Hannah keeps her promise to give her son to the Lord in I Samuel 1:24–28.]

Haran *(huh-RON)*

was a brother of Abraham and the father of Lot.

Haran is also a city in Mesopotamia. Abraham lived in Haran for a while. Abraham's father died in Haran.

[Abraham left Haran in Genesis 12:1–5.]

hardness of the heart (HARD-ness of the HART)

is a stubborn attitude that does not accept God's grace. Pharaoh hardened his heart. He refused to let the Israelites go. We are not to harden our hearts. We are to hear and obey God.

[One of the many times Pharaoh hardened his heart was in Exodus 8:8–15.]

Pharaoh hardened his heart and would not let the Hebrews leave.

harlot (HAR-lot)

is a woman who sells herself to men. Rahab was a harlot in Jericho. She saved the Israelite spies by hiding them on her roof. Joshua saved her and her family when Jericho was destroyed.

[Rahab the harlot saves the spies in Joshua, Chapter 2.]

harp (HARP)

was a musical instrument. It was made of wood. It had about twelve strings. The harp was one of the instruments in the Temple. Harps of today are different than the ones mentioned in the Bible.

[The instruments of the Temple are listed in II Chronicles 29:25–27.]

A harp is a musical instrument.

hart (HART)

is an adult male deer. Our desire for God should be like the thirst of a hart for water.

[A hart's thirst is described in Psalm 42:1.]

A hart is an adult male deer.

harvest (HAR-vest)

is to gather the crops. Wheat, grapes, and olives are common things that were harvested. Jesus spoke of a different harvest. It was the harvesting of souls.

[Jesus needs more people to help with the harvest in Matthew 9:35–38.]

hate (HATE)

is to dislike something very much. Jesus was hated

To harvest is to gather a crop.

The head is the top part of the body.

Peter healed a lame man.

Samuel heard the voice of the Lord.

David was a man after God's own heart.

by many of the religious leaders. God hates sin and idolatry. John tells us that hating another person is as bad as murder. We are not to hate other people.

[John tells us to love our brother in I John 4:16–21.]

hath *(HATH)*

means to have or own. The followers of Christ have eternal life.

[John records who hath eternal life in I John 5:11–12.]

head *(HED)*

is the top part of the body. Head is also the person in charge. Christ is the head of the church. Sadness was shown by putting ashes on the head. Wagging the head mocked or made fun of someone.

[Paul tells us that Jesus is the head of the church in Colossians 1:18.]

heal *(HEEL)*

is to cure sick people. Jesus healed many people during His ministry. Jesus spoke to or touched sick people to heal them. The apostles also healed the sick.

[Peter heals a lame man in Acts 3:1–10.]

hear *(HEER)*

is to listen to the words of another. Jesus used stories to teach His followers. Unbelievers would not understand His stories and teachings.

[Jesus talks about hearing in Mark 4:10–13.]

hearken *(HARK-un)*

means to hear.

*[See **hear**.]*

heart *(HART)*

is the center of the emotions such as love and joy. David was a man after God's own heart. Paul said that a person must believe in the heart to be saved. Christ wants to live in your hearts.

[We can have eternal life by believing with our heart that God raised Jesus from the dead as shown in Romans 10:9–10.]

heaven *(HEV-un)*

is the place above the earth and seas. It is also the home for God and His angels. Jesus promised a heavenly home for His followers.

[Jesus prepares a place in heaven for us in John 14:2–3.]

heavenly Father *(HEV-un-lee FA-ther)*

is the same as God the Father. We have an earthly father and mother. God lives in heaven. He is our heavenly Father.

[The heavenly Father has the power to forgive in Matthew 6:6–15.]

Hebrew *(HEE-broo)*

was a child of Eber. Hebrew is first used for Abraham's family. Anyone related to Eber is a Hebrew. Hebrew is also the language for most of the Old Testament books.

[Hebrew is one of the languages written on the sign on the cross as recorded in John 19:19–20.]

Hebrews, Epistle to the *(HEE-brooz, uh-PIS-ul to the)*

is a New Testament book written to the Jews. Hebrews tells us that Jesus is now our High Priest. It also shows that the Jewish sacrifices were temporary. The sacrifice of Jesus completes God's redeeming work.

[The sacrifice of Jesus is explained in Hebrews 10:4–14.]

heed *(HEED)*

means the same as hear.

*[See **hear**.]*

heir *(AIR)*

is a person who inherits property. Jesus will inherit the entire world when He returns. Christians are to be heirs with Jesus.

[The promise to be an heir with Jesus is found in Romans 8:16–17.]

hell *(HELL)*

is the place where people are separated from God. It is a place for punishment. The ungodly

Heaven is the final home for followers of Christ.

Hebrew is the language of the Old Testament.

Heirs receive property.

Soldiers wore different kinds of helmets.

A woman was healed by touching the hem of Jesus' robe.

A herdsman cares for cattle.

King Herod ordered that babies were to be killed.

and demons are thrown into hell forever.

[The ungodly are separated from God in Revelation 20:10–15.]

helmet *(HEL-mut)*

is a metal hat. Soldiers wear helmets to protect their heads. The armour of God includes the helmet of salvation.

[The armour of God is listed in Ephesians 6:13–17.]

hem *(HEM)*

is the edge of a robe. The hem of the High Priest's robe had gold bells. This was so that the other priests could hear him moving in the Holy of Holies. A woman was healed by touching the hem of Jesus' robe.

[A sick woman touches the hem of Jesus' robe in Luke 8:43–48.]

herdsman *(HERDS-mun)*

is the keeper of cattle. Abraham and Lot were herdsmen. Jacob tended the cattle for himself and his father-in-law. Jacob had a large increase in his cattle.

[Jacob was a herdsmen in Genesis 30:29–31.]

heritage *(HAIR-uh-tuj)*

is the things given to you by your family. This is the same as a birthright. The Promised Land is Israel's heritage from God. Children and the Mosaic Law are also heritages.

[The Promised Land was given as a heritage in Genesis 15:18–21.]

Hermon, Mount *(HERM-un, MOUNT)*

is located north of Israel.

*[See **Mount Hermon.**]*

Herod *(HAIR-ud)*

was king of Judea when Jesus was born. He was also known as Herod the Great. Herod gave the orders to kill the babies of Bethlehem two years old and under. Herod feared the birth of Jesus, the King of the Jews.

[Herod talks to the wise men about baby Jesus in Matthew 2:1–8.]

Herod Antipas *(HAIR-ud ANN-tuh-pus)*

was the son of Herod the Great and also a king of Judea. He promised a dancing woman anything in his kingdom. The dancer wanted the head of John the Baptist. Herod Antipas killed John to keep his promise. Jesus also appeared before him during one of His trials.

[Herod Antipas makes an ungodly promise in Mark 6:21–28.]

Hezekiah prayed to God to be healed.

Hezekiah *(hez-uh-KYE-uh)*

was a King of Judah. Hezekiah destroyed idols in the Temple. Hezekiah was sick and almost died. He prayed to God, and God healed him. God allowed Hezekiah to live fifteen more years.

[Hezekiah was allowed to live longer in Isaiah 38:1–50.]

high place *(HYE PLACE)*

is the top of a hill or mountain. They were used as places for idols. High places were located in a garden or among some trees. The Israelites were told to destroy the high places of the Canaanites.

[Moses tells Israel to destroy the high places of the Canaanites in Deuteronomy 12:1–3.]

Idols were kept in high places.

High Priest *(HYE PREEST)*

is the same as Chief Priest.

*[See **Chief Priest**.]*

hind *(HYND—rhymes with find)*

is a female deer or doe.

[A wife is to be like a loving hind according to Proverbs 5:19.]

holy *(HOE-lee)*

is to be whole and pure. God is holy. Holy is also to be set apart for God's use. Israel was a holy nation. God had selected Israel to be separated from the world. Christians are called to holy living.

[Christians are called to be holy in I Peter 1:15–16.]

Holy Ghost *(HOE-lee GOWST)*

is the same as God the Holy Spirit.

*[See **God the Holy Spirit**.]*

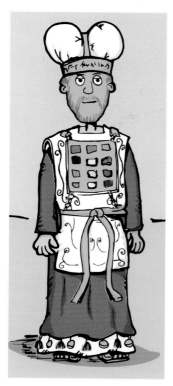

The High Priest was in charge of all the other priests.

103

Holy of Holies

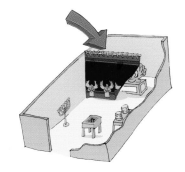

The Holy of Holies was where the Ark of God was kept.

Samson found honey in a dead lion.

To honour is to show respect.

Hophni and his brother took the Ark of God into battle.

Holy of Holies (HOE-lee of HOE-leez)

is the innermost room of the Tabernacle or Temple. The Holy of Holies is also called the most holy place. It was separated by a thick curtain. The Holy of Holies had the presence of Yahweh or God. The Holy of Holies contained the Ark of God. Only the High Priest could enter the Holy of Holies. The Holy of Holies could be entered only on the Day of Atonement.

[The Holy of Holies is described in Exodus 26:31–35.]

Holy Spirit (HOE-lee SPEER-ut)

is the same as God the Holy Spirit.

*[See **God the Holy Spirit**.]*

honey (HUN-ee)

is a sweet fluid made by bees. The Promised Land is called the land of milk and honey. Honey is also part of a riddle made by Samson. Samson had killed a lion. Bees made a nest inside the dead lion. Samson got honey out of this nest. Samson made this into a riddle for the Philistines.

[Samson's riddle can be found in Judges 14:11–14.]

honour (AHN-er)

is to respect someone. God is worthy of honour and glory. One of the Ten Commandments says that we are to honour our father and mother.

[The commandment to honour our parents is found in Exodus 20:12.]

hope (HOPE)

is to expect that God will fulfill His promises to us. The Lord is our hope and salvation.

[God gives us hope in I Peter 1:18–21.]

Hophni (HOFF-nee)

was a son of Samuel. He was a priest of Israel, but he was a wicked man. He and his brother, Phinehas, took the Ark of God into battle. The

Philistines won the battle. Both of Samuel's sons were killed, and the Ark of God was taken.

[The death of Hophni is found in I Samuel 4:3–11.]

Hor, Mount *(HOR, MOUNT)*

is a mountain located in the country of Edom.

*[See **Mount Hor.**]*

hosanna *(hoe-ZANN-uh)*

means, "Pray, save us!" This was the cry of the people as Jesus entered Jerusalem. They were looking for a kingly Messiah.

[Hosanna was shouted in Mark 11:9–10.]

People cried "Hosanna!" as Jesus entered Jerusalem.

Hosea *(hoe-ZAY-uh)*

was a prophet of God. Hosea lived at the same time as the prophets Isaiah and Micah. Hosea gave prophecies to Jeroboam, king of Israel.

[Hosea is called by God to be a prophet in Hosea 1:1–2.]

Hosea, Book of *(hoe-ZAY-uh, Book of)*

is about Israel's disobeying God. Hosea's wife did not honor their marriage. He said Israel was like his wife. Israel did not honor God. Israel had begun to worship idols and make friends with the wicked. God said He would bless the nation if they would obey Him.

[Hosea asks the nation to return to God in Hosea 14:1–9.]

Elisha and his servant looked at the heavenly host.

host of heaven *(HOST of HEV-un)*

is the army at God's command. This army is also called a heavenly host. Elisha asked God to show his army to his servant. Their eyes were opened to the spiritual world. They could then see that the mountains were filled with the host of heaven.

[Elisha's prayer is heard in II Kings 6:14–17.]

household *(HOUSE-HOLD)*

means all the members of a family. It also refers to the home they lived in. The early church met in

One of the early churches met in the household of Lydia.

Huldah

Huldah explained Scripture to the king.

Kneeling while praying to God is part of being humble.

Hunters catch or trap animals.

The husbandman took care of the crops.

households. Many households came to be followers of Christ.

[Lydia and her household became Christians in Acts 16:14–15.]

Huldah (HULL-duh)

was a prophetess. She was the wife of Shallum. The king of Judah found a copy of the Book of the Law. King Josiah talked with Huldah. She said that God was going to judge the nation of Judah.

[King Josiah met with Huldah in II Kings 22:14–20.]

humble (HUHM-bul)

refers to someone who puts others first. Many blessings are promised to those who are humble. We are to be humble when talking to God. Jesus was humble: He became a man and died on the cross.

[The humility of Jesus is recorded in Philippians 2:6–8.]

hunter (HUN-ter)

is a person who kills game for food or pleasure. Some of the famous hunters are Nimrod, Ishmael, and Esau. The tools of the hunter include bows and arrows, nets, snares, or pits.

[Nimrod is called a mighty hunter in Genesis 10:8–9.]

husband (HUZ-bund)

is the male partner in a marriage. Husbands are to give honor to their wives. Christ loves the church. He gave Himself for the church. This is the way a husband is to love his wife.

[Paul tells husbands how to treat their wives in Ephesians 5:25–31.]

husbandman (HUS-bund-mun)

is one who tills the soil. It is the same as a farmer. Farming was important to Israel. A good husbandman cared for his crop. Plowing, pruning, planting, and harvesting were some of the tasks of a husbandman.

[James says that a husbandman needs to be patient in James 5:7–8.]

Hushai *(HOO-shy)*

was David's friend. He belonged to the tribe of Benjamin. David sent him to Absalom. This gave David time to gather his army.

[Hushai talks with Absalom in II Samuel 17:5–14.]

hymn *(HIM)*

is a song of praise to God. The Book of Psalms is a hymn book. Paul and Silas sang hymns in prison. Jesus and His disciples sang a hymn at the end of the Last Supper.

[Jesus and the disciples sang a hymn and went to the Mount of Olives in Matthew 26:30.]

Paul and Silas sang hymns in prison.

hypocrites *(HIP-uh-critts)*

are people who pretend to be something they are not. This applies to people pretending to be followers of Christ. Jesus said hypocrites were like dishes that were clean on the outside and dirty on the inside. Hypocrites try to find fault with others. They ignore their own mistakes.

[Jesus talks of hypocrites in Matthew 23:13–39.]

Hypocrites do the same things they tell others not to do.

hyssop *(HIS-sup)*

was a plant used to purify the Temple. A sponge on top of a hyssop was used to offer vinegar to Jesus on the cross.

[A hyssop is used at the cross of Jesus in John 19:28–29.]

A hyssop was used to offer Jesus some vinegar.

I Am

I Am is the name God used when talking with Moses.

I Am (I AM)

is one name God calls Himself. God has many names. Moses talked to God at the burning bush. The I Am is the name God gave to Moses. Jesus used this title many times in the Gospel of John. This name tells us that God has always existed.

[God reveals His name in Exodus 3:13–14.]

Iconium (eye-KOH-nee-um)

is a city in Asia Minor. Barnabas and Paul preached the Gospel at Iconium. The Jews from Antioch and Iconium stoned Paul. They dragged him outside the city and left him for dead.

[Paul is stoned in Iconium in Acts 14:19–21.]

idle (EYE-dul)

is the same as slothful or lazy.

*[See **slothful**.]*

Paul was stoned at Iconium.

idols (EYE-duls)

are objects of worship. Idols are also called graven images. Idols are made of wood, stone, or metal. The Ten Commandments warn us about idols. We are not to make graven images. We are not to bow down before idols. The Israelites sometimes worshipped idols. One time was when Aaron made a golden calf. This was an idol to a false god.

[The Israelites were warned about idol worship in Exodus 20:3–5.]

idolatry (eye-DOLL-uh-tree)

is the worship of an idol. This is forbidden by the Mosaic Law.

*[See **idols**.]*

Idols are images used for false worship.

image *(IMM-uj)*

is the likeness of something. A graven image is an idol. It is an image of a false god. People are made in the image of God. We were created with a soul, a body, and a spirit.

[God created man in His image in Genesis 1:26–27.]

An image is the likeness of something.

Immanuel *(im-MAN-you-ul)*

means "God with us." It is the Old Testament version of Emmanuel.

*[See **Emmanuel.**]*

immorality *(im-mor-AL-uh-tee)*

is a sin against God.

[Paul warns against immorality in I Corinthians 6:15–20.]

To impute is to take something from one person and to give it to another.

immortal *(im-MORT-ul)*

is to never die. This is the same as eternal life.

*[See **eternal life.**]*

impute *(im-PYUTE)*

is to take something from one person and give it to another. Sin was imputed from Adam to all people. God imputed righteousness to Abraham and David because of their faith. Jesus imputes righteousness to all His followers.

[God imputes righteousness in Romans 4:6 and 22.]

Incarnation was when Jesus became human.

incarnation *(in-car-NAY-shun)*

is God becoming human. Jesus is God. Jesus always existed. The incarnation of Jesus began when Mary became pregnant. Jesus had the same emotions we have. He wept, loved, hungered, and thirsted. Jesus even died. John says that the Word was made flesh and dwelt among us. This is the incarnation of Christ.

[The incarnation of Christ is shown in John 1:14.]

incense *(IN-SENSE)*

is a group of sweet-smelling spices that are burned. Incense was an important part of the sacrifices

Zacharias talked to Gabriel while burning incense.

The altar of incense was a place to burn incense.

made by the Israelites. The smoke that went upward was a picture of our prayers and requests going upward to heaven. The High Priest Zacharias was burning incense in the Temple when the angel Gabriel visited him.

[Aaron was told to burn incense in Exodus 30:7–8.]

incense, altar of *(IN-SENSE, AL-ter of)*

is a golden altar where incense was burned.

*[See **altar**.]*

incorruptible *(in-cor-RUPT-uh-bul)*

refers to someone who remains good and pure. God will give His children a new body. The new body will be incorruptible.

[Paul talks of the day Christians get an incorruptible body in I Corinthians 15:42–54.]

increase *(in-CREESE)*

is to grow in size or number. John the Baptist said that he must decrease and the Messiah must increase. God gives the increase for the Gospel.

[Paul wants Christians to increase in love and faith as shown in I Thessalonians 4:9–12.]

Increase means to grow.

indignation *(in-dig-NAY-shun)*

is the same as wrath.

*[See **wrath**.]*

inherit *(in-HAIR-it)*

is the transfer of property after death. Sons or daughters have their father's inheritance. Many people asked Jesus how to inherit eternal life. Jesus said that those who follow Him shall inherit eternal life.

*[Jesus shows how eternal life is inherited in Matthew 19:27–30. See **birthright**.]*

iniquity *(in-ICK-wuh-tee)*

is the same as sin.

*[See **sin**.]*

Inheritance is the transfer of property when someone dies.

inn *(INN)*

is a place to stay when traveling. Joseph and Mary had to travel to Bethlehem to be taxed by Caesar. Lots of people came into town to be taxed. There was no room in the inn for Joseph and Mary. One innkeeper let them stay in his stable. This is where Jesus was born.

[There was no room at the inn for Joseph and Mary in Luke 2:1–7.]

There was no room at the inn for Joseph and Mary.

inscription on the cross *(in-SCRIP-shun on the CROSS)*

are the words of the sign put on the cross by Pilate. It said, "JESUS OF NAZARETH THE KING OF THE JEWS." It was written in three different languages. These languages were Greek, Latin, and Hebrew. This was to allow all the people who had traveled to Jerusalem for the Passover to read who was on the cross. The priests wanted Pilate to change the words to "He said I am king of the Jews." Pilate refused.

[The inscription of the sign is recorded in John 19:19–22.]

The inscription on the cross of Jesus said, "King of the Jews."

inspiration *(in-spuh-RAY-shun)*

is the act of God leading His people to write each of the books of the Bible. All Scripture is given to us by the inspiration of God. Only God can tell us about God. God is the only witness to the creation of the universe. God has a plan to save people from sin. These things can be revealed only by God. This is called the inspiration of God.

[Paul talks about the inspiration of Scripture in II Timothy 3:16.]

The Bible was written from inspiration from God.

instruct *(in-STRUCT)*

is to teach. Jesus taught in the synagogues. Jesus told his disciples to teach the Gospel to all the nations. Apollos was instructed in the way of the Lord by Priscilla and Aquila. Timothy was instructed in the scriptures by his mother and grandmother.

[Apollos was instructed in Acts 18:24–28.]

Jesus instructed in the synagogues.

Interpretation is to give the meaning of a saying.

An angel kept Abraham from sacrificing Isaac.

Isaiah listened to the voice of the Lord.

intercession (in-ter-SESH-un)

is going between two people. The Holy Spirit goes between God and people. The Holy Spirit makes intercession for our prayers. Jesus makes intercession with God for our sins.

[The intercession of the Holy Spirit and Jesus is shown in Romans 8:26–34.]

interpretation (in-ter-pruh-TAY-shun)

is the meaning of a saying or dream. Daniel gave an interpretation of a dream to the king. He also interpreted the writing on the wall. Joseph interpreted a dream of the Pharaoh. God gave these men the correct interpretations. The Scripture is to be of no private interpretation. This means that all of the Scriptures on a subject are to be looked at together and not separately.

[The idea of no private interpretation is found in II Peter 1:20.]

Isaac (EYE-zuk)

was the only son of Abraham and Sarah. God promised Abraham and Sarah that they would have a son. Abraham was one hundred years old when Isaac was born. Sarah was ninety years old. God told Abraham to offer Isaac as a sacrifice. Abraham obeyed God. God stopped Abraham and provided a ram for the sacrifice. Isaac married Rebekah.

[Abraham is told to offer Isaac as a sacrifice in Genesis 22:1–14.]

Isaiah (eye-ZAY-uh)

was a prophet of God. Isaiah preached the promise of the Messiah. He also talked of the coming kingdom and the fulfillment of God's promises.

[Isaiah is called to be a prophet in Isaiah 6:1–8.]

Isaiah, Book of (eye-ZAY-uh, Book of)

is a book of salvation in the Old Testament. The Israelites were captives in Babylon at the time. Isaiah gave prophecies of the surrounding kingdoms. He also told of the coming Messiah.

[Isaiah said that the Messiah would be born of a virgin in Isaiah 7:14.]

Ishbosheth (ish-BOH-sheth)

was the son of King Saul. Abner made Ishbosheth king of Israel for two years. But Ishbosheth was never anointed king by a priest of Israel. He was murdered by his own captains. David became the true King of Israel.

[Ishbosheth is made king in II Samuel 2:8–10.]

Ishmael (ISH-muh-el)

was the son of Abraham by his concubine Hagar. Ishmael and his mother fled from the camp of Abraham. They were afraid of Sarah. An angel visited Hagar and told her that Ishmael would be a great nation. The Arabs came from Ishmael.

[An angel visited Hagar in Genesis 16:7–14.]

Ishmaelite (ISH-muh-lite)

is someone of the tribe of Ishmael. The Ishmaelites are known today as Arabs.

[See **Ishmael** or **Arabia**.]

Israel (IZ-ray-el)

was another name for Jacob. God changed Jacob's name after he wrestled with an angel. Israel is the name for the Hebrew people led by Moses. Israel split into two nations when King Solomon died. The northern kingdom was called Israel. Ten tribes of Israel made up the new nation of Israel. The southern kingdom was known as Judah.

[Jacob is called Israel in Genesis 32:24–28. See **Jacob**.]

Israel, Twelve Tribes of (IZ-ray-el, TWELVE TRIBES of)

are the tribes that began with the twelve sons of Jacob.

[See **Tribes of Israel**.]

Israelite (IZ-ruh-lite)

is one who lives in Israel.

[See **Israel**.]

Abner made Ishbosheth king of Israel.

Ishmael was the first son of Abraham.

An angel changed Jacob's name to Israel.

Issachar

Issachar was one of the Twelve Tribes of Israel.

Issachar (ISS-uh-car)

was the ninth son of Jacob. His mother was Leah. He began the tribe of Issachar. The tribe of Issachar was in the north part of Palestine. One of the judges for Israel, Tola, was of the tribe of Issachar.

*[The birth of Issachar is recorded in Genesis 30:17–18. See **Tribes of Israel**.]*

Jacob wrestled with the angel.

Jabin (JAY-bun)

was king of Hazor. Jabin was the leader of those who attacked Joshua at the water of Merom. Jabin sent Sisera to fight the army of Deborah and Barak. Jabin and Sisera were defeated and killed. Jabin lost power.

[Jabin's general is defeated in Judges 4:2–16.]

Jacob (JAY-kub)

was the son of Isaac and Rebekah. He was the younger of his twin brother Esau. Jacob bargained for Esau's birthright. Jacob tricked Isaac into giving him the blessing meant for Esau. Jacob worked seven years to marry Rachel. He was tricked into marrying Rachel's older sister, Leah. He worked another seven years to marry Rachel. Jacob wrestled with an angel. God changed his name to Israel. Jacob was the father of twelve sons. These sons became the leaders of the twelve tribes of Israel.

[Jacob is born holding on to his brother's foot in Genesis 25:21–26.]

Jacob's Ladder was a vision unto heaven he saw at Bethel.

Jacob's Ladder (JAY-kub's LAD-er)

is a vision Jacob had at Bethel. There was a ladder going from earth to heaven. Angels were using this ladder. The Lord was at the top of this ladder. The Lord spoke and promised to give land to Jacob and his family.

[The Lord speaks with Jacob in Genesis 28:10–15.]

Jacob's well (JAY-kub's WELL)

is a place in Samaria where Jesus stopped to rest. He offered a Samaritan woman living water. Jesus said she would never thirst after

Jesus offered living water at Jacob's well.

Sisera slept in the tent of Jael.

Jahweh is one of the ways to pronounce the Hebrew name for God.

Jesus healed the daughter of Jairus.

James became the leader of the Jerusalem church.

taking the living water. Jesus said He was the living water.

[Jesus offers living water in John 4:5–14.]

Jael (JAY-ul)

was the woman who killed Sisera. Sisera was the general of the Canaanite army. Deborah and Barak defeated his army. Sisera fled into her tent. Jael killed Sisera when he was asleep. Jael was praised in the Song of Deborah.

[Jael kills Sisera in Judges 4:18–22.]

Jahweh (YAH-weh)

is the name of God. Jahweh means the same as Yahweh.

*[See **Yahweh**.]*

Jairus (JAIR-us)

was a synagogue official. He came to Jesus. Jairus wanted Him to heal his twelve-year-old daughter. The little girl died before Jesus got there. Jesus raised her from the dead.

[Jairus wanted Jesus to heal his daughter in Mark 5:22–23.]

James, Epistle of (JAMES, uh-PIS-ul of)

is a New Testament book written to Jewish believers. James says that good works are important for the believer. Faith without good works is dead. James teaches the practical part of being a Christian.

[James shows his faith by his good works in James 2:17–18.]

James, the half brother of Jesus (JAMES, the half BRO-ther of JEE-zuz)

wrote the New Testament epistle of James. James was one of the elders of the Jerusalem church. James replaced Peter as the leader of the Jerusalem church.

[James becomes leader of the Jerusalem church in Acts 21:17–18.]

James, the son of Alphaeus (JAMES, the son of al-FEE-us)

was one of the Twelve Disciples. Nothing else is said about this James. This may be "James the younger." His mother, Mary, was among the women at Jesus' crucifixion and at the open tomb.

[James, the son of Alphaeus, was given power by Jesus in Matthew 10:1–3.]

James Zebedee saw the transfiguration of Jesus.

James, the son of Zebedee (JAMES, the son of ZEB-uh-dee)

was one of the disciples. James, Peter, and John were the closest disciples to Jesus. Jesus called James and John the sons of thunder. James was present when Jesus raised Jairus' daughter from the dead. He witnessed the transfiguration of Jesus. James went with Christ to the Garden of Gethsemane.

[James, the son of Zebedee, was called to follow Jesus in Matthew 4:18–22.]

Jason paid the bail for Paul and Silas.

Jason (JAY-sun)

was a follower of Paul and Silas. Jason lived in Thessalonica. The Jews were angry at Paul's preaching and arrested Paul and Silas. The Jews made Jason give them bail money before they released Paul and Silas.

[Jason listens to the Gospel in Acts 17:1–9.]

Samson used a jawbone as a weapon.

jawbone of an ass (JAW-BONE of an ASS)

was a weapon in the hand of Samson. Samson killed one thousand Philistines using this jawbone.

[Samson uses a jawbone for a club in Judges 15:15–17.]

jealousy (JELL-uh-see)

is a hateful desire to have the things that someone else has. Joseph's brothers were jealous. They sold their brother into slavery. Christians are to avoid jealousy. Jealousy can also be a demand to be faithful. God is a jealous God. He does not allow the worship of false gods. God is

Joseph's brothers sold him into slavery because they were jealous of him.

Jehoiachin

Jehoiada had the king rebuild the Temple.

jealous for His people, Israel. Israel's enemies are His enemies.

[Jealousy was the reason Joseph is sold into slavery in Genesis 37:11–27.]

Jehoiachin *(juh-HOY-uh-kun)*

was the son of Jehoiakim. Jehoiachin became king of Judah when he was eighteen years old. He ruled only three months before being taken captive by King Nebuchadnezzar of Babylon.

[Jehoiachin became king in II Kings 24:6–15.]

Jehoiada *(juh-HOY-uh-duh)*

led a battle against Queen Athaliah. She had taken the throne of Judah. Joash was made king at the age of seven. Jehoiada was part of the king's council. Jehoiada had the king restore the Temple. King Joash became a bad king when Jehoiada died.

[Jehoiada leads the battle against the queen in II Kings 11:13–16.]

Jehoiakim cut out the parts of Jeremiah's prophecy he did not like.

Jehoiakim *(juh-HOY-uh-kim)*

was the son of Josiah. Jehoiakim became king of Judah. Judah had been conquered by Egypt. Jehoiakim was the name given to him by the Pharaoh. His original name was Eliakim. Jehoiakim took the prophecy of Jeremiah. He cut out the parts he did not like and threw them into the fire. God told Jeremiah to rewrite the prophecy and to include a curse on Jehoiakim.

[Jehoiakim cuts up the prophecy of God in Jeremiah 36:18–30.]

Jehovah *(juh-HOE-vuh)*

is a name for God. It means the same as Yahweh.
*[See **Yahweh**.]*

Jehu *(JEE-hoo)*

was the son of Jehoshaphat. Jehu became king of Israel. Elisha the prophet had him anointed as king at Ramoth-gilead. Jehu killed the wicked

King Jehu destroyed the worship of Baal.

Queen Jezebel. Jehu destroyed the worshipping of Baal in Israel.

[Jehu is anointed king in II Kings 9:1–4.]

Jeremiah (jair-uh-MYE-uh)

was a prophet and priest of Israel. He was the son of Hilkiah. He is known as the weeping prophet. Jeremiah was exiled to Egypt by Jewish officers. He announced that God's judgment was coming to Judah and Jerusalem. Jeremiah also told of the blessings for Judah if they obeyed God.

[The word of the Lord came to Jeremiah in Jeremiah 1:2.]

Jeremiah wept for Jerusalem.

Jeremiah, Book of (jair-uh-MYE-uh, Book of)

is an Old Testament book about the evil in Judah. Judah was to be judged for sin. They were to be taken captive for seventy years. Jeremiah wept for Judah. God promised to deliver them if they obeyed Him.

[Judah can find God as shown in Jeremiah 29:10–14.]

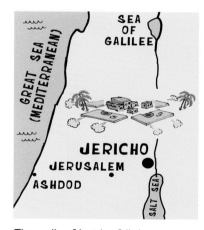

Jericho (JAIR-uh-koe)

was the first city Israel conquered under Joshua. Jericho is located next to the Jordan River. Jericho was like the Garden of Eden. Joshua had the Israelites march around the city for six days in a row. They marched around Jericho seven times on the seventh day. The walls fell when they shouted and blew the trumpets.

[Jericho's walls fall in Joshua 6:1–21.]

The walls of Jericho fell down.

Jeroboam (jair-uh-BOE-um)

was the first king of the northern kingdom. The prophet Ahijah from Shiloh gave ten pieces of his torn coat to Jeroboam. This told him that he was to rule over ten of the twelve tribes. Jeroboam led the ten tribes to revolt when King Solomon died. Jeroboam became king of Israel. He was a wicked king.

[Jeroboam gets pieces of a coat in I Kings 11:29–39.]

Jeroboam got ten pieces of cloth from Ahijah.

Jerusalem

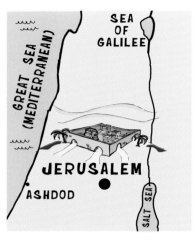

Jerusalem was the capital of Israel.

Jerusalem began the very first church.

Jesse had eight sons.

Jethro was a Median priest.

Jerusalem (juh-ROO-suh-lum)

is a city conquered by King David. Jerusalem is also called Zion, Mount Moriah, and the City of David. It is located next to the Mount of Olives. Jerusalem was made the capital of Israel. King Solomon built the Temple in Jerusalem. The Ark of God was moved into the Temple. Jerusalem became the religious center of Israel.

[King Solomon builds the Temple in Jerusalem as recorded in I Kings 6:1–9.]

Jerusalem, Church of (juh-ROO-suh-lum, CHURCH of)

was the first church. This church began with Pentecost. Peter and the other eleven disciples were the leaders of this church. The church of Jerusalem grew very rapidly. Three thousand men, plus many women and children, became Christians during one occasion.

[The Twelve Disciples select seven men to help minister to the Jerusalem Church in Acts 6:1–7.]

Jesse (JESS-ee)

was the father of eight sons. David was the youngest son. Jesse was the grandson of Boaz and Ruth. He was from the tribe of Judah and lived in Bethlehem.

[Jesse sends David with lunch for his brothers in I Samuel 17:17–18.]

Jesus (JEE-zus)

is the Son of God.

[See God the Son.]

Jesus Christ (JEE-zus CRYSTE)

is the Son of God.

[See Son of God.]

Jethro (JETH-roe)

is the father-in-law of Moses. Jethro was a Median priest. Moses tended the sheep for Jethro while in exile.

[Moses is a shepherd in Exodus 3:1.]

Jew (JOO)

is another name for Hebrew. Jew is short for Judah.

[Jews from around the world came to Jerusalem in Acts 2:5.]

Jezebel (JEZ-uh-bell)

was the wife of King Ahab. Queen Jezebel was wicked. She worshipped Baal. Queen Jezebel tried to kill all the prophets of God. Obadiah saved one hundred prophets from her by hiding them in a cave. Queen Jezebel tried to kill the prophet Elisha.

[Queen Jezebel kills the prophets of God in I Kings 18:4.]

Jezebel worshipped the idol Baal.

Jezreel (JEZ-ruh-el)

is a city north of Jerusalem. King Ahab and Queen Jezebel lived here. Naboth had a vineyard near their palace. The queen had Naboth killed. The king took Naboth's vineyard. Jezebel died in Jezreel.

[King Ahab takes Naboth's vineyard in I Kings 21:1–15.]

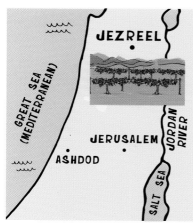

Jezreel is the location of Naboth's vineyard.

Joab (JOE-ab)

was King David's nephew. He was commander of David's army. David told Joab not to kill Absalom, David's son. Joab slew Absalom anyway. Joab rebelled when King David died. King Solomon ordered Joab to be killed.

[Joab kills David's son in II Samuel 18:9–15.]

Joab killed Absalom.

Job (JOBE)

was a man who lived in Uz. Satan was allowed to give pain to Job. Satan gave Job big sores. Satan had all his children killed. Satan had all Job's cattle and sheep killed. Job still worshipped and obeyed God. Job was blessed by God. God restored to Job twice what he began with.

[Job gets boils all over his body in Job 2:7.]

Job, Book of (JOBE, Book of)

is the oldest book in the Bible. It is an Old Testament book about Job. Satan claimed that

Job sat in sack cloth and ashes.

Job worshipped God only because of special favors. God allowed Satan to take all these favors away from Job. Job's life was to be spared. Satan gave Job sores all over his body. Satan killed all Job's children and cattle. Job still loved and trusted God. God restored to Job twice the riches he had before.

[God blessed Job in Job 42:9–17.]

Joel (JOE-ul)

was a prophet of God. The word of the Lord came to Joel. Nothing more is known about Joel.

[The word of the Lord came to Joel in Joel 1:1.]

Joel, Book of (JOE-ul, Book of)

is an Old Testament book written to the southern kingdom, Judah. Judah no longer obeyed and worshipped God. God sent locusts and a drought because of their sin. They still did not obey God. God allowed Judah to go into captivity. God still promises to deliver and bless those who obey Him.

[The plague of locusts are talked about in Joel 1:4–10.]

Fisherman John became an apostle of Jesus.

John Mark (JON MARK)

is another name for Mark. John Mark wrote the Gospel of Mark.

[See Mark.]

John, the apostle (JON, the uh-POSS-ul)

was the son of Zebedee. He was the brother of James. They lived in Galilee. John was a fisherman. John was called to be one of the Twelve Disciples.

[Jesus called John to be an apostle in Mark 1:17–20.]

John the Baptist was the one to baptize Jesus.

John the Baptist (JON the BAP-tist)

was the son of Zacharias and Elisabeth. John baptized Jesus in the Jordan River. John the Baptist preached repentance. He knew that Jesus was the Messiah. King Herod threw John in prison. The

king beheaded John the Baptist because of a promise he made to a dancer. Jesus said that John was the greatest of anyone ever born.

[John baptized Jesus in Matthew 3:13–17.]

John, Epistle of, I, II, and III (JON, uh-PIS-ul of, 1, 2, and 3)

are letters of the New Testament written for believers. These epistles show that God is Life, Light, and Love. John wants Christians to be in fellowship with each other. He also warns of false teachers.

[John talks of false teachers in I John 2:18–23.]

John, Gospel of (JON, GOS-pul of)

is a New Testament book about the life of Jesus. John shows that Jesus was the Son of God. The miracles recorded in John show that Jesus was God.

[God's love is shown in John 3:15–18.]

join (JOIN)

is to put or bring together. A man and a woman are joined in marriage. Jesus said that what God has joined together, let no one separate.

[Jesus talks of the joining of a marriage in Matthew 19:4–6.]

Jonah (JOE-nuh)

was the son of Amihai. Jonah was a prophet of God. God told him to go to Nineveh to preach. He went the other way to Tarshish. God sent a big fish to swallow Jonah. He was inside the fish for three days. The fish vomited him out. Jonah finally went to Nineveh and preached.

[The stories about Jonah can be found in the Book of Jonah.]

Jonah, Book of (JOE-nuh, Book of)

is a story of judgment in the Old Testament. God sent Jonah to tell the city of Nineveh of a coming judgment. Nineveh repented and obeyed God. God did not destroy Nineveh.

[God spares Nineveh in Jonah 3:3–10.]

A man and a woman are joined in marriage.

Jonah spent three days in the belly of a fish.

Jonathan

Peter raised Dorcas from the dead in Joppa.

Elisha was one of the people to part the waters of the Jordan River.

Joseph became a great leader in Egypt.

An angel visited Joseph.

Jonathan (JAH-nuh-thun)

was the son of King Saul. Jonathan and David were close friends. Jonathan saved David from being killed. Jonathan was killed by the Philistines.

[Jonathan is killed in battle in I Samuel 31:1–6.]

Joppa (JAH-puh)

was a town west of Jerusalem. Dorcas lived in Joppa. She got sick and died. Peter went to Joppa. Peter raised Dorcas from the dead. Many people became Christians because of this.

[Peter goes to Joppa in Acts 9:36–42.]

Jordan (JOR-dun)

is a river in Israel. The Jordan River flows from the Sea of Galilee to the Dead Sea. Joshua, Elijah, and Elisha parted the waters of the Jordan River in order to cross. Jesus was baptized in the Jordan River.

[John baptizes Jesus in the Jordan River in Matthew 3:13.]

Joseph (JOE-zuf)

was a young son of Jacob. Jacob loved Joseph the most of all his sons. Joseph was hated by his brothers. They sold Joseph into slavery and then told their father that Joseph had been killed. Joseph became a great leader in Egypt. He was able to save his family from a famine.

[Jacob sent his sons to buy corn from Joseph in Genesis 42:1–3.]

Joseph, husband of Mary (JOE-zuf, HUZ-bund of MAIR-ee)

was visited by an angel. The angel told him that Mary was carrying the Messiah. He also said that it was good for Joseph to take Mary as his wife. Joseph did as the angel had said.

[An angel visits Joseph in Matthew 1:19–24.]

Joseph of Arimathea (JOE-zuf of air-uh-muth-EE-uh)

asked for the body of Jesus from Pilate. Joseph

and Nicodemus put one hundred pounds of myrrh and aloes on the body of Jesus. Joseph wrapped the body of Jesus in clean linen. He laid Jesus in a new tomb and rolled a stone to cover the door.

[Joseph begs Pilate for the body of Jesus in Matthew 27:57–60.]

Joseph of Arimathea asked for Jesus' body from Pilate.

Joshua (JAH-shoo-uh)

was a prophet of God. He was one of ten spies Moses sent into Canaan. Joshua wanted to enter into the land that God promised them. Moses and the people of Israel did not enter the land. God punished them and sent them into the wilderness. Forty years later, Joshua became the leader of the Israelites and led them into Canaan. Jericho was the first city Joshua captured.

[Joshua sent spies into Jericho in Joshua, Chapter 2.]

Joshua, Book of (JAH-shoo-uh, Book of)

is the Old Testament record of Israel entering into the Promised Land. Joshua led the nation across the Jordan River on dry land. God gave Jericho to Israel. God shows us how to be successful in the battle of life.

[God encourages Joshua in Joshua 1:1–9.]

Joshua was one of the spies sent into Canaan.

Josiah (joe-ZYE-uh)

was King of Judah. King Josiah destroyed the idols in Judah. Josiah turned Israel back to God.

[Josiah obeys God in II Kings 23:3–20.]

jot (JOT)

is the smallest letter of the Hebrew alphabet. The jot is much like a period. Jesus said that every jot and tittle of each prophecy was to be fulfilled. This means that every detail was a promise of God and would become true.

[Jesus came to fulfill the law. This includes every jot and tittle as shown in Matthew 5:17–18.]

Jot is a small part of a Hebrew letter.

joy (JOY)

is happiness. Joy is one of the fruits of the Spirit.

Joy is what we feel when we rejoice.

Judah

Judah was a kingdom formed by two tribes.

Judah was one of Jacob's sons.

Judas Iscariot was paid thirty pieces of silver.

God gave us joy that no one can take from us.

[*Joy is promised from God in John 16:20–28.*]

Judah (JOO-duh)

was one of the twelve sons of Jacob. Judah is the father of the tribe of Judah. King David and the Messiah came from the tribe of Judah.

[*Jacob blesses Judah in Genesis 49:8–12.*]

Judah, Kingdom of (JOO-duh, KING-dum of)

is the southern nation formed by the tribes of Benjamin and Judah. The Kingdom of Judah was made when Jeroboam rebelled. This happened when King Solomon died. Judah went into captivity after Israel was conquered.

[*Judah is formed in I Kings 12:21–24.*]

Judas, half brother of Christ (JOO-dus, HAFF BRO-ther of CRYSTE)

was one of the Twelve Disciples. Judas wrote the Epistle of Jude. Judas is also called Jude.

[*Judas was one of Twelve Disciples as shown in Luke 6:16.*]

Judas Iscariot (JOO-dus iss-KAIR-ee-ut)

was one of the Twelve Disciples. Judas took care of the money for Jesus and the disciples, but he was evil. Judas sold Jesus for thirty pieces of silver. When he met Jesus in the Garden of Gethsemane, he betrayed Jesus with a kiss. Judas Iscariot hanged himself.

[*The death of Judas Iscariot is recorded in Matthew 27:3–5.*]

Jude (JUDE)

was another name for Judas, the half brother of Jesus.

[See ***Judas, half brother of Christ.***]

Jude, Epistle of (JUDE, uh-PIS-ul of)

is a New Testament letter written by Jude. Jude warns the Christian church against false teachings.

Christians are to help and pray for each other.

[Jude tells Christians to remain in the faith in Jude 3–4.]

Judea *(joo-DEE-uh)*

means the same as the Kingdom of Judah. It was also a province of Rome.

*[See **Judah, Kingdom of.**]*

Judea is a Roman province.

judge *(JUDGE)*

was the person who made decisions of Law. Israel was ruled by judges before they had a king. Gideon, Deborah, Samuel, and Samson were some of the judges God used.

[Samuel was the last judge as shown in I Samuel 8:1–5.]

Judges, Book of *(JUH-juz, Book of)*

is an Old Testament book recording the first years of Israel in the Promised Land. Israel did not have a king. Israel was ruled by priests and judges.

*[Judges ends with Israel disobeying God in Judges 21:24–25. See **judge.**]*

Deborah was one of the judges of Israel.

judgment seat *(JUDGE-ment SEET)*

is where decisions were made. A judge did not have lawful power until he was seated in the judgment seat. Everyone will stand before the judgment seat of Christ.

[The judgement seat of Christ is shown in II Corinthians 5:10.]

justify *(JUS-tuh-fie)*

is to be freed from guilt. People are guilty of sin. Jesus paid the penalty for our sin. We are justified before God if we are followers of Christ.

[The blood of Jesus justifies sinners as shown in Romans 5:8–10.]

Trials were held at the judgment seat of the city.

Kadesh-Barnea

Spies entered Canaan from Kadesh-Barnea.

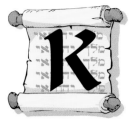

Kadesh-Barnea (KAY-desh bar-NEE-uh)

is the place the Hebrews stayed for thirty-eight years after leaving Mount Sinai. They were to enter the Promised Land from Kadesh-Barnea. Moses sent the twelve spies into Canaan from this place.

[Moses sent out spies from Kadesh-Barnea in Numbers 13:26–27.]

kindness (KIND-ness)

is a loving action. God is love. His kindness is shown by the grace He has offered to sinners. Kindness is one of the things a Christian is to show to others.

[Kindness and other graces of Christians are listed in Colossians 3:12–17.]

A king is the male ruler of a country.

king (KING)

is a male ruler of a country. God ruled Israel through prophets and judges. But the Israelites wanted to have a king. They wanted to be like the other nations. The prophet Samuel anointed Saul as the first king of Israel. The Jews thought Jesus was coming as a king when He entered Jerusalem. They sang "Hosanna" to their new king. Jesus came first to save the world from sin. Jesus will rule as king when He returns.

*[Jesus is greeted as a king in Matthew 21:1–9. See **Kingdom of God**.]*

Kingdom of God (KING-dum of GOD)

is the future rule of God over the Earth. Jesus preached about the Kingdom of God. When Jesus comes back again, He will rule the whole world. The lion and the lamb will be able to lie down together safely. Swords will be beaten into plowshares. There will be true peace everywhere.

Swords will be made into plows during the Kingdom of God.

Jesus died and rose from the dead on the third day. Jesus then went to heaven to prepare a place for believers. Jesus will set up the Kingdom of God when He returns.

[Jesus preached the Kingdom of God in Mark 1:14–15.]

King James Version *(KING JAMES verz-yun)*

is the translation of the Bible paid for by King James of England. It was completed in 1611. The King James Version is also called the Authorized Version. King James of England paid to have a group of scholars translate Scripture into English. These scholars were well educated and learned men. The result is a very accurate translation of the Hebrew, Aramaic, and Greek copies of the Scriptures.

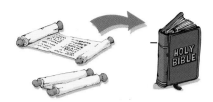

The King James Version is an English translation of the Bible.

Kings, Book of, I and II *(KINGS, Book of, I and 2)*

is a history of the kings of Israel and Judah in the Old Testament. I Kings is a record of King Solomon. Both books show that the sin of the nation comes from the king. Some of the kings were good. Other kings were evil. II Kings records the lives of the prophets Elijah and Elisha. The record of the kings ends when Israel and Judah are taken into captivity.

[The nation is divided into Israel and Judah in I Kings 12:16–20.]

kinsman redeemer *(KINS-mun ree-DEE-mer)*

is someone who buys back property for a relative. This was a duty of a relative by Jewish law and custom. A person may have sold property and land because of poverty. A kinsman, or someone related to the family, has the right to buy back that which was sold. Naomi's family had sold their property and moved to Moab. Ruth was a gentile but had married Naomi's son. Ruth's husband died. Ruth and Naomi moved back to Israel. Ruth met Boaz while she was gleaning his field. Naomi knew that Boaz was a kinsman. Boaz liked

Boaz became the kinsman redeemer for Ruth and Naomi.

Kirjath-Jearim

The Ark of God was returned to Kirjath-Jearim.

Mount Carmel is located near the Kishon River.

Judas betrayed Jesus with a kiss.

People kneel when praying to God.

Ruth and was willing to be a kinsman redeemer for Naomi and Ruth. This was done by marrying the widow of the kinsman. Boaz married Ruth. This restored property back to Naomi.

[Boaz became a kinsman redeemer in Ruth 4:9–12.]

Kirjath-Jearim (KER-ee-uth JAY-uh-rum)

is a city located north of Jerusalem. When the Philistines returned the Ark of God to Israel, it was kept at Kirjath-Jearim.

[The Ark of God is taken to Kirjath-Jearim by the Philistines in I Samuel 6:21–7:2.]

Kishon (KYE-shon)

is a small river that flows through the Valley of Jezreel. It was at Kishon that Deborah and Barak defeated the Canaanite Sisera. Kishon is also where Elijah killed the prophets of Baal.

[The battle of Kishon is recorded in Judges 4:13–16.]

kiss (KISS)

is the touching of the lips to another person. A kiss was a sign of friendship, respect, and honor. A holy kiss was given by the early Christians when they met. Judas betrayed Jesus with a kiss.

[Judas kissed Jesus in the Garden of Gethsemane in Matthew 26:47–49.]

kneel (NEEL)

is to go down on one or both knees. People kneeled when receiving a blessing. Kneeling is also done to show honor and respect. Kneeling was done before a king or when worshipping God. Daniel and Peter kneeled when they prayed.

[Peter kneels in prayer in Acts 9:40.]

Knowledge, Tree of (NAH-luj, TREE of)

was one of the special trees in the Garden of Eden. It is also known as the Tree of Knowledge of Good and Evil.

[See **Tree of Knowledge of Good and Evil.**]

Korah (KOR-uh)

was a leader of an uprising against Moses and Aaron. Israel was in the wilderness of Paran. Korah, Dathan, and Abiram led the revolt against Aaron and Moses. They claimed they had no need for priests. They could do the sacrifices themselves. God caused the earth to open. It swallowed the leaders and their property. A fire from the Lord destroyed the other rebels.

[Korah turns against God in Numbers 16:1–35.]

Korah was swallowed up by the ground.

Laban

Jesus is the Lamb of God.

The names of those going to heaven are in the Lamb's Book of Life.

Laban (LAY-bun)

was Rebekah's brother. He was the father of Leah and Rachel. After Jacob tricked Esau from his birthright, he fled to his Uncle Laban's house. Laban agreed to give his daughter, Rachel, as payment for Jacob's seven years of work. Laban tricked Jacob into marrying the older daughter, Leah. Jacob worked a second seven years to marry Rachel.

[Laban makes Jacob work fourteen years to marry Rachel in Genesis 29:15–30.]

Lamb of God (LAM of GOD)

is one of the names for Jesus. John the Baptist identified Jesus as the Lamb of God who takes away the sin of the world. Isaiah said the Messiah would be an offering for sin. The law for sin offerings prescribed a lamb for atonement to be made before the Lord. The Passover lamb was slain at the sixth hour of the day. This was the same time that Jesus died on the cross.

[The time of Jesus' death is shown in Mark 15:23–37.]

Lamb's Book of Life (LAM's BOOK of LIFE)

is the record of everyone who is a follower of Jesus. The Book of Life is first mentioned in Psalm 139:16. God checks the names of those who are not in the Lamb's Book of Life. They are not allowed into heaven and are separated from God forever.

[The Lamb's Book of Life is opened in Revelation 13:8.]

lame (LAME)

is to be unable to walk. Jesus and the apostles healed lame men. Peter heals a lame man at the

Jesus healed the lame man.

Temple. Many people became Christians when they saw this miracle. The priests arrested Peter for healing the lame man.

[Peter heals the lame man in Acts 3:1–10.]

To lament is the same as having grief.

lament *(luh-MENT)*

is the same as to grieve.

*[See **grieve**.]*

Lamentations, Book of *(lam-in-TAY-shuns, Book of)*

is an Old Testament book about the exile of Israel. Lamentations is written like a song for a funeral. Jeremiah weeps for the nation. Jeremiah wanted to see Israel restored. He prays for mercy from God for the nation.

[Jeremiah offers a prayer of mercy in Lamentations, Chapter 5.]

lamp *(LAMP)*

was a metal or clay bowl that held olive oil and a wick. The wick was made out of twisted flax. The bowl had a pinched spout to hold the wick. The lamp gave a bright light. This was the lighting used inside the homes of the Israelites. Jesus gave a parable of the ten bridesmaids. Five of them had oil for their lamps. They were wise and ready for the bridegroom. The five foolish bridesmaids did not have oil for their lamps. This story tells us to be ready for the return of Jesus. Jesus is the light of the world. God's word is a lamp for the godly.

[God's word is a lamp as shown in Psalm 119:105.]

Lamps were used for light.

lampstand *(LAMP-STAND)*

was a golden lamp used inside the Temple. The lampstand was made out of one piece of gold. It had three branches from both sides and one in the middle. It is also called a menorah or candlestick.

[The golden lampstand is made of gold in Exodus 25:31–40.]

The temple sanctuary was lit by a golden lampstand.

The Promised Land is called the land of milk and honey.

The final meal Jesus ate was the Last Supper.

Lavers are bowls used by priests for washing.

The Ten Commandments and the Torah are called the law.

land of milk and honey (LAND of MILK and HUH-nee)

is another name for the Promised Land.

[See **Promised Land.**]

Last Days (LAST DAYS)

is the time just before the return of Jesus. Jesus will then set up the Kingdom of God. The last days will be filled with wickedness. It will become like the days of Noah.

[Jesus says the last days will be like the days of Noah in Matthew 24:36–41.]

Last Supper (LAST SUPP-er)

is the name given to the Passover meal eaten by Jesus and the Twelve Disciples. It was the last meal Jesus ate before He was crucified. The Last Supper was held in a large furnished room called an upper room.

[The disciples eat the Last Supper in Mark 14:12–25.]

laver (LAY-ver)

is a large bowl used in the Temple. The bronze laver of the Tabernacle was made from metal mirrors given by the Jewish women. The bronze laver was also called the molten sea. The priests washed in the molten sea. Ten smaller lavers were used for washing sacrifices.

[The making of the lavers is shown in Exodus 30:18–21.]

law (LAW)

is a rule that is to be obeyed. Moses gave many laws to the Israelites. The Ten Commandments were some of these. The law is also called the Torah. Jesus came to fulfill the law. Paul showed that the law was given for a good purpose. He also showed that the law could not save. Jesus is the only one who can save.

[Paul talks of the law in Galatians 3:10–13.]

Law of Moses *(LAW of MOE-zuz)*

is the law given to the Israelites by Moses. It is also called the Mosaic Law.

*[See **Mosaic Law**.]*

laying on of hands *(LAY-ing on of HANDS)*

was a way of showing faith in God. The priest laid his hands on the sacrifice. This was to show that sin was being placed on the animal. The animal died because of this sin. Laying on of hands was a way the church ordained and healed people.

[Priests are to lay hands on the sin offering in Leviticus 4:14–21.]

Priests were to lay their hands on the offering.

Lazarus *(LAZ-uh-rus)*

was a person in a parable told by Jesus. Lazarus was sick and poor. The rich man did not help Lazarus. Lazarus died and went to heaven. The rich man died and was tormented in hell. The rich man wanted water, but Lazarus could not help. There is a big gap between the two places. This parable warns the selfish that justice will be done.

[The rich man cries out for water in Luke 16:19–31.]

A sick Lazarus sat outside the gate of the rich man.

Lazarus of Bethany *(LAZ-uh-rus of BETH-uh-nee)*

was a close friend of Jesus. When Lazarus was sick, Martha sent for Jesus to heal her brother. Lazarus died before Jesus arrived in Bethany. Lazarus had been in the tomb for four days. Jesus went to the tomb of Lazarus and raised him from the dead. This shows the power of God.

[Jesus raised Lazarus from the dead in John 11:1–44.]

Leah *(LEE-uh)*

was the older daughter of Laban. Jacob worked seven years to marry Rachel, but Laban tricked Jacob into marrying Leah. Jacob would work another seven years to marry Leah's sister, Rachel. Jacob and Leah had six sons.

[Leah is married to Jacob in Genesis 29:21–28.]

Jesus raised Lazarus from the dead.

To lean is to rest on something.

Leaven is what makes bread rise.

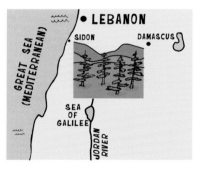

Cedars of Lebanon were used to build the Temple.

Leprosy is a disease that shows white spots on the skin.

lean (LEEN)

is to rest on something. We are to trust in God. We are not to lean on our own understanding. God promises to guide us in our lives.

[We are not to lean on our own understanding as shown in Proverbs 3:5–6.]

leaven (LEV-un)

is what makes bread rise. It takes time for leaven to raise the dough. The Israelites were in a hurry to leave Egypt. There was no time for leavening the bread. The bread they ate was unleavened.

[Leaven is not used in bread as a memorial to God's deliverance of Israel from Egypt as shown in Exodus 12:14–39.]

Lebanon (LEB-uh-nun)

is a small country on the Mediterranean Sea. It was a fertile land. The cedars of Lebanon were used to build the Temple.

[King Solomon orders the cedars of Lebanon in I Kings 5:1–6.]

leprosy (LEP-ruh-see)

is a skin disease. Leprosy was identified as white spots on the skin. The worst cases of leprosy cause the loss of fingers and toes. Leprosy could kill. Leprosy made the Hebrew spiritually unclean. A leper was not allowed to go into the Temple.

[Elisha cures Naaman of leprosy in II Kings 5:1–14.]

Levi (LEE-vye)

was the third son of Jacob and Leah. Levi was the original father of Israel's priests. Moses and Aaron were from the tribe of Levi. Aaron was the first Chief Priest for Israel.

[Levi was born in Genesis 29:34.]

Levites (LEE-vites)

are members of the tribe of Levi. The tribe of Levi was selected to become priests. Levi was the only tribe that stood with Moses against the worship of the golden calf. God chose the Levites

to be priests and to tend to the Tabernacle. The Levites did not get a land inheritance. They were supported by the gifts from the other tribes.

[Levites stand with Moses in Exodus 32:25–32.]

Leviticus, Book of *(luh-VIT-uh-kus, book of)*

is an Old Testament book that describes the purpose of the priests. Levi was the tribe of Israel selected to be priests. Leviticus gives the rules for the priests. Leviticus tells how sinful people can approach a Holy God.

[Sin offerings are made in Leviticus 23:27–32.]

life *(LIFE)*

is what allows us to move and think. God breathed life into Adam. God gives everyone physical life. Jesus came to give us eternal life. Eternal life means spiritual life forever in heaven.

[Jesus offers us life in John 10:10.]

The Tree of Life has twelve different fruits.

Life, Book of *(LIFE, Book of)*

is the same as the Lamb's Book of Life.

*[See **Lamb's Book of Life**.]*

Life, Tree of *(LIFE, Tree of)*

was one of the trees in the Garden of Eden.

*[See **Tree of Life**.]*

light *(LITE)*

is to shine. Light removes and drives out darkness. God is light. Moses glowed from being in the glory of God. Jesus is the light of the world.

[Jesus is the light as shown in John 8:12.]

Lamps give off light.

linen *(LIN-un)*

was a common fabric for the Israelites. It was spun from the flax plant and bleached. This fabric was woven into clothing, bedding, curtains, and burial shrouds. The Tabernacle veil and the High Priest's garments were made of fine linen.

[The Temple veil is made of fine linen as shown in Exodus 26:31–35.]

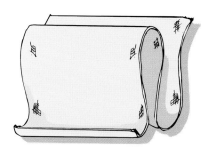

Israelites' clothing was made from linen.

The lintel is the wooden beam over the doorways.

A lion is the symbol for the tribe of Judah.

Jesus is the living water.

John the Baptist ate locusts and honey.

lintel (LIN-tul)

is the wooden beam that goes over a doorway. The last plague God sent against Egypt was the death of their firstborn. God told the Hebrews to sprinkle the blood of a sacrificed lamb on the lintel and doorposts. This was a sign for the Lord to pass by the house. The firstborn of those houses would be saved.

[The Lord passes by the homes with blood on the lintel in Exodus 12:22–23]

lion of Judah (LYE-un of JOO-duh)

is the symbol for this tribe. Jacob blessed Judah. He said that Judah will be like a lion's cub. Judah was to be the royal family of Israel.

[Jacob's blessing is recorded in Genesis 49:8–12.]

living water (LIV-ing WA-ter)

is the eternal life that Jesus gives. Jesus offers living water at Jacob's well. Jesus is the living water.

[Living water is offered in John 4:1–14.]

lo (LOW)

means look. We are to look to God for all our needs. Jesus promises to be there for us. He said, "Lo, I am with you alway, even unto the end of the world."

[Jesus uses "Lo" in His promise in Matthew 28:18–20.]

locust (LOE-cust)

is an insect that looks like a grasshopper. Locusts swarm in large numbers. They can destroy crops in large areas. One of the plagues of Egypt was a swarm of locusts. John the Baptist ate locusts and honey.

[Moses sent the Pharaoh locusts in Exodus 10:3–20.]

loins (LOINS)

are the hips and lower back. A girdle was worn around the waist. Gird up the loins meant folding the robe into the girdle. This was done to fight, run, or work.

[Jesus said to gird up our loins to be ready for His return in Luke 12:36–40.]

long-suffering (long-SUF-er-ing)

means to be patient. God is long-suffering and of great mercy. He is not willing that any should perish. He sent His Son to redeem sinners. Followers of Christ are to be long-suffering.

[Christians are to be long-suffering as shown in the fruits of the spirit Galatians 5:22–25.]

lord (LORD)

is a title for one who has power. Lord is a name used for God. This name shows that God has power and is the ruler of the world.

[God lets Moses know that He is Lord in Leviticus 19:1–4.]

Lord of Hosts (LORD of HOSTS)

is a name for God that shows the power of God. God is the commander of a host of angels. He is the Lord of Hosts.

[The Lord of Hosts is the God of Israel as shown in Isaiah 51:15–16.]

Lord's Day (LORD's DAY)

is the day of the week Jesus rose from the dead. This was on a Sunday. The early church met on the first day of the week. The Lord's Day does not replace the Sabbath.

[John has a vision from God on the Lord's Day in Revelation 1:10–11.]

Lord's Prayer (LORD's PRAY-er)

is an outline for prayer. Jesus used this to teach His followers how to pray. The Lord's Prayer is a prayer of praise and a prayer asking for God's will.

[The Lord's Prayer is recorded in Matthew 6:9–13.]

Lord's Supper (LORD's SUPP-er)

is a memorial started by the early church. The Lord's Supper is based on Jesus' Last Supper. This is a time to remember the Gospel of Jesus.

Jesus is the Lord of Hosts.

The first day of the week is called the Lord's Day.

Jesus taught his disciples how to pray in the Lord's Prayer.

The fruit of the vine and unleavened bread make up the Lord's Supper.

Sheep tend to get lost without a shepherd.

Two angels led Lot and his family out of Sodom.

The soldiers cast lots for Jesus' robe.

God turned Lot's wife into a pillar of salt.

Jesus gave himself for the church. His body died on the cross for our sin. This is shown in breaking the unleavened bread. Jesus shed His blood on the cross. This is remembered by drinking the fruit of the vine.

[Paul talks of the Last Supper in I Corinthians 11:20.]

lost (LOST)

is to be missing and alone. The good shepherd will leave his flock to find a lost sheep. He is joyful when he finds the lost sheep. A woman will search the entire house for a lost coin. She is glad when she finds the lost coin. God is joyful when a sinner repents. Jesus promises that His followers will never be lost.

[The promise that Christians will never be lost is recorded in John 17:12.]

Lot (LOT)

was the nephew of Abraham. Lot settled in the Jordan Valley. Lot moved into the city of Sodom. Sodom was a wicked city. God was going to destroy Sodom. Two angels led Lot and his family out of Sodom before God's judgment.

[Lot is led out of Sodom in Genesis 19:15–16.]

lots (LOTS)

is an old method of gambling. It was like rolling dice. Casting or throwing lots was how some decisions were made. The ship's crew threw lots to find out who was the cause of a storm. This showed that it was Jonah who caused their problem. The Roman soldiers threw lots to see who would get Jesus' robe.

[Lots were thrown in Matthew 27:35.]

Lot's wife (LOT's WIFE)

left Sodom with Lot. She wanted to return to the city. Lot's wife looked back at the city. God turned her into a pillar of salt.

[Lot's wife is turned into salt in Genesis 19:23–28.]

love *(LOVE)*

is to care very much for someone. God is love. Christians are to love each other. They are to also love their enemies. Jesus tells His followers to live in His love.

*[Jesus talks of love in John 15:9–19. See **agape**.]*

Love is to care very much for someone.

Lucifer *(LOO-suh-fer)*

means the morning star. Lucifer was an angel. Lucifer wanted to be worshipped. Lucifer rebelled against God. Other angels joined with him. God threw Lucifer and the fallen angels out of heaven. Lucifer is also called Satan and the Devil.

[Lucifer is thrown out of heaven in Isaiah 14:12.]

God threw Lucifer out of heaven.

Luke *(LUKE)*

was a disciple of Christ. Luke was an eyewitness to the life and ministry of Jesus. Luke wrote the Gospel of Luke and the Book of Acts. Luke was a doctor. Luke was also a gentile.

[Paul calls Luke a doctor in Colossians 4:14.]

Luke was a doctor and an apostle of Jesus.

Luke, Gospel of *(LUKE, GOS-pul of)*

is a New Testament book about the life of Christ. Luke tells us how Jesus was a friend of sinners. Jesus came to save that which was lost. The thief on the cross was the last sinner Jesus talked to. Jesus said that the thief would go to paradise because of his faith.

[Jesus tells the thief that he will go to paradise in Luke 23:39–43.]

lukewarmness *(LUKE-WARM-ness)*

is to be neither hot nor cold. Lukewarmness is how one of the seven churches in the Book of Revelation is described. They know God's truth. They are not obeying God. This church is told to repent and obey God.

*[The lukewarm church can be found in Revelation 3:14–19. See **backsliding**.]*

Lukewarmness is to be neither hot nor cold.

Lydda

Peter healed a lame man in Lydda.

The serpent lied to Eve.

Paul preached in Lystra.

Lydda *(LID-uh)*

was a city north of Jerusalem. Lydda was the capital of Samaria. Lydda is where some of the Jews settled when they returned from exile. Peter helped the church in Lydda.

[Peter heals a lame man in Lydda in Acts 9:32–35.]

Lydia *(LID-ee-uh)*

was the first European Christian. Lydia was a seller of purple cloth. She sold purple cloth to rich people. Lydia and her family became followers of Jesus. The church at Philippi met at the home of Lydia.

[Lydia and her family become Christians in Acts 16:14–15.]

lying *(LYE-ing)*

is to not tell the truth. Satan is the father of lies. God is truth. A righteous man hates lying. Christians are to speak the truth.

[Paul says that the church is not to lie in Ephesians 4:25.]

Lystra *(LIST-ruh)*

is a city in Asia Minor. Lystra was the home of young Timothy. Paul healed a crippled man at Lystra. The people of Lystra thought Paul was a god. Paul preached the Gospel at Lystra. The Jews hated his preaching. The Jews from Antioch and Iconium stoned Paul. They dragged him outside the city and left him for dead. Paul got up and walked back into the city.

[Paul is left for dead in Acts 14:1–20.]

Macedonia is the north part of Greece.

Macedonia *(mass-uh-DOE-nee-uh)*

is the northern part of Greece. Paul had a vision from God. The vision was of a Macedonian inviting him into his country. Paul brought the Gospel to Macedonia. Paul went to Philippi, a city of Macedonia. Lydia was the first person to become a Christian in Europe. The first church in Europe was held in Lydia's home.

[Paul has a vision about Macedonia in Acts 16:9–15.]

Magdala *(MAG-duh-luh)*

was a town in Galilee. Mary Magdalene was from Magdala. Mary was possessed with demons. Jesus called out the seven demons.

[Jesus travels to Magdala in Matthew 15:39.]

Mary Magdalene was from Magdala.

Magi *(MAJ-eye)*

were men who watched the stars. The wise men from the east knew about the promise of a Messiah. They left their home when they saw a sign in the sky. This was the star that came over Bethlehem. The Magi stopped to talk to King Herod. The priests told them that the Messiah was to be born in Bethlehem. King Herod wanted them to return. He said that he wanted to worship the King of the Jews. The Magi brought three types of gifts for Jesus. An angel told the Magi that the king wanted to kill Jesus. The Magi did not return to King Herod.

[The Magi visited King Herod in Matthew, Chapter 2.]

Magi were men who watched and followed the stars.

magnify *(MAG-nuh-fye)*

is to increase in size or power. The Lord magnified Joshua and Solomon in the sight of Israel. David sang many songs that magnified the name

Mary sang a song to magnify God.

Maiden is an unmarried woman.

A man is an adult male.

of God. The angel told Mary that she would be the mother of the Messiah. She sang a song to magnify the Lord. Her song is known as the Magnificat.

[The name of God is to be magnified as shown in Psalm 70.]

Mahlon (MAH-lun)

was the son of Elimelech and Naomi. Mahlon went to Moab because of a famine. Mahlon married a Moabite, Ruth. Mahlon died. Ruth went back to Israel with her mother-in-law, Naomi. Boaz became their kinsman redeemer.

[Mahlon marries Ruth in Ruth 4:9–10.]

maiden (MAY-dun)

is an unmarried woman. A female servant was called a handmaid. An angel told Mary she was to be the mother of the Messiah. Mary called herself a handmaid of the Lord. She was willing to obey God as His servant.

[Mary becomes the handmaid of the Lord in Luke 1:26–38.]

Malachi (MAL-uh-kye)

was a prophet of God. Malachi lived at the same time as Nehemiah. Malachi said Israel robbed God. He called for Israel to obey God.

[Malachi says that Israel robbed God in Malachi 3:8–9.]

Malachi, Book of (MAL-uh-kye, Book of)

is the last book in the Old Testament. The Israelites were discouraged. Malachi brought them the promise of God's blessing. God said that He would bless the children of Abraham. But first Israel had to obey God. Malachi ends with the promise of a Messiah.

[The promise of a Messiah is found in Malachi 3:1–3.]

man (MAN)

means a grown male human being. Man can also mean all people. Sin entered into the world by one man. That man was Adam. Jesus was God. Jesus became a man. Jesus knew no sin. Jesus was the perfect sacrifice for sin. Salvation is offered to all people through the shed blood of Jesus.

[Anyone can come to God as shown in I Peter 1:17–25.]

Manger is a feeding trough for animals.

Manasseh (muh-NASS-uh)

was one of Joseph and Asenath's sons. Manasseh was adopted by Jacob, his grandfather. Jacob gave Manasseh a blessing. Manasseh became the father of one of the Twelve Tribes of Israel. Manasseh, the oldest son, did not receive the blessing of the firstborn. Jacob gave that blessing to Manasseh's brother, Ephraim.

[Jacob adopts and blesses Manasseh in Genesis, Chapter 48.]

manger (MAIN-jer)

is a feeding trough used for farm animals. A manger was made of limestone or bricks. This is where Jesus was laid to sleep when He was born.

[Jesus was laid in a manger in Luke 2:7–16.]

The Israelites picked up manna from the ground.

manna (MAN-nuh)

was a special food given by God when the Israelites were in the desert. It means "What is it?" This is what the Israelites first said when they saw the manna on the ground. Manna was like a grain. Manna was small and was found on the ground every morning. The Israelites were to take only what they needed. The manna bred worms and stank if they took too much. They ground up the manna and made cakes. Manna was also boiled and eaten. The Israelites got tired of manna and began to grumble.

[God supplies manna for the Israelites in Exodus 16:13–36.]

Manoah (man-OH-uh)

was the father of Samson. He was of the tribe of Dan. Manoah prayed for a son. A man visited Manoah during a meal. He said that God would give him a son. He told Manoah that the child was

Manoah saw an angel go to heaven in some smoke.

Elisha parted the Jordan River with the mantle of Elijah.

Maranatha means "Our Lord shall come."

Mark and Paul preached in Cyprus.

to be a Nazarite. The man told Manoah to offer the meal as a burnt offering. The man was an angel from God. He went up to heaven in the smoke of the offering.

[God blessed Manoah with a son in Judges, Chapter 13.]

mantle (MAN-tul)

is a robe or cape worn as an outer garment. Elijah rolled up his mantle and hit the water. The waters of the Jordan River parted and they walked across on dry ground. Elisha was faithful to the calling of God. Elijah left his mantle for Elisha. Elisha received the double blessing of a firstborn son from God. Elisha also hit the Jordan River with his rolled mantle. The water parted for him and he crossed back on dry ground.

[Elijah hits his mantle on the Jordan River in II Kings 2:8.]

Maranatha (MAIR-uh-nuth-AH)

means Our Lord shall come. This is the hope the early Christians had. They expected Jesus to return any day. Maranatha is still the hope for the Christian. Jesus can return at any time. He said that no one would know the hour of His return.

[God the Father knows when Jesus will return as shown in Matthew 24:36.]

Mark (MARK)

was from Jerusalem. He was a close friend of Peter. Mark went with Paul on a missionary trip and later went on a missionary trip with Barnabas.

[Mark and Barnabas took the Gospel to Cyprus in Acts 15:36–39.]

Mark, Gospel of (MARK, GOS-pul of)

is a New Testament book on the life of Christ. Mark shows that Jesus was the perfect servant. Mark also shows that Jesus was God through the power of His works. Mark shows that Jesus was a man through His feelings.

[Mark declares that Jesus is the Son of God in Mark 1:1.]

marriage (MAIR-uj)

is the joining of a man and a woman together as a family. Adam and Eve were the first married people. Jesus taught that marriage was to be forever. He said that no one should break up what God has joined. Moses had given the Jews a way to divorce. Jesus said that Moses did this because people had hardened their hearts.

[The Pharisees questioned Jesus about marriage and divorce in Mark 10:2–12.]

Marriage is the joining of a man and a woman as a family.

marriage supper (MAIR-uj SUPP-er)

is a feast that celebrates a wedding. This was a day of celebrating. John tells us of the marriage supper of the Lamb. This is when Jesus and His church are joined together. It is a time of celebration.

[The marriage supper of the Lamb begins in Revelation 19:7–9.]

The marriage supper is a banquet for newlyweds.

Mars Hill (MARS HILL)

was a hill in Athens. Idols to all the pagan gods were located on Mars Hill. One of the idols was to the unknown god. Paul said he knew who the unknown god was. Paul said that Jesus was the God they should worship. Many Greeks became followers of Christ.

[Paul preaches on Mars Hill in Acts 17:22–34.]

Idols to pagan gods were located on Mars Hill.

Martha (MARTH-uh)

was the sister of Mary and Lazarus of Bethany. She was a close friend of Jesus. Martha and Mary were the ones who sent for Jesus when Lazarus was sick. Martha was working in the house during one visit by Jesus. She complained that Mary was not helping. Jesus reminded Martha that following Him was more important than housework.

[Martha met Jesus on the road in John 11:20–22.]

martyr (MAR-ter)

is someone who dies for a cause. Early Christians were killed for following Jesus. Saul arrested and

Martha wanted her sister to help clean.

Mary Magdalene

Jesus cast seven demons out of Mary Magdalene.

Mary, mother of James, was a witness for Christ.

Mary went to Bethlehem to be taxed.

The Jerusalem church met in the home of Mary, the mother of Mark.

killed Christians. John shows that God will remember the deaths of those martyred in His name.

[The blood of martyrs of Jesus is shown in Revelation 17:6.]

Mary Magdalene *(MAIR-ee MAG-duh-leen)*

was from Magdala. Mary Magdalene was controlled by seven demons. Jesus threw them out. Mary Magdalene became a follower of Christ. She became one of the closest friends of Jesus. Mary Magdalene was a witness to the death, burial, and resurrection of Jesus.

[Mary was present at the cross of Christ in John 19:25.]

Mary, mother of James *(MAIR-ee, MO-ther of JAMES)*

was a follower of Christ. She was also the mother of Joses and Salome. Mary was from Galilee. She was a witness to the death and resurrection of Jesus.

[Mary went to the tomb to anoint the body of Jesus in Mark 16:1–8.]

Mary, mother of Jesus *(MAIR-ee, MO-ther of JEE-zuz)*

was a cousin to Elisabeth, the mother of John the Baptist. The angel Gabriel visited Mary and told her that she would be blessed among all women. Gabriel said that she would give birth to the Messiah. Mary asked how that could be possible. She was a virgin. The angel said that all things were possible with God. God was the Father of Jesus. Joseph and Mary went to Bethlehem to be taxed. Mary gave birth to Jesus in a stable. She saw Jesus' first miracle. Mary also saw the death and burial of Jesus. She was one of the women to find that Jesus had risen from the grave.

[Mary talks to an angel in Luke 1:26–38.]

Mary, mother of John Mark *(MAIR-ee, MO-ther of JON MARK)*

was the owner of a house in Jerusalem. The early church met in her house. Her son, John

Mark, eventually became a disciple of Paul and Barnabas.

[The church met in Mary's house in Acts 12:12.]

Mary of Bethany (MAIR-ee of BETH-uh-nee)

was the sister of Martha and Lazarus. Mary, Martha, and Lazarus were close friends of Jesus. Mary spent time listening to Jesus teach. Mary anointed Jesus' feet with costly ointment. Judas Iscariot wanted to sell the ointment. He wanted to give the money to the poor. Jesus reminded Judas that He would not be with them always. He said Mary did a good thing.

[Mary anoints the feet of Jesus in John 12:1–8.]

Mary of Bethany anointed Jesus' feet.

master (MAST-er)

is a person in charge. People have one of two masters. People can choose to obey God or to live without God. One of these choices becomes a person's master. We cannot have two masters.

[Jesus talks of two masters in Luke 16:13.]

Two masters cause confusion.

Matthew (MATH-you)

was one of the Twelve Disciples. Matthew's brother James was also one of the Twelve Disciples. Matthew is also called Levi. Matthew was a tax collector. He collected taxes from people who used the Damascus Road.

[Matthew is called to be an apostle in Matthew 9:9.]

Matthew was a tax collector.

Matthew, Gospel of (MATH-you, GOS-pul of)

is a New Testament book of the life of Christ. Matthew was written to show that Jesus was the kingly Messiah. Matthew shows that the promised king had come. The Kingdom of God was ready to begin. But many people rejected Jesus.

[Jesus said the kingdom was shut up for Israel until they turned to God as recorded in Matthew 23:13–39.]

Matthias witnessed the ascension of Jesus into heaven.

Matthias (muh-THY-us)

was a disciple who followed Jesus. Matthias was with Jesus and the Twelve Disciples from the time of Jesus' baptism. Matthias witnessed the ascension of Jesus into heaven. The eleven disciples selected Matthias to replace Judas Iscariot as one of the Twelve Disciples.

[Matthias is selected as an apostle in Acts 1:22–26.]

mediator (MEE-dee-ay-ter)

is someone who counsels between two people. Mediators are used to make agreements. God gave the law to Israel. He made a covenant with Abraham. Jesus made a new covenant. It is a promise of grace. Jesus mediates this covenant before God.

[Jesus is the mediator of the new covenant as shown in Hebrews 12:24.]

Christians are to meditate on God's word.

meditate (MED-uh-tate)

is to think and study. Isaac and David went alone to meditate. Christians are to meditate on God's word. Timothy was told to meditate on being an example of Christ.

[Paul tells Timothy to meditate in I Timothy 4:4–16.]

meek (MEEK)

refers to someone who is gentle and humble. Meekness does not mean weakness. Meekness is allowing God to control our lives. Meekness is a fruit of the Spirit. Christians are to be meek.

[Jesus talks of the meek at the Sermon on the Mount as shown in Matthew 5:5.]

Megiddo (muh-GID-oh)

is the valley near Mount Megiddo.

*[See **Mount Megiddo.**]*

Melchisedec (mel-KIZ-uh-dek)

is the same as Melchizedek.

*[See **Melchizedek.**]*

To be meek is to be gentle.

Melchizedek (mel-KIZ-uh-dek)

was a priest and king of Salem. Abraham gave Melchizedek a tenth of everything. This was a tithe to God. Melchizedek and Abraham both worshipped the true God.

[Abraham gives his tithe to Melchizedek in Genesis 14:17–20.]

Abraham gave an offering to Melchizedek.

memorial (muh-MOR-ee-ul)

is something that serves as a reminder. The bronze serpent was a memorial to God's deliverance from the poison snakes. Aaron's rod was a memorial to God's selection of the priests. Many men of God built altars as a memorial of thanksgiving. Joshua took twelve stones from the Jordan River bed. He made a memorial to God's deliverance from the wilderness. The Lord's Supper is a memorial to Jesus' death on the cross.

[Joshua makes a memorial in Joshua 4:1–9.]

Joshua set up twelve stones as a memorial for crossing the Jordan River.

mene, mene, tekel, upharsin (MEN-uh, MEN-uh, TECK-ul, you-FAR-sun)

were the words written on the palace wall. When King Belshazzar of Babylon had a party, a hand wrote these words. Daniel was brought in to tell the meaning of this message. Daniel told the king that God was going to judge his kingdom. It was going to be divided. The king lost his life and kingdom that very night.

[A hand writes on the palace wall in Daniel, Chapter 5.]

"Mene, mene, tekel, upharsin" was written on the palace walls.

Mephibosheth (muh-FIB-oh-sheth)

was a son of Jonathan. A nurse helped the young Mephibosheth flee from the Philistines when he was five years old. She dropped him. The fall crippled him in both feet.

[Mephibosheth is hurt in II Samuel 4:4.]

Mephibosheth was hurt when he was dropped.

mercy (MER-see)

is to show kindness or compassion by not judging or punishing. God's mercy is eternal. His mercy is

The mercy seat was the lid to the Ark of God.

The king threw Meshach into a fiery furnace.

A messenger is someone who carries a message.

Messiah means the anointed one.

without limit. God's mercy has forgiven sin. God's mercy allows us to go to heaven.

[God's mercy can save us as shown in Titus 3:5.]

mercy seat (MER-see seet)

was a plate of pure gold. The mercy seat was the lid to the Ark of God. The High Priest sprinkled the blood on the mercy seat on the Day of Atonement. This was to ask for forgiveness for the sins of the nation.

[The mercy seat was the cover for the Ark of God as shown in Exodus 25:17–22.]

Meshach (MEE-shack)

was one of Daniel's three friends. They were taken as slaves to Babylon. His Hebrew name was Mishael. Shadrach, Meshach, and Abednego refused to worship an idol. The three were thrown into a fiery furnace. God saved these men.

[Shadrach, Meshach, and Abednego are thrown into the furnace in Daniel 3:8–28.]

messenger (MESS-un-jer)

is someone who carries a message. Angels are messengers of God. John the Baptist was God's messenger. He prepared the way for the Messiah.

[God sent Israel a messenger in Matthew 11:7–15.]

Messiah (mus-EYE-uh)

means the anointed one. The Greek word is Christ. Kings and priests were anointed with oil. The Messiah was to be king of Israel and sit on the throne of David. The Old Testament prophecies about the Messiah also show His suffering. This is how Jesus came the first time. Jesus will come as the kingly Messiah when He returns.

*[See **Christ**.]*

mete *(MEET)*

means to measure and give out. Jesus warns us not to judge others. The measure we judge will be meted back.

[Jesus talks of meting out judgment in Matthew 7:2.]

Methuselah is the oldest man that ever lived.

Methuselah *(muh-THOO-zuh-luh)*

was a son of Enoch. Methuselah was the grandfather of Noah. Methuselah is the oldest man that ever lived. He was nine hundred sixty-nine years old when he died. Methuselah is the oldest person recorded in the Bible. God sent the Flood in the same year that Methuselah died.

[Methuselah died in Genesis 5:25–27.]

Micah *(MYE-kuh)*

was a prophet of God. He lived at the same time as the prophets Hosea, Amos, and Isaiah.

[Micah is called to be a prophet in Micah 1:1.]

Micah, Book of *(MYE-kuh, Book of)*

is an Old Testament book written to Israel and Judah. Micah condemns the sins of the nation. God promises deliverance to those who obey Him. Herod asked where the King of the Jews was to be born. The chief priests and scribes found the answer in Micah.

[The Messiah was to be born in Bethlehem as shown in Micah 5:2.]

Satan held Michael back for twenty-one days.

Michael *(MYE-kul)*

is an archangel of God. God sent Michael to answer Daniel's prayer. Michael was held back twenty-one days by Satan.

[Michael brings Daniel a vision in Daniel 10:10–12:4.]

millennium *(muh-LEN-ee-um)*

is a Latin word that means a thousand years. A thousand years is mentioned as the length of the Kingdom of God. Christ will rule as king on the earth during the millennium. Many of God's

Jesus will rule the earth during the millennium.

Millstone is one of the two big stones used to grind grain.

To minister is to help those in need.

Pharaoh's priests performed miracles.

Miriam did a victory dance when the Egyptians were defeated.

promises for the Jews will be fulfilled during the millennium.

[Jesus rules the world for a millennium in Revelation 20:1–7.]

millstone (MILL-STONE)

is one of the two big stones used to grind grain. The grain is fed between the stones. The stones are turned and grind the grain. This makes the grain a coarse meal or flour. Samson had to turn a millstone when he was captured.

[Samson works a grindstone in Judges 16:21.]

minister (MIN-is-ter)

is to help those in need. Ministering is a gift of God. Paul was a minister to the gentiles. The church chose seven men to minister to the needs of the widows.

[Jesus sends Paul to be a minister to the gentiles in Acts 26:14–18.]

miracle (MEER-uh-kul)

is something that happens that could not normally occur. Jesus and the apostles performed many miracles. These miracles included walking on the water, feeding thousands of people, and healing the sick. Not all miracles come from God. Satan turned the staffs of the Pharaoh's magician into snakes. The false prophet will come with signs and lying wonders.

[The false prophet will perform miracles as shown in Revelation 16:13–14.]

Miriam (MEER-ee-um)

was the sister of Moses and Aaron. She led the women in a song of victory when the waters drowned Pharaoh's army. She rebelled against Moses. Moses cursed her with leprosy. Moses healed her after seven days.

[Miriam sings of the victory in Exodus 15:20-21.]

mist (MIST)

is a fog or a spray of water. A mist watered the

plants in the days of Noah. Saul was blinded in a mist. A mist of darkness is waiting for the ungodly.

[Peter says that a mist of darkness waits for the ungodly in II Peter 2:13–17.]

The mite is a small coin.

mite *(MITE)*

was the smallest coin in Israel. Five mites is the same as one penny. The poor widow gave two mites to the Temple. Jesus said she had given more than the rich people at the Temple. This was because she gave all she had while the rich gave just a portion.

[Jesus talks of the widow's mite in Mark 12:41–44.]

mitre *(MITE-er)*

is a head covering for the High Priest. Aaron wore the mitre. It was a sign of power and honor. The mitre was made of fine linen with a golden plate on its front. The gold plate had the words "Holiness to the Lord" engraved on it.

[The mitre of Aaron is described in Exodus 28:36–38.]

Mitre is the special hat that the priest wore.

Moab *(MOE-ab)*

was the son of Lot's older daughter. Moab is the father of the Moabites. The Moabites would not let Israel pass through their land. Israel had to go around. Israel fought the Moabites. Ruth was a Moabite.

[The birth of Moab is recorded in Genesis 19:30–37.]

Molech *(MOE-lek)*

is the name of a false god. People were sacrificed to honor Molech. Some of the Israelites put their children through the fire of Molech. God tells us not to worship false gods. God also says it is a sin to kill. Worshipping Molech was a great sin.

[God told Israel not to worship Molech in Leviticus 20:2–5.]

Moloch *(MOE-luk)*

is the same false god as Molech.

*[See **Molech**.]*

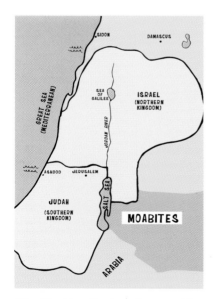

The Moabites lived on the east side of the Jordan river.

The molten sea rested on the backs of twelve brass oxen.

Jesus cast out the moneychangers from the Temple.

Mordecai warned Queen Esther of a plot to kill the Jews.

Abraham was to sacrifice Isaac on Mount Moriah.

molten sea (MOL-tun SEE)

was a large bronze bowl that stood in the courtyard of the Temple. It was fourteen feet across. The molten sea rested on the backs of twelve brass oxen. The priests washed in the molten sea to purify themselves.

[The molten sea is put on twelve oxen in I Kings 7:23–26.]

moneychanger (MUH-neeCHAIN-jer)

was a person who sold or exchanged money. The Jews were to offer only Jewish money at the Temple. The moneychangers were not honest. The moneychangers and the sellers of animals had turned the Temple court into a wicked marketplace. Jesus turned their tables over. He said they had turned God's house into a den of thieves.

[The moneychangers are chased out of the Temple in Matthew 21:12–13.]

Mordecai (MOR-duh-kye)

was the uncle of Esther. Mordecai had adopted Esther. He told Esther what to do before the king. The king was looking for a queen. The king selected Esther. Haman hated Mordecai. Haman tried to have Mordecai and all the Jews killed. Mordecai told Queen Esther of this evil plot. The king had Haman killed instead.

[Mordecai adopted Esther as his daughter in Esther 2:7.]

Moriah (muh-RYE-uh)

is a rocky area north of Jerusalem. Moriah is where God told Abraham to sacrifice Isaac. God provided a ram for the sacrifice at the last moment. Solomon's Temple was built on Moriah.

[Abraham and Isaac climb Moriah in Genesis 22:1–14.]

Morning Star (MORN-ing STAR)

was a name for Lucifer. Lucifer is a fallen angel. He is also known as Satan and the Devil.

[The Morning Star is thrown out of heaven in Isaiah 14:12–15.]

Mosaic Law (moe-ZAY-ick LAW)

is the law God gave to Moses. The Mosaic Law is the same as the Ten Commandments.

*[The Mosaic Law is found in Exodus, Chapter 20. See **Ten Commandments**.]*

Moses (MOE-zuz)

was a Levite. Baby Moses was put into a little boat to hide him from the Pharaoh. The Pharaoh's daughter found and adopted Moses. Moses visited the Hebrews when he was forty years old. He killed an Egyptian who was beating a Hebrew. Moses left Egypt and lived in the land of Midian. Forty years later, Moses came upon a burning bush. God talked to Moses and told him to lead the Hebrews out of Egypt. God used Moses to get the Pharaoh to let His people go. God had to send ten plagues against Egypt. Pharaoh finally let the Hebrews leave. Moses led the Hebrews into the wilderness. Moses was the leader of the Israelites for forty years.

[Moses sees the Promised Land but is not allowed to enter it in Deuteronomy 34:1–5.]

God used Moses to get Pharaoh to let the Israelites go.

mote (MOTE)

is a speck of dust or dirt. Jesus said that we should remove the beam in our eye before we try to remove the mote in our friend's eye. Jesus was telling us that we need to be pure before we start judging others.

[Jesus talks of motes in Matthew 7:1–5.]

A mote can be a speck in the eye.

mother (MO-ther)

is a woman who carries, gives birth, and cares for a child. The sin of Adam and Eve introduced pain in childbirth. Jesus had an earthly mother when He became flesh. His mother was Mary. Mary was the mother to other sons and daughters after the birth of Jesus.

[Mary becomes a mother in Bethlehem in Luke 2:1–7.]

Mothers give birth to babies.

The ark landed on Mount Ararat.

Elijah challenged the prophets of Baal on Mount Carmel.

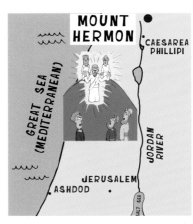

The transfiguration of Jesus happened on Mount Hermon.

Mount Ararat (MOUNT AIR-uh-rat)

was the final resting place for Noah's ark. Noah left the ark on the mountain and came down the mountain. They made a sacrifice on Mount Ararat. They gave thanks to the Lord for delivering them from the Flood.

*[Noah's ark rests on Mount Ararat in Genesis 8:1–5. See **Ararat.**]*

Mount Carmel (MOUNT CAR-mul)

is located in Palestine on the Mediterranean Sea. Mount Carmel was where Elijah challenged the prophets of Baal. Both Elijah and the prophets took fatted calves and put them on separate altars. Elijah told the prophets of Baal to have their gods honor their sacrifice. The prophets of Baal jumped around and yelled. Nothing happened. Elijah built a trench around his altar and had twelve barrels of water poured on his sacrifice. The water filled the trench. Elijah asked God to accept his offering. Fire from heaven came down. It burned up the offering and lapped up the water in the trench.

[Elijah challenged the prophets of Baal in I Kings 18:17–39.]

Mount Hermon (MOUNT HER-mun)

is located north of Israel. Mount Hermon is the place where Jesus was transfigured. This was when the glory of God shone through Jesus. Peter, James, and John were with Jesus on Mount Hermon.

*[Jesus is transfigured at Mount Hermon in Matthew 17:1–9. See **transfiguration.**]*

Mount Hor (MOUNT HOR)

is a mountain located in the country of Edom. This is the place where Aaron died.

[The death of Aaron is recorded in Numbers 33:38–39.]

Mount Megiddo (MOUNT muh-GID-oh)

is the mountain that oversees a great valley. This valley is the place where a big battle will be fought. All of the nations will fight against God. This is called the Battle of Armageddon.

[All the armies of the world will gather at Mount Megiddo in Revelation 16:14–16.]

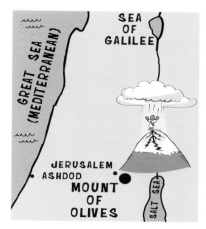

Jesus will split the Mount of Olives.

Mount Nebo (MOUNT NEE-boe)

is a mountain near Jericho. This is the place the Israelites entered into the Promised Land. God shows Moses the land of milk and honey from Mount Nebo. This is the mountain where Moses died.

[Moses sees the Promised Land from Mount Nebo in Deuteronomy 34:1–4.]

Mount of Olives (MOUNT of AH-livz)

is the mountain east of Jerusalem. The Garden of Gethsemane was on the Mount of Olives. Jesus gave the Olivet Discourse from here. The ascension of Jesus took place at the Mount of Olives.

*[The Mount of Olives will split in two when the Lord returns as shown in Zechariah 14:3–5. See **Olivet Discourse**.]*

Mount Sinai (MOUNT SYE-nye)

is the place where God revealed Himself to Moses. God gave Moses two tablets of stone. These were written with the finger of God. These tablets contained the Ten Commandments. Moses returns from Mount Sinai to find the Hebrews worshipping a golden calf.

[Moses returns from Mount Sinai in Exodus 32:15–18.]

Mount Sinai is where God gave Moses the Ten Commandments.

mourning (MORN-ing)

is being very sad. Mourning is the same as having grief.

*[See **grieve**.]*

multiply (MUL-tuh-ply)

is to increase in number. God told Adam and Eve to go out and multiply. This was a command to populate the earth. God told Noah the same thing after the Flood.

[God told Adam and Eve to be fruitful and multiply in Genesis 1:27–28.]

God told Adam and Eve to multiply.

Cain murdered his brother Abel.

I'M TIRED OF EATING ONLY MANNA!

ME, TOO!

The Israelites murmured to God about the manna.

A small mustard seed grows into a large plant.

Myrrh is a scented spice used to anoint the dead.

murder *(MER-der)*

is killing someone. Killing is a sin. Murder breaks one of the Ten Commandments. Sometimes murder is an accident. God provided six cities of refuge. A person could go to one of these cities and be safe if a death was accidental. Jesus said that hating someone was like murder.

["Thou shalt not kill" is listed in Exodus 20:13.]

murmur *(MER-mer)*

is to mumble and complain. The Israelites kept murmuring against God. They murmured when they got thirsty. They murmured when they were hungry. They murmured when they were tired of eating manna. God supplied all their needs. God made the Israelites wander in the wilderness for forty years. This was because they murmured and disobeyed God.

[The Israelites murmured in Numbers 14:1–37.]

mustard seed *(MUST-erd SEED)*

is a seed that produces a large plant. Mustard seeds are very small. Jesus said that faith the size of a mustard seed could move mountains. Mustard plants grow fast and large. Jesus said the Kingdom of God will grow like a mustard seed. This meant that it would start small and grow fast. The church at Jerusalem started small and added thousands.

[Faith the size of a mustard seed can be found in Matthew 17:20.]

myrrh *(MERR)*

is a scented resin. Myrrh was traded along with spices. Myrrh was used in anointing oil, as perfume, and to preserve dead bodies. Myrrh was one of the three gifts that baby Jesus received from the wise men. Joseph and Nicodemus anointed the body of Jesus with myrrh and aloes.

[One hundred pounds of myrrh is put on the body of Christ in John 19:38–42.]

mystery (MIS-tuh-ree)
is an unknown. The age of grace was a mystery until Jesus revealed it. Much about God is a mystery. We know only that which God has revealed to us in the Bible.

[Paul shows us that grace was a mystery in Ephesians 3:2–19.]

Mystery is something unknown.

Naaman

Naaman cured his leprosy in the Jordan River.

Naaman (NAY-uh-mun)

was a captain in Syria. He was a leper. His captive servant girl told him about God and the prophet Elisha. Naaman went to the prophet Elisha to be healed. Elisha told him to wash in the Jordan River seven times. Naaman got angry. He felt the rivers of Syria were better. But Naaman washed in the Jordan River. God healed Naaman of his leprosy.

[Naaman is cured in II Kings 5:1–14.]

Naboth (NAY-buth)

was the owner of a vineyard. The vineyard was next to the palace of King Ahab. The king wanted the land for a vegetable garden. Naboth refused to sell his land. King Ahab got mad and did not eat. Queen Jezebel had Naboth killed. The king then took the vineyard.

[Naboth is killed for a vineyard in I Kings 21:1–16.]

Naboth owned a vineyard.

Nadab (NAH-dab)

was the oldest son of Aaron. Nadab had a brother, Abihu. They were priests of Israel. Nadab did not obey God. Nadab and Abihu offered strange fire before the Lord. A fire from God destroyed both of them.

[God's judgment of Nadab may be found in Leviticus 10:1–7.]

Nahum (NAH-hum)

was a prophet of God. Nahum was an Elkoshite. Nahum had a vision from God. This vision told of the destruction of Nineveh.

[Nahum had a vision from God in Nahum 1:1.]

Nadab offered strange fire before the Lord.

Nahum, Book of *(NAH-hum, Book of)*

is an Old Testament book of judgment. The Lord sometimes takes a long time to show His anger. But God will judge the wicked. Nineveh was a wicked nation and destroyed many surrounding nations. God was going to destroy Nineveh. God also promised to deliver Judah.

[Nineveh is to be scattered in Nahum 3:18–19.]

nails *(NAILS)*

are large iron spikes. They were used to crucify Jesus. These nails were five to seven inches long. The nails were driven into the hands and feet of the person crucified and held the body firmly to the cross.

[Thomas wanted to see the nail holes in Jesus's hands as recorded in John 20:24–29.]

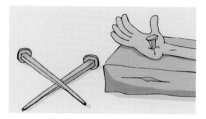

Large iron spikes were used as nails.

name *(NAME)*

is what something is called. Adam gave names to all the animals. A child's mother usually gives her baby a name. The names of people in the Bible had special meanings. This lets us know more about a person. Kings sometimes changed the names of their captives. Daniel and his friends were given new names in Babylon. God sometimes changed a person's name. Part of the reason is that the person had changed. Everyone that follows God is a changed person.

[Jesus has a name above all other names as shown in Philippians 2:9–10.]

People have names.

Naomi *(nay-OH-mee)*

was the wife of Elimelech. She was the mother-in-law to Orpah and Ruth. Naomi's husband and sons died in Moab. Naomi and Ruth returned to Israel. Naomi told Ruth what to say and do for Boaz. Boaz became the kinsman redeemer for Naomi.

[Naomi's property is returned to her in Ruth 4:9.]

Naomi's husband Mahlon and her two sons died in Moab.

Naphtali

Napthali was the sixth son of Jacob.

The path to God is a narrow path.

Joseph, the husband of Mary, was a carpenter in Nazareth.

Naphtali *(NAFT-uh-lye)*

was the sixth son of Jacob. His mother was Bilhah. Naphtali was the father of one of the Twelve Tribes of Israel.

[Naphtali is born in Genesis 30:6–8.]

narrow *(NAIR-oh)*

means thin. Jesus talked about two paths for life. The path that leads to destruction is broad. This is the path most people take. The path to God is narrow. Few people choose to follow this path.

[Jesus talks of the narrow path in Matthew 7:13–14.]

Nathan *(NAY-thun)*

was a prophet of God. King David sinned by taking Uriah's wife and then killed Uriah to hide his sin. God sent Nathan to judge King David. Nathan told the king about a rich man. The rich man had lots of sheep. This man took the only lamb of a poor man. Nathan was talking of the sin of King David.

[Nathan talks to King David in II Samuel 12:7–11.]

Nathanael *(nath-ANN-yul)*

was one of the Twelve Disciples. He is also called Bartholomew. Philip told Nathanael about the Messiah. Nathanael did not believe Philip. He said nothing good comes from Nazareth.

[Nathanael hears of the Messiah in John 1:43–49.]

Nazarene *(naz-er-EEN)*

is a person from Nazareth. Jesus was called a Nazarene.

[Jesus is called a Nazarene in Matthew 2:23.]

Nazareth *(NAZ-uh-reth)*

is a small town in Galilee. Nazareth was not the best city in Israel. Nathanael said that nothing good comes from Nazareth. Jesus lived in Nazareth. His family moved there after returning from Egypt.

[Jesus was thrown out of the synagogue at Nazareth in Luke 4:16–30.]

Nazarite *(NAZ-er-ite)*

was someone dedicated to God by a special oath. A Nazarite would not cut his hair. They were not to drink wine or touch the dead. Famous Nazarites are Samson, Samuel, and John the Baptist.

[A Nazarite gets a haircut in Judges 16:17–21.]

Nazarites did not cut their hair.

Nebo *(NEE-boh)*

is a mountain near the Jordan River.

*[See **Mount Nebo**.]*

Nebuchadnezzar *(neb-uh-kud-NEZZ-er)*

was king of Babylon. Daniel interpreted two of the king's dreams. King Nebuchadnezzar made a gold statue. All the people were to worship the statue. Daniel's friends did not bow down to the image. The king threw the three Hebrews into a fiery furnace. God protected these men. King Nebuchadnezzar praised the God of the Hebrews.

[King Nebuchadnezzar and the fiery furnace is recorded in Daniel 3:1–28.]

Daniel told Nebuchadnezzar about his dreams.

Nehemiah *(nee-uh-MYE-uh)*

was a prophet of God. Nehemiah was the cupbearer to the king. Nehemiah rebuilt the walls of Jerusalem.

[Nehemiah was allowed to go to Jerusalem in Nehemiah 2:1–13.]

Nehemiah was a cupbearer to the king.

Nehemiah, Book of *(nee-uh-MYE-uh, Book of)*

is an Old Testament book about rebuilding. The Jews went back to Jerusalem. The walls of the city were broken down. Nehemiah rebuilt the walls of Jerusalem. The Jews had a lot of problems trying to build the walls. God shows that His work will be completed.

[The enemies of the Jews see the hand of God in the building of the walls as shown in Nehemiah 6:1–16.]

neighbour *(NAY-ber)*

is a person who lives nearby or in the same area. The Mosaic Law says to love your neighbour. The

Anyone in need is a neighbour.

Nero

Nero played while Rome burned.

Pharisees said a neighbour was a Jew who strictly observed Mosaic Law. Jesus tells us who our neighbour is in the parable of the Good Samaritan. A neighbour is anyone who needs help. Christians are to love their neighbours.

[Jesus gives a lesson on neighbours in Luke 10:25–37.]

Nero (NEE-roh)

was a Roman emperor. Nero was the Caesar Paul appealed to.

[Paul was brought before Nero as shown in II Timothy 4:22 (but this is not in all copies of the Bible).]

New Covenant (noo CUH-vuh-nunt)

is a new promise made by God.

[See New Testament.]

There are twenty-seven books in the New Testament.

New Testament (noo TEST-uh-ment)

is a group of books written after Jesus returned to heaven. There are twenty-seven books in the New Testament. These books tell of the new promise given by God. This promise was made possible by the birth, death, and resurrection of Jesus. The New Testament is a promise of the grace of God. God's grace is available to everyone.

[The New Testament is described in Hebrews 9:15–28.]

Nicodemus came to Jesus at night.

Nicodemus (nick-uh-DEE-mus)

was a Pharisee and a ruler of the Jews. Nicodemus came to Jesus by night and asked how he could be born again. Jesus said that he had to believe in the Son of God.

[Nicodemus visits Jesus in John 3:1–18.]

nigh (NYE)

means near. Christians are to draw nigh to God. God will draw nigh unto them. There will be warnings when the Kingdom of God draws nigh.

[Jesus tells us when the Kingdom of God will draw nigh in Luke 21:25–31.]

Nigh is to be near.

Nimrod *(NIM-rod)*

was a mighty hunter. Nimrod built the Tower of Babel and the city of Babylon.

[Nimrod was a hunter as shown in Genesis 10:8–10.]

Nineveh *(NIN-uh-vuh)*

was the capital of Assyria. It was a wicked city. Nineveh was an enemy city of Israel. God told Jonah to preach to Nineveh. The whole city turned to God, but they became wicked again. Then God sent Nahum to preach his judgment. Nineveh was destroyed.

[Nineveh obeyed God in Jonah 3:5–10.]

Noah *(NOE-uh)*

was a preacher. Noah and his family obeyed God. Everyone else in the world was wicked. God told Noah to build an ark. God sealed Noah and his family inside the ark. They were the only people saved from the Flood.

[Noah walked with God in Genesis 6:8–9.]

Noah's ark *(NOE-uhs ARK)*

was a large boat built by Noah. It saved Noah and seven people from the Flood. It also saved two animals of each kind. Noah was inside the ark for almost one year. There was no sail, no oars, and no rudder on the ark. The ark went where God wanted it to go. It stopped on top of Mount Ararat.

[The story about Noah, the ark, and the Flood begins in Genesis 6:1.]

northern kingdom *(NOR-thern KING-dum)*

was made up of ten tribes of Israel. These tribes divided from the nation when King Solomon died. The northern kingdom is also called Israel.

[The northern kingdom rebels in I Kings 12:16–19.]

numbers *(NUM-bers)*

occur in different patterns in the Bible. These patterns give added meaning to Scripture. Three

Nimrod built the tower of Babel.

Noah was a preacher.

Noah built a large boat for his family and two of each animal.

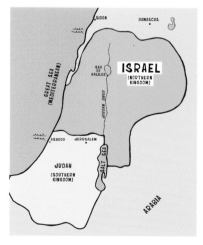

Northern kingdom is one of the names for ten of the tribes of Israel.

Numbers, Book of

The number seven means complete.

is the number for God. Six is for man. Seven is a number of completion and perfection. God's creation took seven days. It was complete and perfect. Many other numbers, like twelve or forty, also have special meanings in the Bible.

[God takes seven days for creation in Genesis 1:1–2:3.]

Numbers, Book of (NUM-bers, Book of)

is a history of Israel's wandering in the wilderness. God provided manna and water for them. God also provided quail for meat. The Israelites grumbled against God. Their unbelief prevented them from entering the Promised Land the first time.

[The Israelites are kept from the Promised Land in Numbers 14:22–25.]

oath (*OATH*)

is a promise. Oaths were binding. An oath was made in front of witnesses. Jesus said a legal oath should not use God's name. The High Priest made an oath to God when questioning Jesus.

[Jesus talks of swearing an oath in Matthew 23:16–22.]

An oath is a binding promise.

Obadiah (*oh-buh-DYE-uh*)

was the name of many people. Obadiah was a prophet of God. He wrote one of the books in the Old Testament. Another Obadiah saved one hundred prophets from wicked Queen Jezebel.

[Obadiah saves the prophets in I Kings 18:3–6.]

Obadiah hid one hundred prophets in a cave.

Obadiah, Book of (*oh-buh-DYE-uh, Book of*)

is the shortest book in the Old Testament. Obadiah talks of God's judgment on Edom. The Edomites would not let Israel pass through their land. It was the easiest way into the Promised Land. God will judge Edom. God also promised to deliver Israel.

[Israel is promised the land of the Canaanites in Obadiah 20–21.]

Obed (*OH-BED*)

was the son of Boaz and Ruth. Obed was King David's grandfather.

[Obed is born in Ruth 4:13–17.]

obey (*oh-BAY*)

is to do what you are told to do. Children are to honor and obey their parents. Israel was to obey the Mosaic Law.

[Obeying the Lord is better than making offerings to the Lord as shown in I Samuel 15:22.]

To obey is to listen to your parents.

An offering is a gift to God.

Og was the last of the giants.

Oil was used for fuel in lamps.

A woman put ointment on Jesus' feet.

oblations (oh-BLAY-shuns)

are sacrifices or offerings made to God.

*[See **sacrifice**.]*

offering (OFF-er-ing)

is a gift to God. Offerings are made to praise, give thanks, or ask for forgiveness. Some of the important offerings were the burnt offerings, the peace offering, and the sin offering. Jesus' death on the cross is the last sin offering that is needed. The early Christian church gave freely and cheerfully every week.

[The offering of the body of Christ is shown in Hebrews 10:8–10.]

Og (AWG—rhymes with hog)

was the Amorite king of Bashan. Israelites defeated Og and his army before they crossed the Jordan. Og was the last of the giants. His bed was made of iron and was over thirteen feet long. Og was the tallest person in the Bible.

[Og was the last of the giants as shown in Deuteronomy 3:11.]

oil (OIL)

was obtained by crushing olives. Oil was used for cooking and anointing. It was also used as an offering and a fuel for lamps. Oil sometimes stands for the presence of the Holy Spirit. Jesus gave a parable of the ten bridesmaids. The five foolish virgins did not have oil in their lamps. The wise ones had oil and could go into the wedding.

[Oil for lamps is a part of a parable in Matthew 25:1–13.]

ointment (OINT-ment)

was olive oil mixed with spices. Ointments were used as medicine and for cleaning and anointing. A sinful woman put ointment on the feet of Jesus.

[Jesus' feet were covered with ointment in Luke 7:36–46.]

Old Covenant (OLD CUH-vuh-nunt)

is the promises God made to Abraham, Moses, and David. These promises are made to the Jews.

The Old Covenant promised land, riches, a Messiah, and God's blessing.

[God made a Mosaic Covenant with Abraham in Genesis 15:18–21.]

Old Testament *(OLD TEST-uh-ment)*

is the first part of the Christian Bible. There are thirty-nine books in the Old Testament. It is the Jewish Scripture, and most of it was written by Jews. The Old Testament has three main parts. These parts are the Law, the Prophets, and the Writings. Jesus quoted a lot from the Old Testament.

[The Old Testament ends with the promise of a Messiah in Malachi 4:5–6.]

Olives, Mount of *(AH-liv, MOUNT of)*

is the mountain east of Jerusalem.

*[See **Mount of Olives**.]*

olive trees *(AH-liv TREES)*

grow up to forty feet and live for hundreds of years. They were important to Israel. Olives were a source of food and oil. Olive groves had an oil press. A heavy stone wheel crushed the fruit and its hard kernel to release oil. Olive oil made a bright flame when lit. The olive tree also refers to the nation Israel. Gentiles have been grafted into this olive tree.

[Gentiles can become part of the olive tree in Romans 11:13–17.]

Olivet Discourse *(AH-luh-vet DIS-CORSE)*

is the sermon Jesus preached on the Mount of Olives. This was the message given to His Twelve Disciples about the last days. Jesus told of the destruction of Jerusalem and His second coming.

*[See **Sermon on the Mount**.]*

omer *(OH-mer)*

was a Hebrew measure of about two quarts. An omer was also the first sheaf of barley that was offered to the Lord.

[An omer of barley was an offering as shown in Leviticus 23:9–15.]

There are thirty-nine books in the Old Testament.

Olive trees grow to forty feet.

An omer is two quarts.

Jesus told His disciples of the last days in the Olivet Discourse.

Jesus is the only begotten Son of God.

The Jerusalem church ordained the first deacons.

Baptism and the Lord's Supper are ordinances of the church.

Orpah stayed in Moab.

only begotten (OWN-lee be-GOT-un)

means the only one of a kind or unique. Only begotten Son refers to Jesus. Jesus is the one and only Son of God.

[Jesus is declared to be the only begotten Son of God in John 1:9–14.]

ordained (or-DAINED)

is to appoint someone to the service of God. Moses ordained seventy elders to assist him. The Twelve Disciples ordained seven holy men to help the people of the church.

[The Jerusalem church ordains seven men in Acts 6:1–6.]

ordinances (OR-duh-nun-suz)

are ceremonies that stand for something. The Jewish priests had ordinances for washing, offerings, and circumcision. The early Christian church observed the ordinances of baptism and the Lord's Supper. These ordinances show the Gospel of Christ. Baptism shows the death, burial, and resurrection of Christ. The Lord's Supper shows that Christ died for us.

[The ordinance of the Lord's Supper began in I Corinthians 11:23–26.]

Orpah (OR-puh)

was a daughter-in-law of Naomi. Her husband died in Moab. Naomi and Ruth returned to Israel. Orpah stayed in Moab.

[Orpah returned to her people and her gods in Ruth 1:12–15.]

palm *(PALM)*

is a tree that grows in warm areas. The leaves of the palm were laid on the ground as Jesus entered Jerusalem. The people thought Jesus was coming to set up His kingdom. This was the Sunday before Jesus was crucified. It is called Palm Sunday.

[Palms were laid on the road in John 12:12–13.]

palsy *(PAWL-zee)*

is a disease that causes the loss of muscle. Someone with the palsy could not walk. The friends of a man with the palsy took the lame man to see Jesus. There was no room at the door. The friends opened the roof and lowered him to Jesus. Jesus healed the man.

[Jesus heals the man with the palsy in Mark 2:1–12.]

Paphos *(PAFF-us)*

is a city in Cyprus. Paul preached the Gospel in Paphos. A sorcerer tried to keep Paul quiet. Paul cursed the sorcerer with blindness.

[Paul visits Paphos in Acts 13:6–12.]

papyrus *(puh-PYE-rus)*

is a reed that grows at the edge of water. Papyrus is the same as a bulrush.

*[See **bulrush**.]*

parable *(PAIR-uh-bul)*

is a story used to teach. A parable may or may not be a true event. Some parables were riddles. A rabbi sometimes teaches his students using parables. Much of the teachings of Jesus were done through parables. His famous parables

They laid palm branches before Jesus.

The man with the palsy was let down through the roof.

Paul preached in Paphos.

Reeds that grow in the water are papyrus.

Jesus said the thief would be with Him in paradise.

Very good paper is parchment.

Moses parted the Red Sea.

Passover was the tenth plague.

include the Good Samaritan [*Luke 10:30–37*], the rich fool [*Luke 12:16–21*], and the wheat and the tares [*Matthew 13:24–30*].

paradise (PAIR-uh-dise)

is a perfect place to live. The Garden of Eden was paradise. Heaven is a paradise. Jesus promised the thief that he would go to paradise.

[Paradise is promised to the thief in Luke 23:39–43.]

parchment (PARCH-ment)

is very good paper. Parchment was made using papyrus. The parchment would be sewed together in long strips. These were rolled into scrolls.

[Paul asks Timothy to bring the parchment of the Old Testament in II Timothy 4:13.]

pardon (PARD-un)

is the same as forgiveness.

*[See **forgive**.]*

part (PART)

is to separate. Moses parted the waters of the Red Sea. Joshua, Elijah, and Elisha parted the waters of the Jordan River. God used these miracles to allow people to cross the waters.

[Joshua parts the Jordan River in Joshua 3:14–17.]

partake (par-TAKE)

is to share or take part in. Paul teaches about the Lord's Supper. Only Christians can partake in the meaning of the Lord's Supper.

[Partakers of the Lord's Supper are described in I Corinthians 10:15–21.]

Passover (PASS-oh-ver)

was the last plague sent against Egypt. The Hebrews were slaves to the Egyptians. Moses kept asking the Pharaoh to let his people go. The Pharaoh would not release them. God sent plagues against Egypt. The passover was the tenth plague. This was a plague that caused the death of the firstborn son in each family. The Hebrews had to put the blood of a lamb on the doorpost as a sign. The Lord passed over these homes and the firstborn was spared. This is called the Passover.

[The Lord passed over the doorposts of the Hebrews in Exodus 12:21–23.]

Unleavened bread was eaten during Passover Feasts.

Passover Feast *(PASS-oh-ver FEEST)*

is a Hebrew feast celebrating the Passover. The Passover Feast was also called the feast of unleavened bread. Unleavened bread was eaten during the Passover. The Hebrews did not have time to leaven their bread when they left Egypt. The Last Supper was a Passover Feast for Jesus and the Twelve Disciples.

[Jesus celebrated the Passover in Luke 22:7–14.]

path *(PATH)*

is a small road. Paths are also the way we live our lives. Those who obey God are to follow the paths of righteousness.

[God leads us in paths of righteousness in Psalm 23:3.]

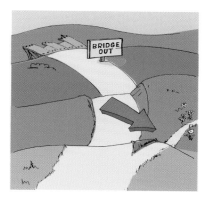

A path is a narrow road.

Patmos *(PAT-mus)*

is a small island near Greece. The Romans sent prisoners to Patmos. The apostle John was sent to Patmos. It was at Patmos that John wrote the Book of Revelation.

[John has a vision from God while at Patmos as shown in Revelation 1:9.]

The apostle John had a vision on the Isle of Patmos.

patriarchs *(PAY-tree-ARKS)*

are the fathers that began the nation of Israel. These men include Abraham, Isaac, and Jacob.

[Jacob's sons were twelve patriarchs as shown in Acts 7:8.]

Paul *(PAWL)*

was the apostle to the gentiles. He was also called Saul. Paul was born in Tarsus. Paul knew the Scriptures because he had studied under Gamaliel.

Paul met Jesus on the road to Damascus.

peace

Peace is part of the armour of God.

A peacemaker keeps people from fighting.

The penny had a graven image of Caesar.

Pentateuch is the first five books of the Bible.

Paul met Jesus on the Damascus Road and was blinded. Paul became a follower of Christ. Ananias healed Paul of his blindness three days later. Paul took the Gospel to Asia Minor and Europe.

[Paul met Jesus in Acts 9:1–9.]

peace (PEESE)

occurs when there are no struggles. Peace is a blessing from God. Jesus can be our peace. Peace is a fruit of the spirit. Peace is part of the armour of God.

[Peace from God shall protect us as shown in Philippians 4:7.]

peacemakers (PEESE-may-kers)

are people who work to bring peace. God blesses peacemakers.

[Peacemakers are part of the Beatitudes listed in Matthew 5:9.]

penny (PEN-ee)

was a small silver coin. The penny was a day's pay. The image of Caesar was on one side of the penny. A penny could not be given at the Temple. It had a graven image on it. Moneychangers traded Roman coins for Hebrew coins.

[The parable of the vineyard paid the workers a penny a day in Matthew 20:2.]

Pentateuch (PENT-uh-tuke)

means five scrolls. Pentateuch means the same as Torah. The Pentateuch is the first five books of the Old Testament. These books are Genesis, Exodus, Leviticus, Numbers, and Deuteronomy.

*[See **Torah**.]*

Pentecost (PENT-uh-cawst)

is a Jewish feast. It is celebrated fifty days after Passover. Pentecost is also called the Feast of Weeks and the Feast of Firstfruits. Today the Jews call it Shavuot. Most of the first Christians were Jews. All the disciples gathered together on the day of Pentecost for this feast. The Holy

Spirit then filled all of the believers. Today Christians still call this day Pentecost.

[The disciples gathered together on the day of Pentecost in Acts 2:1–21.]

perfect *(PER-fect)*

is being pure and without sin. Only God is perfect. Jesus was perfect. People cannot be perfect without God.

[The gifts from God are given for the perfecting of Christians as shown in Ephesians 4:7–16.]

To perish is to die.

perish *(PER-ish)*

is to die. God does not want people to perish. God sent Jesus to save us. People who follow Jesus will not perish.

[Peter reminds us that God does not want us to perish in II Peter 3:9.]

persecute *(PER-suk-yute)*

is to give pain to others because they are different. Saul persecuted David. Shadrach, Meshach, and Abednego were persecuted by the king. Jezebel persecuted the prophets of God. Saul persecuted the Christians.

[Jesus asked Saul why he persecuted Him in Acts 9:3–5.]

The king of Persia gave back the Temple treasures.

Persia *(PERZ-yuh)*

was a great nation. King Cyrus of Persia allowed the Jews to return to Israel. He gave supplies for rebuilding the Temple. King Ahasuerus of Persia married Esther.

[A Persian king selected a Hebrew wife in Esther 2:17.]

pestilence *(PEST-uh-lunse)*

is a disease that kills a lot of people. Pestilence is the same as a plague.

*[The last days will have war and pestilence as shown in Matthew 24:7. See **plague**.]*

Lice was sent to the Egyptians as a pestilence.

Peter, Epistle of, I and II *(PEET-er, uh-PIS-ul of, I and 2)*

are letters written to the Christian Jews. The first letter encourages the church. The second

Peter, the apostle

Peter walked on the water to Jesus.

An Egyptian ruler was a Pharaoh.

Philemon's slave ran away.

letter warns about false teachers. There was suffering caused by following Christ. Peter reminds Christians of their new inheritance. Christians will become part of the Temple of God.

[Jesus and Christians are living stones for the Temple as shown in I Peter 2:5–6.]

Peter, the apostle *(PEET-er, the uh-POSS-ul)*

was a fisherman. Peter is also called Simon, Simon Peter, and Cephus. Jesus called Peter and his brother, Andrew, to follow Him. Peter was one of the Twelve Disciples. Peter became the teacher and leader of the first church.

[Peter walks on the water in Matthew 14:28–31.]

Pharaoh *(FAIR-oh)*

was the ruler of Egypt. Moses asked the Pharaoh to let God's people leave Egypt. The Pharaoh would not let them go. God sent ten plagues against Egypt. The Pharaoh finally told them to leave.

[The Pharaoh lets the Hebrews leave in Exodus 12:31–33.]

Pharisees *(FAIR-uh-sees)*

were religious leaders. They obeyed and protected the Mosaic Law. They added more laws. These extra laws became traditions. Jesus preached that He came to fulfill the law. Many of the Pharisees hated Jesus. The Pharisees, Sadducees, and Romans had Jesus killed.

[Jesus tells the Pharisees that He was to fulfill the law in Matthew 5:17–20.]

Philemon *(fye-LEE-mun)*

was a friend of Paul. Philemon was a Christian. A slave of Philemon ran away. Paul told him that the slave was now a Christian, too. Paul asked Philemon to forgive the slave.

[Paul wrote his friend in the Epistle of Philemon.]

Philemon, Epistle to *(fye-LEE-mun, uh-PIS-ul to)*

is a letter written to the owner of a slave. Onesimus had run away from Philemon. He became a Christian when he met Paul. Paul told him to go back to Philemon. Paul asks Philemon to forgive Onesimus.

[Paul talks of brotherly love in Philemon 15–16.]

Philip *(FILL-ip)*

was chosen by the church at Jerusalem. Philip was one of the first seven deacons.

[Philip was selected to serve in Acts 6:1–6.]

Philip was a deacon for the Jerusalem Church.

Philip, the apostle *(FILL-ip, the uh-POSS-ul)*

was one of the Twelve Disciples. Philip led his brother, Nathanael, to Jesus. Philip knew Jesus was the Messiah.

[Philip brings Andrew to Christ in John 1:43–51.]

Philippi *(FILL-up-eye)*

was a city of Macedonia. Paul and Silas visited Philippi. They were arrested, beaten, and jailed. Paul told them he was a Roman citizen. Paul demanded to be released. The city asked them to leave the jail and Philippi.

[Paul leaves Philippi in Acts 16:38–40.]

Paul and Silas were thrown into jail in Philippi.

Philippians, Epistle to the *(fill-IPP-ee-unz, uh-PIS-ul to the)*

is a letter written by Paul to the church at Philippi. It is a letter of victory and joy. These are given to those who follow Jesus.

[Paul says that all things can be done when Christ is in it as shown in Philippians 4:13.]

Philistines *(FILL-us-tins)*

were a nation of warriors. They worshipped false gods. Israel fought them many different times. The Philistines captured Samson. The giant Goliath was a Philistine. Israel never fully conquered the Philistines.

[The Philistine giant challenges Israel in I Samuel 17:1–10.]

Phinehas *(FINN-ee-us)*

was a son of Eli. He was a priest of Israel.

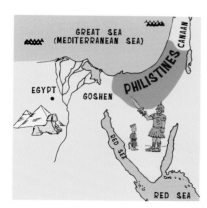

Goliath was a Philistine.

Pilate

Pilate offered to free one prisoner.

The Israelites were led by a pillar of cloud by day and a pillar of fire by night.

Jonah had pity on the gourd plant.

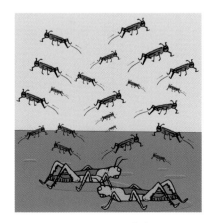

Locusts are one type of plague.

Phinehas was a wicked man. He and his brother, Hophni, took the Ark of God into battle. The Philistines won the battle. Both of Eli's sons were killed, and the Ark of God was taken.

[The death of Phinehas is found in I Samuel 4:3–11.]

Pilate *(PYE-lut)*

was a Roman ruler of Judea. The Chief Priests, rulers, and people of Jerusalem brought Jesus to Pilate. They wanted Pilate to convict Jesus and sentence Him to death. Pilate said he found no fault in Jesus. Pilate sentenced Jesus to death anyway.

[Pilate sends Jesus to His death in Luke 23:13–25.]

pillars of fire and cloud *(PILL-ers of FIRE and CLOUD)*

were columns that showed the presence of God to Israel. These pillars were over the Ark of God. A pillar of cloud went before the Israelites during the day. This was how God guided them in the wilderness. The pillar of fire showed them that God was with them at night.

[God guided the Israelites using these pillars as recorded in Exodus 13:21–22.]

pity *(PIT-ee)*

is to feel sorry for someone. Jonah had pity for a gourd that died. Jonah had no pity for a whole city. God has pity for every soul.

[Jonah shows pity for a gourd in Jonah 4:4–11.]

plagues *(PLAYGZ)*

are diseases or judgments that affect a lot of people. Plagues are sometimes given as God judges a nation. There are many plagues given during the last days. The most famous plagues are the ten plagues given to Egypt.

*[God promises plagues to the sinner in Leviticus 26:21. See **ten plagues of Egypt**.]*

pleasure *(PLEZ-yur)*

is bringing delight. God takes pleasure in righteousness. The ungodly seek after their own pleasures. Christians are to seek the pleasure of God's goodness.

[All things were created to bring pleasure to God as shown in Revelation 4:11.]

pluck (PLUCK)

is to rob, pick, or take. God gives believers eternal life. No one can pluck the Christian out of God's hand. No one can pluck the Christian out of Jesus' hand.

[Christians cannot be plucked away from God as shown in John 10:27–29.]

To pluck is to pick.

Pontius (PON-tus)

was the Roman ruler of Judea. He was very cruel. He was also known as Pilate or Pontius Pilate.

[See **Pilate.**]

Pool of Bethesda (POOL of buth-EZ-duh)

was a pool in Jerusalem. An angel would stir the waters of Bethesda. The first person into the pool was healed. It was here that Jesus healed a man who had been sick for thirty-eight years.

[Jesus heals at the Pool of Bethesda in John 5:2.]

An angel stirred the water at Bethesda.

poor (PORE)

refers to people in need. The Mosaic Law allowed the poor to glean the harvests. The law gave many other rights to the poor and widows. Jesus said we would always have the poor with us. The early church helped the poor and the widows. Christians and Jews are to remember and care for the poor.

[Paul says we need to help the poor in Galatians 2:10.]

To be poor is to not have anything of value.

portion (POR-shun)

is a share of goods or property. A portion was the son's part of his inheritance. God's chosen people are called God's portion. The Twelve Tribes of Israel each received a portion of the land of

A portion is part of something.

Potiphar

Potiphar bought Joseph as a slave.

Canaan. Levi did not get a portion. They were the tribe of priests. Their portion was the tithe.

[The firstborn son was to get a double portion according to Deuteronomy 21:15–17.]

Potiphar (POT-uh-far)

was the Egyptian captain of the guard who purchased Joseph. Joseph had been sold to the Midianite traders. Joseph was put in charge of Potiphar's house. Potiphar's wife tried to seduce Joseph. Joseph refused her. Potiphar had Joseph thrown in prison.

[Joseph is sold to Potiphar in Genesis 37:36.]

power (POW-er)

is the ability to act or produce. God has power to create. God has power to judge. God has power to forgive sin. All power was given to Jesus. Miracles are examples of the power of God.

[All power is given to Jesus as shown in Matthew 28:18–19.]

Prayer is talking to God.

praise (PRAIZ)

is to give glory and admiration to God. God is worthy to be praised. People can praise God in word, deed, or songs. Many of the psalms of the Bible are songs of praise.

[Peter says Jesus is worthy to be praised forever in I Peter 4:11.]

prayer (PRAY-er)

is talking to God. Prayer can be praise, honor, being thankful, or asking. Prayer is to be a private talk between a person and God. Jesus taught His disciples how to pray. Christians are told to pray without stopping. This means that we should be able to talk to God about anything and at anytime.

[Jesus taught His disciples how to pray in Matthew 6:5–15.]

preach (PREECH)

is to give a speech that has a message. King Solomon called himself a preacher. John the

Paul and Silas preached the Gospel to the world.

Baptist preached repentance to Israel. Jesus preached the coming of the Kingdom. Jesus told His disciples to go into all the world and preach the Gospel.

[*The Gospel is to be preached to every creature as shown in Mark 16:15.*]

precious (PRESH-us)

is having a high value. The breastplate of the High Priest had twelve precious stones. The Glory of the City of God will shine like a precious stone. Jesus is precious to the believer.

[*Peter shows how precious Jesus is in I Peter 2:1–7.*]

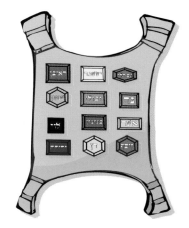

The breastplate had twelve precious stones.

prepare (pree-PARE)

is to make ready. Noah prepared an ark. King David prepared to build the Temple. God's judgment is prepared for sinners. Jesus went to heaven to prepare a place for believers.

[*Jesus has gone to prepare a place for us in heaven as shown in John 14:3.*]

Noah prepared an ark.

pride (PRIDE)

refers to thinking too highly of oneself. Pride was the first sin. Lucifer wanted to be worshipped like God. Christians are not to be lifted up with pride. King Solomon said pride will lead to destruction.

[*Pride goes before destruction as shown in Proverbs 16:18.*]

Pride was the first sin.

priest (PREEST)

is the person who makes sacrifices and offerings. The tribe of Levi was selected to be the priests for Israel. They were to make all the sacrifices for the nation. The High Priest was the only one who could go into the Holy of Holies. Jesus has become the High Priest for the Christian.

[*Jesus is our High Priest as shown in Hebrews 4:14–16.*]

prince (PRINCE)

is a male ruler. A prince is the son of the King. The Messiah is the Prince of Peace. Satan is the

Priests led the worship and sacrifices for Israel.

The prodigal son spent all his money and ended up with the pigs.

A promise is an agreement.

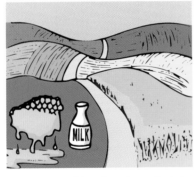

The Promised Land is also called the land of milk and honey.

There are many prophecies about a suffering Messiah.

prince of devils. Satan is also prince of the world. Daniel calls God the Prince of Princes.

[Isaiah calls the Messiah the Prince of Peace in Isaiah 9:6.]

Priscilla *(pruh-SILL-uh)*

was the wife of Aquila.

*[See **Aquila and Priscilla**.]*

prodigal son *(PROD-uh-gul SON)*

was one of the parables of Jesus. Prodigal means reckless and wasteful. The youngest son took his inheritance and moved away. He spent all his money. The son ended up poor and decided to go back home. The son thought that it would be better for him to be a slave to his father. But his father was glad when his son returned. He had a party for the prodigal son.

[The parable of the prodigal son is found in Luke 15:11–32.]

profit *(PRAH-fut)*

is making money or gain. Good works is the profit of being a Christian. Jesus said there is no profit that is worth losing your soul.

[Jesus talks of profit in Mark 8:36.]

promise *(PROM-iss)*

is an agreement between two people. It is the same as a covenant.

*[See **covenant**.]*

Promised Land *(PROM-ist LAND)*

was all the land that God promised to give to Abraham. The Promised Land is also called the land of milk and honey. God showed Moses the Promised Land from Mount Nebo.

[God showed Abraham the Promised Land in Genesis 13:14–18.]

prophecy *(PRAH-fuh-see)*

is the telling of the future. A lot of the prophecies tell of a kingly Messiah. They also tell of a suffering Messiah. Jesus is the Messiah. He fulfilled the prophecies of a suffering Messiah. He will fulfill the prophecies of the kingly Messiah.

[The first prophecy is found in Genesis 3:15.]

The test of prophet or prophetess was to be correct all of the time.

prophets and prophetesses (PRAH-futs and PRAH-fuh-tuh-suz)

are those people called to speak for God. There are many prophets of God listed. Some of these are Elisha, Elijah, Nathan, and Ezekiel. Deborah, Miriam, and Anna are prophetesses of God. God has a test for a true prophet. A prophecy from God is correct all the time. A false prophet may be correct some of the time.

[The test for a prophet of God is found in Deuteronomy 18:15–22.]

King Solomon gave us many proverbs.

prosper (PROSS-per)

is to succeed or grow. God wants His people to prosper. The Israelites would prosper when they followed God's commandments. The wicked prosper for a little while. Joseph obeyed the Lord. The Lord made everything that Joseph did prosper.

[Joseph prospers even in jail as shown in Genesis 39:22–23.]

proverb (PRAH-verb)

is a short truthful saying. King Solomon was the wisest man that ever lived. A lot of his proverbs are found in the Book of Proverbs.

*[See **Proverbs, Book of.**]*

Proverbs, Book of (PRAH-verbs, Book of)

are a collection of wise sayings. Most of the sayings are from King Solomon. He was the wisest man that ever lived.

[The purpose of Proverbs is found in Proverbs 1:1–9.]

psalm (SALM)

is a song. The Book of Psalms is a collection of psalms. King David wrote many psalms.

*[King David wrote a psalm of thanksgiving in II Samuel, Chapter 22. See **Psalms, Book of.**]*

Psalms are songs of praise and rejoicing.

A Publican collected taxes.

Pur is the same as casting lots.

To purchase is to buy something.

To purge is to make something pure.

Psalms, Book of (SALMZ, Book of)

is the longest book in the Old Testament. Psalms is a Hebrew song book. There are songs of praise, joy, and thanksgiving. The psalms were sung to worship God. Jesus and the Twelve Disciples sang a psalm at the Last Supper. Jews and Christians are to sing psalms.

[Jesus quoted from Psalm 22:1 in Matthew 27:46.]

Publican (PUB-luh-kun)

was a tax collector. Most Publicans were not honest. They took more money than they were supposed to take. The Hebrews thought they were great sinners. Matthew and Zacchaeus were Publicans.

[Jesus ate with Publicans and sinners in Matthew 9:10–13.]

Pur (POO-er)

means "lots" or lottery. Haman was going to destroy the Jews. Haman threw lots to find out the best day to carry out his plot.

*[See **Purim** or **lots**.]*

purchase (PER-chus)

is to buy something. A kinsman redeemer can purchase property that had once belonged to their relatives. Jesus purchased salvation for believers.

*[See **kinsman redeemer**.]*

pure (PURE)

is to be perfect or clean. Jesus said, "Blessed are the pure in heart." Christians are to keep themselves pure. They are to be pure like Jesus was pure.

[John calls Christians to be pure in I John 3:1–3.]

purge (PERJ)

is to clean out. Gold is purged by fire. Christians are to purge their minds of ungodly thoughts. Following Christ purges us from sin.

[Christians are not to forget that they are purged of old sin in I Peter 1:4–9.]

purify (PURE-uh-fye)

is to make clean or whole. There were many things that would make a Jew unclean. This meant that he was defiled and could not worship God. The Jew that became unclean had to purify himself. This included fasting, prayer, washing, sacrifices, and isolation. Each reason for uncleanness had a different way to purify the person. One of the reasons to purify was to make sure diseases were not spread in the camp. Purifying was also an outward sign of obeying God.

[Purifying for touching a dead person lasted seven days as shown in Numbers 19:11–22.]

Priests purified themselves by washing.

Purim (POO-er-im)

means "lots" or lottery. This is the name of a feast that Queen Esther began. It is in celebration of God's deliverance of His people. Purim is named after the habit of the enemy Haman. He threw lots when he was making decisions. Haman wanted to destroy the Jews. Queen Esther found out his plot. Haman was killed instead.

[The feast of Purim began in Esther 9:26–32.]

Haman cast lots.

purse (PURSE)

is a leather or cloth pouch to hold money. Jesus sent the seventy disciples two by two. Jesus told his disciples to take no money with them. They were not to take a purse or supplies with them. God would supply their needs. Judas carried the purse for Jesus and the other disciples.

[Jesus says not to take a purse or extra things in Matthew 10:1–9.]

A purse is a leather pouch for money.

pursue (per-SOO)

means to chase after something. Pharaoh's army pursued the Hebrews. God drowned them in the Red Sea.

[The Egyptian army pursues the Israelites in Exodus 14:23–31.]

The pursuing Egyptian army was drowned in the Red Sea.

quail

Quail was a food God provided for Israel.

quail (KWAIL)

was a food provided by God to the Israelites. The Hebrews complained about having only manna to eat. They wanted meat to eat. But they were in the middle of the wilderness. God gave them quail for meat.

[The quail enter into the Israelite camp in Exodus 16:13 and Numbers 11:31–32.]

queen (KWEEN)

is the wife of a king or a female ruler. Some of the queens were evil. Jezebel was an evil queen. She tried to murder all the prophets of God. Athaliah murdered her own grandsons so she could remain queen. Some of the queens were good. Queen Esther saved all the Hebrews from being killed.

[Obadiah hid one hundred prophets from Queen Jezebel in I Kings 18:4.]

A female ruler is sometimes called a queen.

queen of heaven (KWEEN of HEV-un)

is an idol worshipped by the women in Judah. They hoped to have children and wealth by worshipping this idol. This broke one of the Ten Commandments. God said that His people were to have no other gods before Him.

[God was not pleased with the worship of the queen of heaven in Jeremiah 7:17–20.]

Queen of Sheba (KWEEN of SHEE-buh)

was the ruler of a land far to the south of Israel. She came to King Solomon because she heard of his wisdom. She had to see if all the things she heard were true. The queen asked King Solomon many hard questions. He answered all of them.

The Queen of Sheba asked King Solomon many questions.

The Queen of Sheba then glorified God.

[The Queen of Sheba visited King Solomon in I Kings 10:1–13.]

quench *(KWENCH)*

is to put out. A camp fire is quenched by pouring water on it. The shield of faith quenches the fiery darts of the wicked. Christians are not to quench the Holy Spirit. This means that they are to allow the Holy Spirit to control our lives.

[Paul asks us not to quench the Holy Spirit in I Thessalonians 5:16–18.]

quicken *(KWICK-un)*

means to make alive. God quickened Adam when He formed him out of the dust of the ground. Sin has separated people from God. This is spiritual death. Believing in Jesus can make us alive spiritually.

[Jesus offers to quicken us in John 5:21–24.]

Quench is to pour water on a fire.

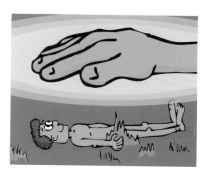

God quickened Adam.

A Rabbi is a Jewish teacher.

Rahab helped two spies escape.

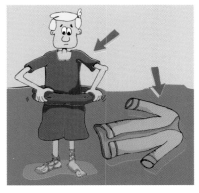

Raiment is the same as clothes.

Rabbi *(RABB-eye)*

means "my master." Rabbi is a title given to Jewish teachers. Jesus said that we are not to call anyone Rabbi. All followers of Christ are equal. Christ is the only master.

[Jesus talks about Rabbis in Matthew 23:7–8.]

Rabboni *(ruh-BOH-nee)*

is another word for Rabbi.

*[See **Rabbi**.]*

Rachel *(RAY-chul)*

was the younger daughter of Laban. Jacob saw Rachel when she brought the sheep to water. Jacob loved her and agreed to work for Laban for seven years to marry Rachel. Laban tricked Jacob into marrying Leah. Jacob worked another seven years for Rachel. She was his second wife. Rachel was the mother of Joseph and Benjamin.

[Rachel and Jacob were married in Genesis 29:16–28.]

Rahab *(RAY-hab)*

was a harlot who lived in Jericho. Rahab was the mother of Boaz. Rahab was great grandmother to King David. She hid the Israelite spies. Rahab and her family were saved when Jericho fell.

[Rahab hid the Israelite spies in Joshua, Chapter 2.]

raiment *(RAY-ment)*

are any clothes that are worn. The raiment of Jesus became white as the light when He was transfigured. Followers of Christ will be clothed in white raiment.

[Jesus' raiment turns white in Matthew 17:1–2.]

rainbow (RAIN-boh)

is the colored light in the sky after a rain. A rainbow is a sign from God. The rainbow reminds us of God's promise never to destroy the world by water again.

[The first rainbow is recorded in Genesis 9:8–17.]

A rainbow is a sign from God.

raise (RAIZ)

is to bring to life or to lift up. Jesus and the apostles raised people from the dead. Paul says that the dead will be raised with a new body. Jesus was raised from the dead. This is the resurrection of Christ.

[The raising the dead to a new life is found in I Corinthians, Chapter 15.]

ram's horn (RAMZ HORN)

was a trumpet used to call the people of Israel together. Joshua had the priests blow a ram's horn as they marched around Jericho.

[The sound of the ram's horn helped make the walls of Jericho fall in Joshua 6:5.]

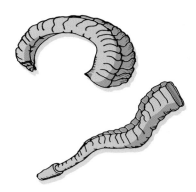

Trumpets were made out of a ram's horn.

ransom (RAN-sum)

is payment for the release of a prisoner. People are prisoners of sin. Jesus paid the ransom to set us free from the penalty of sin.

[Jesus paid the ransom in I Timothy 2:3–6.]

rapture (RAP-chur)

is a Latin word meaning caught up. Rapture is not in the Bible but is used to describe a special event. The rapture talks of believers being caught up to meet the Lord in the air.

[The rapture refers to believers being caught up as shown in I Thessalonians 4:14–17.]

A ransom is money paid to set people free.

raven (RAY-vun)

is a black bird. The raven is a member of the crow family. The raven was the first bird Noah sent out of the ark after the Flood. God sent ravens to feed

Raven is a black bird.

razor

Delilah used a razor to shave Samson's head.

Reap is to harvest grain.

Jesus rebuked Satan.

Rebekah helped Isaac cover his arms with wool.

Elijah by the brook Cherith during the famine.

[Elijah is fed by ravens in I Kings 17:4–6.]

razor (RAY-zer)

was used to shave the face and head. The beard was a sign of manhood. The head was shaved when someone was sad. People who took the Nazarite oath never shaved their heads. Samson was put under an oath before he was born. A razor was not to touch his head. Samson lost strength when Delilah put a razor to his head.

[Samson was under oath to avoid razors as recorded in Judges 13:5.]

reap (REEP)

is to harvest grain using a sickle. Gleaning is reaping the leftovers. The seed sowed is the seed reaped. Paul says if we sow to the spirit we shall reap eternal life.

[Reaping is shown in Galatians 6:7–8.]

Rebekah (ruh-BECK-uh)

was the daughter of Bethuel. Rebekah was Isaac's wife. She was the mother of Jacob and Esau. Rebekah helped Jacob trick Isaac into receiving the firstborn's blessing.

[Rebekah is married in Genesis 24:61–67.]

rebuke (reb-YUKE)

is to blame or scold. Jesus rebuked Satan when He was tempted. Jesus rebuked the wind and it calmed. Christians are to be a light to the world without rebuke.

[Christians are to be without rebuke as shown in Philippians 2:15.]

receive (re-SEEVE)

is to take or accept something offered. Christians receive everlasting life. They also receive the Holy Spirit. The ungodly will receive eternal separation from God.

[The Christian receives an eternal inheritance in Hebrews 9:14–15.]

Red Sea (RED SEE)

is a large body of water near Egypt. Moses parted the waters of the Red Sea. The Hebrews crossed on dry ground. Pharaoh's army chased them. God closed the waters of the Red Sea. The entire Egyptian army was drowned.

[Pharaoh's army is drowned in the Red Sea in Exodus 14:23–30.]

redeem (re-DEEM)

is to buy back property or to pay a ransom. God redeemed His people from Egypt. Jesus redeems us from sin. The New Testament tells how Jesus is able to be our redeemer.

*[Jesus redeems us as shown in Galatians 3:13. See **kinsman redeemer**.]*

redemption (re-DEMP-shun)

is to redeem or pay a ransom.

*[See **redeem** or **ransom**.]*

reeds (REEDS)

are the same as bulrushes.

*[See **bulrush**.]*

refuge (REF-yooj)

is a place of safety. Israel had six cities of refuge. These were cities a person could go into and be safe. They would go to a city of refuge if they had accidentally killed somebody.

*[The Lord is our refuge and strength is shown in Psalm 46:1. See **city of refuge**.]*

regeneration (re-gen-er-AY-shun)

is to be given a new life in Christ. The mercy of God regenerates the sinner. Regeneration is the same as being born again.

*[God's mercy regenerates the sinner as shown in Titus 3:5. See **born again**.]*

Rehoboam (ray-huh-BOH-um)

was a son of King Solomon. Rehoboam was to become king of Israel when King Solomon died.

The Red Sea divides Africa from Asia.

To redeem is to buy something back.

Refuge is a place of safety.

Rehoboam added more taxes.

King Solomon reigned over Israel.

Rehoboam was asked to remove some of the taxes, but he increased the taxes instead. The people rebelled. Ten of the twelve tribes formed Israel. Rehoboam became king of the remaining two tribes. He was the first king of Judah.

[Rehoboam increases taxes in I Kings 12:9–11.]

reign (RAIN)

is to rule. The Israelites wanted a king. They wanted Saul to reign over them. David and Solomon also reigned over Israel. Jesus will return to set up His kingdom. Jesus will then reign over the whole world.

[Many believers will reign with Jesus for a thousand years as shown in Revelation 20:4–6.]

Christians are to rejoice in the Lord.

rejoice (re-JOYCE)

is to be full of joy. The godly rejoice in the Word of God. The Hebrews rejoiced in being delivered from Egypt. They sang a joyful song of victory led by Miriam. Jerusalem rejoiced when Jesus entered into the city. They thought that the Messiah would set up His kingdom.

[Christians are to rejoice in the Lord always as shown in Philippians 4:4. See joy.]

remembrance (re-MEM-brunse)

is thinking of something more than once. The Israelites set up memorials to remember important events. Joshua set up twelve large stones to remember the crossing of the Jordan River. Christians are to eat the Lord's Supper. This is to remember the sacrifice that Jesus made for us.

[Jesus told us to eat the Lord's Supper in remembrance of Him as recorded in Luke 22:19–20.]

Remembrance is to recall past events.

remission (re-MISH-un)

is forgiveness or pardon. There is no remission of sin without the shedding of blood. This was one of the reasons for the animal sacrifices in the Old

Testament. Jesus died on the cross for the remission of sin. The remission of sins is available to all who believe in the name of Jesus.

[Jesus said that His shed blood was for the remission of sin in Matthew 26:28.]

remnant (REM-nunt)

is something left over. Noah and his family were a remnant after the world was destroyed. Israel and Judah went into captivity. God allowed a remnant to return to Jerusalem. This remnant rebuilt Jerusalem and the Temple. A remnant will survive God's judgment in the last days.

[God always has a remnant as shown in Isaiah 10:20–23.]

God saved a remnant from the Flood.

rend (REND)

is to tear apart. People who were sad would rend their clothes. Sometimes they would rend their clothes in anger. Jesus told Caiaphas that He was the Son of God. The High Priest rent his clothes. He said that Jesus blasphemed God.

*[Caiaphas rends his clothes in Matthew 26:57–65. See **rent**.]*

render (REND-er)

is to give. Jesus was asked if it was lawful to pay taxes. Jesus took a coin. The coin had a picture of Caesar on it. Jesus said to render to Caesar that which belonged to Caesar. He also said to render to God that which belonged to God.

[Jesus says to render taxes in Matthew 22:17–21.]

People who were sad would often rend their clothes.

rent (RENT)

is to have torn your clothes.

*[See **rend**.]*

repent (re-PENT)

is to regret a sin or crime. God wants all people to repent and come to Him. John the Baptist preached repentance to Israel. Jesus said repentance and the remission of sin should be preached

Jesus told us what to render to Caesar.

reproach

Queen Esther made a request to King Xerxes.

Resist is to push away.

A dove found no rest and returned to the ark.

to the whole world. Peter and Paul preached the Gospel of repentance.

[All heaven rejoices when one person repents as shown in Luke 15:4–7.]

reproach (re-PROACH)

is to blame or find fault. Elisabeth was the mother of John the Baptist. She said that her son took away her reproach of being childless. Jesus bore the reproach of all our sin. Christians are to avoid reproach.

[An elder is to avoid reproach as shown in I Timothy 3:7.]

request (re-KWEST)

is asking for something. Queen Esther made a request of the King. Her request was that the Hebrews would not be killed. Christians can make requests directly to God. Paul says to let our requests be known to God. Christians make requests to God by prayer.

[We can make requests to God as shown in Philippians 4:6.]

resist (re-ZIST)

is to push away. People who resist God will be separated from Him forever. Christians are to resist the Devil. He will flee from those with faith.

[Christians can resist the Devil as shown in I Peter 5:8–9.]

respecter of persons (re-SPECT-er of PER-suns)

is to have a favorite person. God is not a respecter of persons. All people are equal. All people are sinners and need Jesus. Everyone becomes a Christian the same way.

[God is not a respecter of persons as shown in Romans 2:10–11.]

rest (REST)

is to sleep or not work. Noah released a dove from the ark. The dove found no rest and returned. God offers us rest. Jesus promised to ease our load and give us rest. God made the Sabbath a day of rest.

[Jesus gives us rest in Matthew 11:28–30.]

restoreth (re-STOR-uth)

is to return. The Mosaic Law required a theft to be restored to the owner. Jesus restored the health of many sick people. The Lord can restore your soul.

[The Lord restoreth your soul in Psalm 23:3.]

Stolen property was to be restored to its owner.

resurrection (rez-uh-RECK-shun)

is to come back to life. Lazarus and Jairus' daughter were two people Jesus raised from the dead. Many people were resurrected after Jesus rose from the dead. The resurrection can also mean life after death. Jesus taught that those who were born again would have eternal life. This was eternal life in heaven with Jesus after we die. Jesus is the resurrection and the life. The Sadducees did not believe in the resurrection of the dead. They got mad when Peter preached the resurrection.

[The Sadducees arrested Peter for preaching the resurrection in Acts 4:1–3.]

Lazarus and Jairus' daughter were two people who were resurrected.

resurrection of Christ (rez-uh-REK-shun of CRYSTE)

is Jesus rising from the dead. This showed that Jesus had power over death. The resurrection of Jesus also shows that He was the Son of God. Hundreds of people touched and talked with Jesus after His resurrection. Several women went to the tomb of Jesus. They found the tomb empty. These women were the first to tell others about Jesus' being raised from the dead.

[The angels tell the women at the tomb that Jesus has risen in Luke 24:1–7.]

return of Christ (re-TURN of CRYSTE)

is when Jesus comes back to the earth. This was a promise made by Jesus and His angels. This is also called the second coming of Jesus or the blessed hope. Jesus will set up His Kingdom when He returns.

*[See the **Second Coming of Christ**.]*

An angel told the women of Christ's resurrection.

Reuben

Reuben began one of the Twelve Tribes of Israel.

Reuben *(ROO-bun)*

was the oldest son of Jacob and Leah. Reuben was the father of one of the tribes of Israel. Reuben saved the life of his youngest brother Joseph. The brothers threw Joseph into a pit and later sold him to a trader.

[Reuben saves Joseph's life in Genesis 37:18–22.]

revelation *(rev-uh-LAY-shun)*

is knowledge given by God. All knowledge of God comes by way of revelation. The Holy Spirit explains mysteries to us through revelations.

[A revelation of Jesus Christ was given to John in Revelation 1:1–3.]

Revelation is how God tells us about Himself and the future.

Revelation, Book of *(rev-uh-LAY-shun, Book of)*

is a New Testament book about the end of the world. John is given a special revelation from God. Revelation tells how a false Christ will come to rule the earth. The world will become evil. It will be just like the days of Noah. God will judge the world again. He will use fire and brimstone. Revelation also tells us of the coming blessings for those who obey God.

[Paradise is given to the followers of Christ for eternity as shown in Revelation 22:1–5.]

revenge *(re-VENJ)*

is the same as vengeance.

*[See **vengeance**.]*

Rhoda *(ROH-duh)*

lived in the same house as Mary, the mother of John Mark. When Peter was in prison, the people in Mary's house prayed for him. Peter was freed and went to Mary's house. Rhoda answered the door. She was surprised when she saw Peter. Rhoda shut the door and ran to tell the others. Rhoda forgot to let Peter into the house.

[Rhoda sees Peter in Acts 12:12–16.]

Rhoda was surprised to see the apostle Peter.

riddles (RID-ulz)

are puzzles or sayings with a hidden meaning. Samson had a riddle about honey. A sign of wisdom is to be able to solve riddles. The Queen of Sheba tested King Solomon with hard questions or riddles. The king was able to answer all her questions.

[The Queen of Sheba gave riddles to King Solomon in I Kings 10:1–3.]

Samson had a riddle about honey.

righteous (RYE-chus)

is to be right. God is righteous. Jesus allows us to have the righteousness of God.

[The righteousness of God is given to people in II Corinthians 5:17–21.]

A robe is an outer garment.

robe (ROBE)

is a long outer garment. Sleeveless robes of blue or purple were worn by royalty, prophets, and the wealthy. A great number of people will wear white robes at the throne of God. The robes are white because they are washed in the blood of the Lamb.

[White robes are worn in Revelation 7:9–14.]

Peter is a name that means rock.

rock (ROCK)

is a large stone. Gideon put an offering on a rock. An angel struck the rock with a staff. Fire came out of the rock. Peter's name means rock. The rock with which Jesus built His church was the fact that He is the Son of God. Moses struck a rock with his staff. Water came out of the rock. Jesus is the rock that gives living water.

[Jesus is the rock of living water as shown in I Corinthians 10:4.]

rod (ROD)

is a long piece of wood. Rod is the same as staff. A rod was used for walking. Rods were also used to guide sheep. God's rod can guide and comfort us.

[The Lord's rod is a source of comfort as shown in Psalm 23:4.]

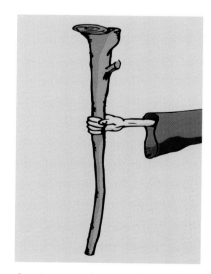

A rod was used as a walking stick.

Paul made an appeal as a Roman citizen.

A root is the part of the plant that is in the ground.

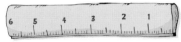

DO UNTO OTHERS AS YOU WOULD HAVE OTHERS DO UNTO YOU

Jesus gave us the golden rule.

Ruth gleaned the fields of Boaz.

Roman (ROH-mun)

was a citizen of Rome or the Roman empire. Paul was a Roman. Paul had more rights as a Roman citizen. Paul appealed to Rome when he was arrested.

[*Paul uses his Roman rights in Acts 25:11. See **appeal**.*]

Romans, Epistle to the (ROH-muns, uh-PIS-ul to the)

is a New Testament book written to the church at Rome. Romans clearly shows God's plan for salvation. Salvation is a free gift. Anyone who calls on the name of the Lord shall be saved. Romans also lists the duties for Christians.

[*God's plan of salvation is listed in Romans 10:9–13.*]

root (RUTE)

is the part of a plant that is buried. The plant can live and grow only if the root is healthy. Seeds must take root before they can grow. Jesus said the same is true for God's Word. The Word of God must take root in our heart before we can come to God. Satan can take away the Word. False teachings can choke out the Word of God. A hardened heart will keep the Word from being able to take root.

[*Jesus talks of God's word taking root in Mark 4:3–20.*]

rule (RULE)

is to have power over. Rule means the same as reign.

[*See **reign**.*]

rule, golden (RULE, GOLD-un)

is a rule for living given by Jesus.

[*See **golden rule**.*]

Ruth (ROOTH)

was a Moabite. Ruth married a Hebrew. When her husband died, she went to Israel with her mother-in-law, Naomi. Ruth was poor and was

gleaning the fields of Boaz. Boaz saw her and loved her. He married Ruth and became the kinsman redeemer for Ruth. Ruth became the great grandmother of King David.

[Ruth was married in Ruth 4:13.]

Ruth, Book of (ROOTH, book of)

is an Old Testament book about a kinsman redeemer. Ruth was a gentile. She married a Jew. She had all the promises given to God's chosen people. Boaz became the kinsman redeemer for Naomi and Ruth.

[Boaz becomes a kinsman redeemer in Ruth 4:9–15.]

Sabbath

God told the Israelites to honor the Sabbath.

Sabbath (SAB-uth)

is a day of rest. The Sabbath is holy to God. It honors the fact that God rested on the seventh day after creation. Honor the Sabbath was one of the Ten Commandments.

[The Sabbath was made holy in Exodus 31:13–17.]

sackcloth (SACK-CLOTH)

are clothes made from coarse material. Wearing sackcloth was a sign of mourning or anguish.

*[See **grieve**.]*

Sackcloth is a coarse fabric used to hold grain.

sacrifice (SACK-ruh-fyse)

is making an offering to God. Sacrifices were made by the rule of the Mosaic Law. The animals had to be clean types. They had to be perfect and without defects. Sacrifices are also called offerings. Sacrifices were made to God for several reasons. Some were made for thanksgiving. The most important reason is to show sadness for sin. A sin offering was made to ask God to forgive sin. God forgave the sin of Israel for one year on the Day of Atonement. Jesus was the Lamb of God. He was sacrificed for our sin. Jesus was the perfect sacrifice.

[Jesus is the perfect sacrifice as shown in Hebrews 10:8–14.]

A sacrifice is an offering to God.

Sadducees (SAD-juh-seez)

was a religious group in Israel. They believed only in the Mosaic Law. They did not believe in the resurrection. Many of the Sadducees opposed Jesus and the apostles.

[The Sadducees arrested Christians in Acts 5:17–18.]

saint (SAINT)

is someone set apart or holy. The New Testament says that anyone who believes in Jesus as Lord is a saint. Millions of saints will be killed in the last days.

[Followers of Christ are called saints in I Corinthians 1:2.]

Salt is a mineral of life.

Salem (SAY-lum)

is a short form of Jerusalem. Salem means peaceful.

*[See **Jerusalem**.]*

salt (SALT)

is a mineral needed for life. Christians are the salt of the world. Lot's wife was turned into a pillar of salt. She wanted to go back to the wicked city of Sodom.

[Lot's wife was turned into salt in Genesis 19:23–26.]

Salvation is to be saved from danger.

Salt Sea (SALT SEE)

is the same as the Dead Sea.

*[See **Dead Sea**.]*

salvation (sal-VAY-shun)

is to keep someone from harm. It is the same as saving a life from death. Salvation is also called being born again. It delivers us from sin. Salvation comes from believing in Jesus. Salvation allows people to go to heaven.

*[See **born again**.]*

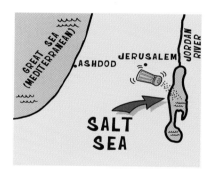

Salt Sea is the old name for the Dead Sea.

Samaria (suh-MAIR-ee-uh)

was the area given to the tribes of Manasseh and Ephraim. Samaritans believed that Mount Gerizim is God's chosen place. They believed that Adam worshiped God there. The Jewish people in Samaria combined the worship of God with the worship of idols. The rest of the Jews knew this was wrong. They called Samaritans dogs. They would not talk with or touch Samaritans. Jesus talked and ate with Samaritans. This made the priests very mad.

[Jesus stayed in Samaria for two days in John 4:39–42.]

Samaria was a province of the Roman Empire.

A Samaritan helped a man who was beaten.

Samaritan *(suh-MAIR-uh-tun)*

is someone who is from Samaria. The most famous Samaritan is the one in the parable told by Jesus. A Samaritan was the only healed leper to give thanks to God. Jesus talked to a Samaritan at Jacob's well. He offered the living water.

*[See **Good Samaritan**.]*

Samson *(SAM-sun)*

was the last major judge of Israel. He was the son of Manoah. He was also of the tribe of Dan. Samson was dedicated to be a Nazarite. God gave him great strength. Samson fought the Philistines. Samson was betrayed by Delilah.

[The story of Samson is found in Judges 13:24–16:31.]

Samuel *(SAM-you-ul)*

was born to Hannah. He was raised by the Prophet Eli at the Shiloh sanctuary. God talked to Samuel when he was a boy. Samuel became a priest and a prophet of Israel. He anointed the first two Kings of Israel.

[God talks to Samuel in I Samuel 3:1–14.]

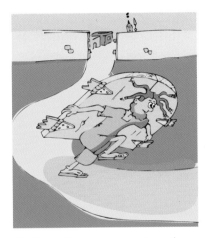

God gave Samson great strength.

Samuel, Book of, I and II *(SAM-you-ul, Book of, I and 2)*

is a record of the lives of the prophet Samuel, King Saul, and King David. Samuel was the last judge for Israel. Saul and David were the first two kings for God's people. Samuel anointed both of these men.

[David's song of thanksgiving is recorded in II Samuel, Chapter 22.]

sanctified *(SANK-tuh-fide)*

means to be set apart as holy. The Temple and the Tabernacle are sanctified by God's glory. The things inside the Temple and the priest are also sanctified. Christians are to be sanctified and useful servants of God.

[Christians are sanctified in Hebrews 10:8–14.]

Samuel answered God's call.

sanctuary (SANK-choo-air-ee)

is a holy place. Sanctuaries include shrines, the Tabernacle, and the Temple. Jesus is the high priest of the heavenly sanctuary.

[Jesus ministers in the heavenly sanctuary in Hebrews 8:1–2.]

sandals (SAND-ulz)

are types of shoes worn to protect the feet. Thongs or laces held the sandal on the foot. Sandals were removed before entering a tent or house. Sandals were also removed when walking on holy ground.

[John the Baptist said he was not worthy to unloose the shoe of the Messiah in Luke 3:15–18.]

Sanhedrin (san-HEED-run)

is the Greek word for council. This council was the high Jewish council. They ruled over the religious issues of Israel. The council had seventy-one members. The High Priest was the head of the Sanhedrin. The Sanhedrin began when Moses selected seventy elders plus Aaron, the High Priest. The Sanhedrin plotted to kill Jesus. The council tried to keep the Gospel from being told.

[The Sanhedrin seeks to kill Jesus in John 11:47–54.]

Sapphira (suh-FIRE-uh)

and her husband Ananias sold a belonging. They were going to give all the money to the church, but they hid some of the money. Peter asked if they had given all they promised. Sapphira was struck dead when she lied to God.

[Ananias and Sapphira lie to the Holy Spirit in Acts 4:32–5:10.]

Sarah (SAIR-uh)

was the name of Abraham's wife. God promised Sarai a son. God then changed Sarai's name to Sarah.

*[See **Sarai**.]*

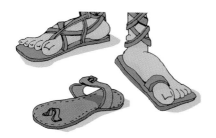

Sandals are types of shoes.

The Sanhedrin were seventy religious leaders.

Sapphira and her husband hid money from God.

Sarah was ninety years old when she became a mother.

Satan is one of the names for Lucifer.

Saul was anointed as the first King of Israel.

The smoke of the incense offering is a sweet savour.

Sarai (suh-RYE)

was Abraham's wife. She had traveled with Abraham from Ur to Haran. Sarai did not have children. God talked with Abraham. God promised Abraham that He would give Sarai a son. God changed her name to Sarah. Sarah was ninety years old when she had her first child. She was the mother of Isaac.

[God makes a promise to Sarai in Genesis 17:15–22.]

Satan (SAYT-un)

means adversary. The name Satan also means enemy. Satan is one of the names used for Lucifer. Satan is a fallen angel. He disobeyed God.

*[See **Lucifer**.]*

Saul (SAUL)

was the son of Kish. He was of the tribe of Benjamin. Saul was the tallest person in Israel. He was anointed by Samuel to be the first king of Israel. King Saul led Israel in battle against the Philistines. Another Saul was a person who killed Christians. He was later called Paul. He became the apostle to the gentiles.

*[See **Paul**.]*

saved (SAVED)

is the same as salvation.

*[See **salvation**.]*

Saviour (SAVE-yur)

is the person who saves. Saviour is one of the names for the Messiah. Sin separates people from God. A Saviour is needed to bring people back to God. Jesus was the Messiah and is the Saviour.

[God sent Jesus to be the Saviour of the world in I John 4:14–15.]

savour (SAVE-ur)

is the same as a smell. Incense was burned on the altar of incense. There was also smoke when a burnt offering was made. The smoke of both of these was called a sweet savour. This smoke represented the prayers of God's people going up to heaven.

[A sin offering made a sweet savour before the Lord in Exodus 29:37–42.]

A scepter is a small staff of a king.

scepter (SEP-ter)

was a small staff of a king. A scepter was a sign of the king or a queen. It was a sign of power. Queen Esther touched the top of a scepter of gold. This showed that she respected the king. Joshua promised that the scepter shall not depart from the tribe of Judah. This meant that the king of Israel would always be of the tribe of Judah. King Saul and King David were of the tribe of Judah. The Messiah will set up a kingdom on Earth. The Messiah has to come from the tribe of Judah. Jesus is of the tribe of Judah.

[Joshua makes the promise of the scepter in Genesis 49:8–10.]

scorn (SCORN)

is to hate or mock. Jarius' daughter died. Jesus went to his house. Jesus was laughed to scorn when He said she was just asleep. Jesus raised her from the dead.

[Jesus was laughed to scorn in Mark 5:21–24 and Mark 5:35–43.]

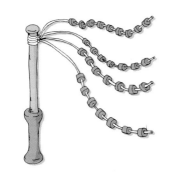

A scourge is a whip with glass or metal in the ends.

scourge (SKERJ)

is to be beaten with a whip. Sometimes the whip had glass or iron pieces in it. Pilate had Jesus scourged before He was crucified.

[Jesus was scourged in Matthew 27:19–26.]

scribes (SCRIBES)

are people trained to write. A scribe was used to record business or decisions made by the king. Scribes were used to copy the Scripture carefully. The prophet Ezra was a scribe. The scribes helped the chief priest make plans to kill Jesus.

[The scribes seek to destroy Jesus in Luke 19:47–48.]

Scribes copied the books of the Bible.

Scripture

The Scriptures were written on scrolls.

Scripture (SCRIP-cher)

is the written Word of God. There are sixty-six books in the Christian Scripture called the Bible.

*[See **Word of God**.]*

scrolls (SCROLLZ)

are made of long sheets of papyrus. They are rolled at each end. Scrolls were used to record important things. The Scriptures were recorded on scrolls.

[The heavens will be rolled back like a scroll in the last days as shown in Isaiah 34:1–8.]

seals (SEELS)

were special marks made in soft clay. The clay hardened and could not be changed. The seal told who sent a message. It also showed that the message had not been opened. The tomb of Jesus had a seal put on the doorway.

[The tomb is sealed by Pilate in Matthew 27:62–66.]

Seals are special marks that tell who sent the message.

seat (SEET)

is a place to sit. It is a type of chair. Decisions are made from a judgment seat. The mercy seat was the top of the Ark of God. God talked with the High Priest from the mercy seat.

[The details of the mercy seat are found in Exodus 25:17–22.]

Second Coming of Christ (SE-cund COME-ing of CRYSTE)

is the return of Jesus to the earth. This is also called the blessed hope. Jesus will set up His kingdom when He returns. Two angels declared that He would return when Jesus went to heaven. No one knows when Jesus will return.

[The angels promise that Jesus will return in Acts 1:6–11.]

seek (SEEK)

is to look for something. The ungodly seek after pleasures and wealth. Jesus said we are first to seek the Kingdom of God. God will then supply all our needs.

[Jesus talks of seeking in Matthew 6:31–34.]

To seek is to look for something.

separate *(SEP-er-ATE)*

is to set apart or be removed from something. A person sometimes separates himself so he can seek God. The Israelites were a separate nation. They were set apart for God. Nothing can separate us from the love of Christ.

[It is impossible to be separated from Christ's love as shown in Romans 8:35.]

Shepherds separate sheep from goats.

sepulchre *(SEP-ul-ker)*

is the same as tomb or grave. Jesus' body was placed in a sepulchre.

*[See **grave**.]*

A sepulchre is a tomb.

seraphim *(SAIR-uh-fim)*

are winged beings that attend the throne of God. A seraph has six wings. They flew above the throne of God. Seraphim sing praises to God. A seraph purified Isaiah.

[Isaiah meets a seraph in Isaiah 6:1–8.]

Seraphim are a six-winged type of angel.

Sermon on the Mount *(SER-mun on the MOUNT)*

is the message given by Jesus to His Twelve Disciples. The mount was located near Capernaum. This message told His disciples how to live godly lives. The Sermon on the Mount begins with the Beatitudes. Jesus taught with power on how the godly are to live.

[The Sermon on the Mount can be found in Matthew, Chapters 5 to 7.]

The serpent had legs before God cursed it.

serpent *(SER-pent)*

is a poisonous snake. The serpent walked on legs in the Garden of Eden. It was the prettiest of all the animals. Satan used the serpent to cause Eve to sin. God cursed the serpent to go on its belly.

[The serpent lies to Eve in Genesis 3:1–7.]

servant *(SER-vunt)*

is a paid worker. Servants helped with the harvest. Foot washing was a lowly job done by servants. Jesus washed the feet of the disciples. He was

The Sermon on the Mount began with the Beatitudes.

To serve is to help or to work for someone.

God created the world in seven days.

The seven churches of the Book of Revelation.

Jesus had seven recorded sayings before He died on the cross.

showing that He came as a servant. Paul said he was a slave or servant of Jesus Christ.

[Peter says we are servants of God in I Peter 2:13–17.]

serve (SERVE)

is to help or work for someone. Jesus says we can serve only one master. We will either serve God or serve the world. Christians are to serve Jesus.

[Jesus talks of serving in Matthew 6:24.]

Seth (SETH)

was the third son of Adam and Eve. Seth was the father of Enos. Seth began a tribe of godly men. Prayer began with Seth.

[Seth's birth is recorded in Genesis 4:25–26.]

seven (SEV-un)

is a number for perfection and completeness. God created for six days and rested on the seventh day. This showed that creation was perfect and complete. Joshua marched around Jericho once each day for six days. They marched around the city seven times on the seventh day. The priests blew seven trumpets made from rams' horns. Their victory was complete. God's final judgment will come in three groups of seven judgments. God's judgment will be perfect and complete.

[Joshua marches around Jericho seven days in Joshua 6:1–20.]

seven churches (SEV-un CHUR-chuz)

were the churches in Asia Minor. These seven churches were Ephesus, Smyrna, Pergamos, Thyatira, Sardis, Philadelphia, and Laodicia. There are some good and bad things said about most of these churches. They are presented to us as examples for churches to follow or avoid.

[These churches are listed in Revelation 1:4–3:22.]

seven sayings from the cross (SEV-un SAY-ings from the CROSS)

are the last things Jesus said before He died.

1. He asked God to forgive those who put Him on the cross [*Luke 23:34*].
2. He promised that the thief would be with Him in paradise [*Luke 23:43*].
3. He told John to care for Mary [*John 19:26–27*].
4. He quoted Psalm 22:1 [*Matthew 27:46*].
5. He said He thirsted [*John 19:28*].
6. He said "It is finished" [*John 19:30*].
7. He quoted Psalm 31:5 [*Luke 23:46*].

Shadrach refused to worship the idol.

seventy weeks (SEV-un-tee WEEKS)

refers to a prophecy made by Daniel. This was seventy weeks of events that would happen before the Messiah came. The Messiah would then set up His kingdom. This will be the Kingdom of God.

[Daniel talks of the seventy weeks in Daniel 9:24–27.]

Shadrach (SHAD-rack)

was one of Daniel's three friends. They were taken as slaves to Babylon. His Hebrew name was Hananiah. Shadrach, Meshach, and Abednego refused to worship an idol. The three were thrown into a fiery furnace. God saved these men.

[Shadrach, Meshach, and Abednego are thrown into the furnace in Daniel 3:8–28.]

Sheba is a country that is south of Israel.

Sheba (SHEE-buh)

was a country to the south of Israel. Sheba was located on the Arabian peninsula. The Queen of Sheba visited King Solomon.

*[See **Queen of Sheba**.]*

sheepfold (SHEEP-FOLD)

is where sheep are kept safe. Some sheepfolds were made of stone fences. Others were attached to houses. Jesus says that a thief does not use the door to enter a sheepfold. This is talking of false prophets. They try to find another way to God. But Jesus is the only way to come to God.

[The sheepfold is talked about in John 10:1–9.]

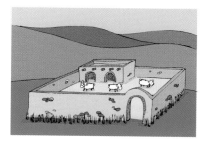

A sheepfold kept sheep safe.

A shekel is a small coin.

A shepherd was one who took care of the sheep.

Shewbread was a special bread that was sprinkled with frankincense.

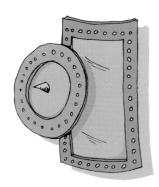

A shield was worn in battle.

shekel (SHAY-kul)

is a Hebrew weight that was about half an ounce. It is also a small coin that was worth one day's pay. Absalom trimmed his long hair once a year. The hair that was cut off weighed two hundred shekels.

[Absalom weighs his hair in shekels in II Samuel 14:25–26.]

Shem (SHEM)

was the name of Noah's oldest son. Shem was one of eight people that entered the ark. These were the only people saved from the Flood.

[Shem entered the ark in Genesis 7:13–17.]

shepherd (SHEP-erd)

is one who watches and takes care of sheep. A good shepherd knows each of his sheep by name. Jesus is the Good Shepherd. He knows His sheep and laid down His life for them.

[Jesus is a good shepherd as shown in John 10:7–18.]

shewbread (SHOE-BRED)

are the twelve cakes put in the Temple of God. Frankincense was put on these cakes. These cakes were put on the Table of Shewbread every week. The shewbread were to be eaten by the priests. The twelve cakes of shewbread was a memorial of the covenant between God and the Twelve Tribes of Israel.

[The shewbread is described in Leviticus 24:5–9.]

shield (SHEELD)

is a device worn on the arm. It is used to protect a person from a sword or arrows. It was made of hard leather or brass. A strap held it firmly on the arm. The other arm was free to use a sword. The shield of faith protects us from the fiery darts of Satan.

[The shield of faith is listed in Ephesians 6:11–19.]

Shiloh *(SHY-loh)*

was a city north of Jerusalem. Shiloh had a sanctuary or a safe place to go. This is where Eli and Samuel lived and worshipped God. The Ark of God was kept at Shiloh from the time of Joshua until Eli's sons lost it in a battle.

[Eli's sons take the Ark of God from Shiloh in I Samuel 4:4–11.]

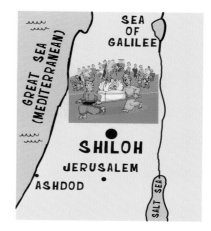

Shiloh was where Eli's sons took the Ark of God into battle.

Shittim *(SHI-tum)*

is a dense wood used in making things for the Tabernacle and the Temple. Shittim was usually covered with gold or brass. Shittim is also called acacia wood.

[Shittim wood was used in building the Tabernacle in Exodus 25:1–9.]

Shittim is the same as acacia wood.

shod *(SHOD)*

is to wear shoes or sandals. This was done to prepare for battle or work or to run. Christians are told to have their feet shod with the Gospel. This means that they are to be ready to take the Gospel anywhere.

[Christians are to have their feet shod in Ephesians 6:11–17.]

signs *(SINES)*

are miracles that prove God is at work. Jesus and the apostles performed signs and wonders. Jesus said the only sign that He was the Messiah would be the sign of Jonah. Jonah was in the belly of the fish for three days and three nights. This sign was that Jesus would be dead for three days and nights and then resurrected. It was a sign that proved He was the Messiah.

[Jesus tells us the sign that He is the Messiah in Luke 11:29–32.]

To shod is to put on sandals.

Silas *(SY-lus)*

was also called Silvanus. He was a leader in the early Jerusalem church. He went with Peter and Paul on missionary trips. Paul and Silas were imprisoned in Philippi. God delivered them from prison with an earthquake. They won the jailer and his family to the Lord.

[Paul and Silas are freed from jail in Acts 16:19–33.]

Paul and Silas were freed from jail.

King Hezekiah made a tunnel to the pool of Siloam.

Simeon praised God when he saw baby Jesus at the Temple.

Simon the Cyrene carried the cross for Jesus.

To sin is to disobey God.

Siloam (sye-LOH-um)

was a pool in Jerusalem created by King Hezekiah. The king made a tunnel to the Siloam pool to help protect the city from an enemy. Jesus used the Siloam pool to give sight to a blind man. He had the blind man wash his eyes in the pool.

[Jesus heals at the Siloam pool in John 9:1–11.]

Simeon (SIM-ee-un)

was one of Jacob's sons. He began the tribe of Simeon. Joseph kept Simeon bound in Egypt. His brothers had to bring Benjamin to free Simeon. Simeon was also a devout Jew who lived in Jerusalem. God promised Simeon that he would see the Messiah. Joseph and Mary brought Jesus to the Temple eight days after His birth. Simeon praised God. Simeon blessed Joseph and Mary.

[God's promise to Simeon is recorded in Luke 2:25–35.]

Simon (SYE-mun)

was a popular name. Simon Peter was one of Jesus' disciples. He was the son of Jonah. Simon Peter was also the brother of Andrew. Jesus changed his name to Peter. Simon of Cyrene was made to carry the cross of Jesus to Golgotha. One of the half brothers of Jesus was named Simon. Jesus visited the house of Simon the leper in Bethany.

*[Simon of Cyrene was made to carry the cross in Matthew 27:31–33. See **Peter, the apostle**.]*

sin (SIN)

is to disobey God or break one of His commandments. Sin began with Adam and Eve. Death started with sin. Sin separates us from God. Jesus paid the penalty for sin. Trusting in the work that Jesus did allows us to go to heaven.

[Jesus paid for our sins in II Corinthians 5:17–21.]

Sinai, Mount (SYE-NYE, MOUNT)

is where Moses received the Ten Commandments.

*[See **Mount Sinai**.]*

Sisera *(SIS-uh-ruh)*

was the captain of the Canaanite army. A heavy rain got all Sisera's chariots stuck in the mud. Deborah and Barak defeated Sisera. Sisera fled to the tent of Jael. Jael killed Sisera in his sleep.

[The death of Sisera is recorded in Judges 4:17–21.]

The chariots of Sisera got stuck in the mud.

skull, place of *(SKULL, PLACE of)*

is what Golgotha means. It was the place Jesus was killed.

*[See **Golgotha**.]*

slave *(SLAVE)*

is a person owned by a master. Paul and Peter said that Christian slaves are to obey their masters. Paul said he was a slave or servant of Jesus Christ. Onesimus was a slave to Philemon. He had run away. Paul met Onesimus and led him to Christ. Paul helped Onesimus return to Philemon.

[The story of the runaway slave is found in Philemon 10–19.]

A slave has no freedom.

sleep *(SLEEP)*

is the rest one gets at night. Sleep sometimes refers to death. Paul says that those who sleep in death shall live with Christ.

[Those who are alive and those who are asleep meet Jesus in I Thessalonians 4:13–18.]

Sleep is a time of rest.

slew *(SLOO)*

is the same as killed. David slew Goliath. Samson slew the Philistines. The Romans and Pharisees slew Jesus.

[Peter told the priest that they slew Jesus in Acts 5:28–33.]

sling *(SLING)*

is a weapon carried by shepherds and soldiers. David used a sling to kill lions and bears. A sling was a long leather strap used to throw stones. David killed the giant Goliath with a stone from a sling.

[David used a sling in I Samuel 17:38–51.]

A sling was a weapon that threw stones.

To smite is to strike another person.

Snares are traps set by hunters for animals.

God destroyed Sodom with fire.

slothful (SLAWTH-ful)

is to be slow and lazy. A slothful servant wastes time. The slothful person does not earn a fair day's pay. Christians are to do work with energy. They are not to be slothful since they serve the Lord.

[Christians are not to be slothful as shown in Romans 12:11.]

sluggard (SLUG-erd)

is the same as slothful.

*[See **slothful**.]*

smite (SMITE)

is to hit or strike. The Lord smote Pharaoh with ten plagues. God will smite the earth with plagues in the last days.

[The two witnesses are given power to smite the earth in Revelation 11:3–6.]

snares (SNAIRS)

are traps used by hunters to catch birds and animals. Elders of the church are to have a good reputation. This allows them to avoid the snares of the devil.

[Reproach is a snare of the devil in I Timothy 3:1–7.]

sober (SOH-ber)

refers to someone who is awake and clear minded. The day of God's judgment can come at any time. Paul says that Christians are to be sober. Christians are to wear the armour of God.

[Paul tells Christians to watch and be sober in I Thessalonians 5:2–9.]

Sodom (SAH-dum)

was a wicked city. It was located next to Gomorrah. God destroyed both of these cities. God rained fire and brimstone. The smoke of God's wrath went up like a furnace.

*[Sodom and Gomorrah are destroyed in Genesis 19:12–28. See **Gomorrah**.]*

Solomon *(SAH-luh-mun)*

was the tenth son of David. He was the second son of Bathsheba. Solomon became the third king of Israel. God asked King Solomon what he desired. King Solomon asked for wisdom, and God gave him wisdom. He sat in judgment for the people of Israel. King Solomon was wise enough to determine who was the real mother of a baby boy.

[King Solomon tests the women in I Kings 3:16–28.]

Solomon was the wisest man that ever lived.

Son of God *(SON of GOD)*

is another name of Jesus. This shows that Jesus was God. God the Father called Jesus His Son when He was baptized. An angel called Jesus the Son of God prior to His birth.

[God said He was pleased with His Son in Mark 1:9–11.]

Son of Man *(SON of MAN)*

is a name for Jesus. This shows that Jesus was a true man. Jesus was God in the flesh.

*[See **Emmanuel**.]*

Jesus, the Son of God, loves children.

Song of Solomon *(SONG of SAH-luh-mun)*

is a love poem. It shows the love of a husband for his wife. The Song of Solomon shows God's love for Israel. This poem is also a picture of the love Jesus has for His church.

[Mutual love is shown in Song of Solomon 2:16–17.]

sons of thunder *(SONS of THUN-der)*

was the name Jesus gave to the brothers James and John. This name may have meant that they were loud. Perhaps they were rough in doing things. James and John had short tempers. A village in Samaria rejected Jesus. The sons of thunder wanted Jesus to call fire down from heaven to destroy them. Sons of thunder was a name that matched their actions.

[Jesus names James and John the sons of thunder in Mark 3:17.]

James and John were called the "sons of thunder."

Southern kingdom is one of the names
for two of the Tribes of Israel.

To sow is to scatter seeds on the
ground.

A sow is a female pig.

sorrow (SAR-roh)

is sadness or grief.

[See **grieve**.]

soul (SOUL)

is the part of a person that is not seen. The soul
lives forever. Your soul will be with God or will
be separated from God. Jesus says that all the
wealth in the world is not worth losing your
soul.

[Jesus talks of the value of a soul in Matthew 16:26.]

southern kingdom (SUH-thern KING-dum)

is the two tribes of Judah and Simeon. Israel split
into two parts when King Solomon died. The
southern kingdom is known as Judah. The northern kingdom is known as Israel. Solomon's son
Rehoboam is the first king of Judah.

[The nation is divided in I Kings 12:16–24.]

sow (SOW—rhymes with low)

is to scatter seeds on the ground. The husband-
man would sow his fields and take care of them.
He would harvest the field if all went well.
Sharing the Gospel is like sowing seeds.

[Jesus gave the parable of the sower in Matthew 13:3–23.]

sow (SOW—rhymes with cow)

is a female pig. A pig is also called a swine. Swine
were unclean animals to the Jews. A sow will
always return to her mud. This was a way to find
false teachers. They will return to their ungodly
ways.

[Peter talks about sows in II Peter 2:22.]

spare (SPAIR)

is to keep from judgment. Nineveh was wicked.
God sent Jonah to tell them to repent. Nineveh
obeyed God. God spared Nineveh.

[God spared Nineveh in Jonah 3:5–10.]

spies *(SPIZE)*

are people sent into a country to gather facts. Spies are sent in secret. Moses sent twelve spies into the Promised Land. Joshua sent two spies into Jericho.

[The story of the two spies is found in Joshua, Chapter 2.]

Moses sent twelve spies into the Promised Land.

spirit *(SPEER-ut)*

is the part of man that gives life. People were created in the image of God. We have a soul, a body, and a spirit. This is much like the three persons of the Trinity: God the Father, God the Son, and God the Holy Spirit.

[Paul wants our spirit to be set apart for God in I Thessalonians 5:23.]

Spirit, Holy *(SPEER-ut, HOE-lee)*

is the same as God the Holy Spirit.

*[See **God the Holy Spirit.**]*

Achan hid the spoils of war in his tent.

spiritual gifts *(SPEER-ut-chul GIFTS)*

are skills God has given to all who obey God. Each Christian has been given different gifts. Love is the greatest of all these gifts.

[The spiritual gifts of God are listed in Romans 12:6–8.]

spoils *(SPOY-ulz)*

are things taken in war. God told Israel not to take spoils when they took Jericho. Achan hid clothes, silver, and gold in his tent. God made Israel lose their next battle.

[Achan takes spoils in Joshua 7:1 and 7:16–25.]

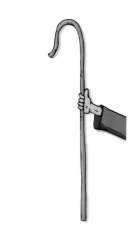

A staff was used by shepherds.

staff *(STAFF)*

is a wood stick. It is used to help walk or climb. A staff is also used for tending sheep. A staff is the same thing as a rod.

*[See **rod.**]*

star of the east *(STAR of the EAST)*

is the sign that brought the wise men to Bethlehem.

The magi saw the star of the east.

Stephen

Stephen saw heaven as he died.

This star went before them and stood over where baby Jesus was.

[The star of the east is a guiding light in Matthew 2:2–10.]

Stephen (STEE-vun)

was one of the seven deacons chosen for the Jerusalem church. Stephen preached the Gospel. The priests arrested Stephen. They stoned Stephen to death. Saul held the clothes of those that were throwing stones.

[The story of Stephen is found in Acts 6:5–7:60.]

steward (STOO-erd)

is a person in charge of another's property. Christians are to be good stewards of the gifts God gives them.

[Christians are to be faithful stewards as shown in I Corinthians 4:1–2.]

Stocks were used to hold prisoners.

stocks (STOCKS)

are wooden frames that hold the head, hands, and feet. Prisoners were jailed and put in stocks.

[Paul and Silas were thrown in jail and bound in stocks in Acts 16:16–24.]

stone (STONE)

is a rock. Stones were used for city walls, dwellings, palaces, and roads. David used a smooth stone to kill Goliath.

[David uses a stone in I Samuel 17:49.]

stoning (STONE-ing)

is a Hebrew death sentence. The condemned person was led outside of the city. Then the people of the city circled the condemned person. They threw large rocks until the condemned person died. Stephen was stoned to death in Jerusalem. Jesus stopped the stoning of an adulterous woman. He said, "He that is without sin among you, let him first cast a stone at her."

[The stoning of Stephen is found in Acts 7:58–60.]

Stoning was a type of death sentence.

storehouse (STORE-HOUSE)

is a stone building used to keep harvested crops. This protected the crops from pests, the weather, and thieves. Obeying God has many blessings. A full storehouse is one of these blessings.

[The storehouse blessing is found in Deuteronomy 28:1–8.]

A storehouse is where grain was kept.

strike (STRIKE)

is to hit. The priests covered Jesus' head and struck him. Then they demanded that He tell them which of them struck Him.

[The priests strike Jesus in Mark 14:65.]

stripes (STRIPES)

are the long wounds made by a whip or scourge. Jesus was scourged. Isaiah prophesied of the stripes of the Messiah. He said that we are healed because of His stripes.

[Isaiah talks of the stripes of the Messiah in Isaiah 53:4–12.]

Stripes refer to the wounds from scourging.

stubble (STUBB-ul)

is the stalks of grain left after the grain is removed. It is sometimes called straw or chaff. Stubble is easily burned.

[Our works for God may contain wood, hay, and stubble as shown in I Corinthians 3:9–15.]

study (STUH-dee)

is to read and learn. Christians are to study God's Word. This helps them to understand His truths correctly.

[Paul says that we are to study in II Timothy 2:15.]

Stubble is leftover stalks of grain.

stumbling block (STUM-bling BLOCK)

is anything that causes a person to stumble or fall. The prophet Malachi said that corrupt priests were a stumbling block to the people. The Gospel of Jesus is a stumbling block to the ungodly.

[Jesus is a stumbling block as shown in I Corinthians 1:22–25.]

People can trip over stumbling blocks.

To suffer is to have pain.

submit *(sub-MITT)*

is to yield or give in. Christians are to submit themselves unto God.

[James tells us to submit to God in James 4:7–8.]

suffer *(SUFF-er)*

is to have a hurt or pain. The Hebrews thought suffering was punishment for sin. Jesus suffered because of our sin.

[Peter talks of the suffering of Christ in I Peter 2:21–24.]

Supper, Last *(SUPP-er, LAST)*

is the last meal that Jesus ate before He died.

*[See **Last Supper**.]*

Supper, Lord's *(SUPP-er, LORD's)*

is done in memory of the death of Jesus.

*[See **Lord's Supper**.]*

supplication *(suh-pli-CAY-shun)*

is asking humbly. Supplications to God are done in prayers.

[Supplications are to be made for all people as shown in I Timothy 2:1.]

swaddling *(SWODD-ling)*

are long narrow pieces of linen. Babies and broken bones were wrapped in swaddling. The cloth was wrapped tightly to prohibit movement. Mary wrapped Jesus in swaddling clothes.

[Jesus is put in swaddling clothes in Luke 2:7.]

Broken bones can be wrapped in swaddling clothes.

swear *(SWAIR)*

is to say foul things. Swear is also to make an oath. Peter swore as he denied knowing Jesus.

[Peter cursed and swore in Mark 14:66–72.]

swine *(SWINE)*

are pigs. Swine are unclean animals for the Jews. The Jews were not to use them for sacrifice or for food. Jesus sent thousands of demons

A swine is a pig.

into a herd of swine. The swine jumped off a cliff and died.

[The death of two thousand swine is recorded in Mark 5:2–13.]

sword (SORD)

is a weapon with a long sharp blade. The Word of God is sharper than a two-edged sword. The entrance to the Garden of Eden is guarded with a flaming sword.

[A flaming sword guards the tree of life in Genesis 3:24.]

A sword is a weapon with a long blade.

sycomore (SICK-uh-more)

is a tree much like a combined fig and mulberry tree. Holes were made in the fruit before it could be eaten. Sycomores were planted along roads to provide shade. Zacchaeus was a very short man. He climbed up a sycomore tree in order to see Jesus.

[Zacchaeus climbs a sycomore in Luke 19:1–5.]

Zacchaeus hid in a sycomore tree.

synagogue (SIN-uh-gogg)

is the local meeting place for Jewish people. The synagogue was where the Scriptures and the law were taught. Jesus read and taught in the synagogues.

[Jesus went into the synagogues as shown in Matthew 9:35.]

Jesus read Scripture in the synagogue.

Tabernacle

The Tabernacle was a tent used for worship.

Table of Shewbread held twelve loaves of bread.

The first set of tables was the Ten Commandments.

One talent weighs about one hundred pounds.

Tabernacle (TAB-er-nack-ul)

was a sacred tent used for worship. God told Moses how to build the Tabernacle. The Tabernacle had two rooms. One was called the Holy Place. The other was the Holy of Holies. The Ark of God was placed in the Holy of Holies. There was a fence around the Tabernacle. A pillar of cloud or fire stood over the Ark of God. The Tabernacle was used for worship until King Solomon built the Temple.

[Moses begins using the Tabernacle in Exodus 33:7–9.]

Tabitha (TAB-uth-uh)

is another name for Dorcas.

[See Dorcas.]

Table of Shewbread (TAY-bul of SHOE-BRED)

is a gold-plated table. This table held the twelve cakes of the shewbread. The Table of Shewbread was placed in the Tabernacle and the Temple.

[Things that go on the Table of Shewbread are listed in I Kings 7:48–50.]

tables of law (TAY-buls of LAW)

are flat pieces of stone made by God. God wrote his law on two tablets. Moses broke the first two tablets. He saw Israel worshipping an idol. God gave Moses two more tablets. The two tables of law are kept in the Ark of God.

[The first set of tables was given to Moses in Exodus 24:12–14.]

talent (TAL-ent)

is a weight of one hundred pounds. The foolish steward buried the talent given to him. His master punished him for not using the talent. God wants us to use all that we have for Him. He does not want us to waste our abilities.

[Parable of the talents is found in Matthew 25:14–30.]

tares *(TAIRS)*

are a grassy weed. Young tares look just like young wheat. Tares do not produce useful grain. Pulling up the tares before the harvest can damage the wheat crop.

[Jesus gives the parable of the tares in Matthew 13:25–30.]

Tares are a type of weed that look like wheat.

tarry *(TAIR-ee)*

is to wait. Young Jesus tarried in Jerusalem. Mary and Joseph left the city without Him. Jesus and three of His disciples went into the Garden of Gethsemane. Jesus told the disciples to tarry and watch. The disciples tarried but did not watch. They fell asleep.

[The disciples tarried in Gethsemane in Matthew 26:36–46.]

Paul was born in Tarsus.

Tarsus *(TAR-sus)*

is located near the Mediterranean Sea. Tarsus is the capital of the Roman province of Cilicia. Tarsus is the birthplace of Paul.

[The birthplace of Paul is found in Acts 9:11.]

tax *(TACKS)*

is money paid to the king. Jesus talks of paying taxes to Caesar. Joseph and Mary went to Bethlehem to pay taxes.

*[Jesus used a fish to pay taxes in Matthew 17:24–27. See **render.**]*

Tax is money paid to the king.

teacher *(TEE-chur)*

is a person who instructs. Teacher is the same as Rabbi.

*[See **Rabbi.**]*

tempest *(TEM-pest)*

is a terrible storm at sea. Jonah was caught in a tempest. A fish swallowed Jonah, and the tempest

Tempest is a storm at sea.

Temple

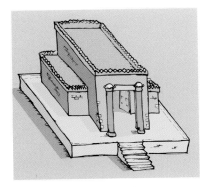

The Temple is where Israel worshipped.

To be tempted is to have a desire to do wrong.

Satan tempted Jesus three times in the wilderness.

calmed. The disciples were in a tempest on the Sea of Galilee. Jesus spoke and the wind calmed. Paul was in a tempest when sailing near Crete. He was shipwrecked.

[Paul is caught in a tempest in Acts 27:13–44.]

Temple *(TEM-pul)*

was a place of worship. The Temple was built like the Tabernacle. King David wanted to build the Temple. God said that a man of war would not build His house. King Solomon built the first Temple. The Temple was very beautiful. The Holy Spirit was present in the Holy of Holies. The Holy Spirit lives in the hearts of Christians. Paul says that our bodies are the temples of God.

[King Solomon builds the Temple in I Kings 6:1–2.]

tempt *(TEMPT)*

is to try to make someone do wrong. Satan tempted Eve in the Garden of Eden. Satan told Eve to eat the fruit, and she ate it.

[Satan uses a serpent to tempt Eve in Genesis 3:1–6.]

temptations of Christ *(temp-TAY-shuns of CRYSTE)*

are the attempts of Satan to destroy Jesus' ministry. Jesus went into the wilderness to fast and pray. Satan first tempted Jesus to turn stones into bread. But Jesus is the bread of life. The second temptation was to jump off a tall point of the Temple. Satan said the angels would save Him. Jesus said, "Thou shalt not tempt the Lord thy God." Satan offered Jesus all the kingdoms of the earth. Jesus told Satan to leave Him. Satan did not want Jesus to be the Messiah. Jesus was able to be tempted because He was fully human.

[The temptations of Christ are listed in Matthew 4:1–11.]

Tempter *(TEMP-ter)*

is another name for Satan.

*[See **Satan**.]*

Ten Commandments *(TEN cuh-MAND-ments)*

are the writings on the tables of stone. The Ten Commandments are part of the Mosaic Law. The Israelites were to obey the Ten Commandments. These Commandments are:

1. to have no other gods,
2. to not make graven images,
3. to not take God's name in vain,
4. to honor the Sabbath,
5. to honor your father and mother,
6. to not kill,
7. to not commit adultery,
8. to not steal,
9. to not be a false witness, and
10. to not covet.

[The Ten Commandments are found in Exodus 20:1–20.]

God gave Moses the Ten Commandments.

ten plagues of Egypt *(TEN PLAYGZ of EE-jipt)*

are the judgments God gave to Egypt in the Book of Exodus. Moses asked the Pharaoh for the release of the Hebrews. Pharaoh would not let them go. God sent ten plagues against Egypt. Pharaoh's magicians copied the first two plagues. The ten plagues God sent were:

1. blood *[Exodus 7:14–25];*
2. frogs *[Exodus 8:1–15];*
3. locusts *[Exodus 10:1–20];*
4. lice *[Exodus 8:16–19];*
5. flies *[Exodus 8:20];*
6. darkness *[Exodus 10:21–23];*
7. cattle die *[Exodus 9:1–7];*
8. boils and blains *[Exodus 9:8–12];*
9. hail *[Exodus 9:18–34];* and
10. death of the firstborn *[Exodus 11:4–6].*

Pharaoh finally let Moses and the Hebrews go.

God cursed Egypt with ten plagues.

tent *(TENT)*

is a shelter made of cloth or skin supported by poles. Abraham lived in a tent. The Israelites lived in tents in the wilderness. Paul was a tent maker.

[Paul made tents in Acts 18:3.]

A tent was a portable house.

The Tabernacle was a Tent of Meeting.

A testament is the same as a promise.

Testimony is to give evidence.

Thaddeus was one of the Twelve Disciples.

Tent of Meeting (TENT of MEET-ing)

is a chosen tent used for a meeting place. Tent of Meeting is the same as the Tabernacle.

*[See **Tabernacle**.]*

testament (TEST-uh-ment)

is a promise. Testament means the same as covenant.

*[See **covenant**.]*

testimony (TEST-uh-moh-nee)

is to give proof or evidence. Testimony is also a public showing of faith. Peter declared the testimony of God to the followers of Christ.

[The Testimony of God is recorded in I Corinthians 2:1–2.]

Thaddeus (THAD-ee-us)

was one of the Twelve Disciples. He is also called Judas the Son of James.

[Thaddeus is listed as a disciple in Mark 3:13–19.]

thanksgiving (thanks-GIVE-ing)

is being grateful for things received. Thanksgiving is part of prayer and worship. All things and blessings we receive come from God. Christians are to give thanksgiving to God.

[Paul tells us to give thanksgiving in Philippians 4:6.]

Thessalonian (thess-uh-LONE-ee-un)

is someone from Thessalonica.

*[See **Thessalonica**.]*

Thessalonians, Epistle to the, I and II (thess-uh-LONE-ee-uns, uh-PIS-ul to the, I and 2)

are New Testament letters written by Paul to the church at Thessalonica. Both letters talk about the ministry of Jesus. These letters tell of His return. Paul gives Christians a hope for the future.

[Believers in Christ will live with Jesus as shown in I Thessalonians 5:9–11.]

Thessalonica (thess-uh-LAH-nuh-kuh)

was the biggest city in Macedonia. Paul preached the Gospel in Thessalonica. A large church was started in this city.

[Paul visited Thessalonica in Acts 17:1–2.]

thief (THEEF)

is someone who steals. Stealing broke one of the Ten Commandments. The thief on the cross went to heaven. The second coming of Jesus will be like a thief in the night. A thief steals when no one is looking. Jesus will return when people are no longer looking for Him.

[Jesus will come like a thief as shown in II Peter 3:10.]

A thief takes what does not belong to him.

thirst (THIRST)

is to have a need for water. Jesus met a woman at the well. He told her that if she drank from the living water she would never thirst. Jesus was thirsty on the cross.

[Jesus takes care of thirst in John 4:13–15.]

thistle (THISS-ul)

is a plant with small spikes or thorns. Thistles had their beginning with Adam's sin. Thistles are a part of Adam's curse. God cursed the ground and made thorns and thistles.

[God created thistles in Genesis 3:17–19.]

A thistle has many tiny thorns.

Thomas (TOMM-us)

was one of the Twelve Disciples of Jesus. Thomas is also known as doubting Thomas. This is because he did not believe that Jesus was alive. Thomas had to touch the nail prints in Jesus' hands to believe.

[Jesus told Thomas to put his finger into His hand in John 20:24–29.]

thorn (THORN)

is a sharp leafless branch. Thistles have small thorns. The thorns used to make the crown that

Thomas had to see the holes in Jesus' hands.

A thorn is a sharp leafless branch.

Thummin was one of the stones used by the High Priest.

Timbrels are musical instruments.

Sundials are an old way of keeping track of time.

Timothy was taught Scripture by his mother and grandmother.

was put on Jesus' head were about three inches long.

*[See **crown of thorns** or **thistle**.]*

thorns, crown of (THORNS, CROWN of)

was a ring of thorns put on Jesus' head to mock Him. They called Him the King of the Jews after they put the crown of thorns on His head.

*[See **crown of thorns**.]*

Thummim (THUMB-im)

was one of the objects used by the High Priest. It was used with the Urim to make decisions.

*[See **Urim and Thummim**.]*

tidings (TIDE-ings)

is the same as news. The angel of the Lord brought glad tidings of great joy to the shepherds. These tidings told of the birth of the Saviour.

[Glad tidings are given in Luke 2:1–20.]

timbrel (TIM-brul)

is a musical instrument. A timbrel looks much like a tambourine. A timbrel was used to sing and praise the Lord.

[Miriam used a timbrel in her victory song in Exodus 15:20.]

time (TIME)

is the measure of the moments of existence. There is a time and purpose for everything.

[King Solomon talks of time in Ecclesiastes 3:1–8.]

Timothy (TIM-uth-ee)

was the son of Eunice. Timothy was from Lystra. He was a young pastor. Paul had led Timothy to the Lord. His mother Eunice and his grandmother Lois taught him the Scriptures when he was a boy.

[Timothy was taught the Scriptures in II Timothy 3:15.]

Timothy, Epistle to, I and II *(TIM-uth-ee, uh-PIS-ul to, I and 2)*

were New Testament letters written by Paul. These letters were to instruct and comfort Timothy. Timothy was a young pastor. II Timothy is the last writings of the apostle Paul.

[Paul tells Timothy to preach the mystery of godliness as recorded in I Timothy 3:14–16.]

tithe *(TITHE)*

means one tenth. A tithe of the increase in crops and livestock was to be given to the Lord under the Mosaic Law. Abraham gave a tithe of his possessions to the Priest Melchizedek.

[The first tithe is recorded in Genesis 14:18–20.]

tittle *(TIT-ul)*

is a small mark in making a Hebrew letter. Tittle is much like crossing a *t* in our alphabet.

[See jot.]

Titus *(TITE-us)*

was a gentile companion of Paul (Galatians 2:3). Paul led Titus to the Lord. Titus and Paul preached the Gospel together.

[Titus brought comfort to the church at Corinth in II Corinthians 7:5–7.]

Titus, Epistle to *(TITE-us, uh-PIS-ul to)*

is a New Testament letter written by Paul. Paul tells Titus to go do good work. Paul also teaches duties and doctrines of Christ.

[Good works are to be maintained in Titus 3:8.]

tomb *(TOOM)*

is a place to keep the dead. Jesus was placed in a tomb. The tomb of Jesus was located outside the city walls of Jerusalem. It was a new tomb cut in the rock. The tomb was owned by Joseph of Arimathea.

[The tomb of Jesus is described in Matthew 27:57–60.]

A tithe means the one-tenth portion that belongs to God.

דְּבוֹרָה

TITTLE

Tittle is the smallest Hebrew letter.

A tomb is where dead people were placed.

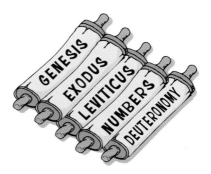

The Torah is the first five books of the Old Testament.

Nimrod tried to build the Tower of Babel.

Transfiguration is when the glory of God shown in Jesus.

tongues of fire (*TUNGZ of FIRE*)

was a visible sign given by God. The Holy Spirit filled all the people present at Pentecost. Tongues of fire sat on each believer. These people could now speak foreign languages. This gift allowed the Christians to tell the Gospel to the foreigners visiting Jerusalem.

[Tongues of fire are found in Acts 2:1–4.]

Torah (*TOR-uh*)

is the first five books of the Old Testament. Torah means the law or the law of Moses. Torah is also called the Pentateuch.

*[See **Pentateuch**.]*

Tower of Babel (*TOW-er of BAY-bel*)

was built to reach God. Nimrod was building the Tower of Babel. God was not pleased with this. God gave these people different languages. This made them scatter around the world. The tower was never finished.

[The story of the Tower of Babel is found in Genesis 11:1–9.]

traditions (*truh-DISH-uns*)

are rules added to the law of Moses. The Pharisees obeyed the Mosaic Law through traditions. Jesus and the disciples disobeyed the traditions of the Pharisees by plucking and eating corn on the Sabbath.

[Jesus and the disciples disobeyed the traditions of the Pharisees in Matthew 12:1–8.]

transfiguration (*trans-fig-yur-AY-shun*)

is when the glory of God was shown in Jesus. Jesus, Peter, James, and John went up Mount Hermon. Elijah and Moses appeared with Jesus. Jesus shone white as snow. God the Father called Jesus His beloved Son.

[Jesus is transfigured in Matthew 17:1–8.]

transgression (trans-GRES-shun)

is breaking a law. Transgression is the same as sin.

[See **sin**.]

treasure (TREZ-yur)

is the storage of valuables. Our heart is where our treasure is located. Jesus says that earthly treasures can be stolen. Jesus tells us to store up heavenly treasures.

[We are to lay up treasures in heaven as shown in Matthew 6:19–21.]

Treasure is the storage of valuables.

Tree of Knowledge of Good and Evil (TREE of NAH-luj of GOOD and EE-vul)

was one of the trees in the middle of the Garden of Eden. Adam and Eve were not to eat of this tree. Satan tempted Eve to eat of this tree. The first sin was when Adam and Eve ate the fruit of the Tree of Knowledge of Good and Evil.

[Tree of Knowledge of Good and Evil is forbidden as shown in Genesis 2:16–17.]

Adam and Eve ate fruit from the Tree of Knowledge.

Tree of Life (TREE of LIFE)

was one of the trees in the Garden of Eden. Eating of this tree gives eternal life. Jesus is the Tree of Life. Followers of Jesus have access to the Tree of Life.

[The Tree of Life is shown in Revelation 22:14.]

The Tree of Life has twelve different fruits.

trials of Jesus (TRY-uls of JEE-zuz)

was the way the Jews had Jesus sentenced to death. Jesus was tried before the Romans. Jesus appeared before Pilate, Herod Antipas, and a second time before Pilate. Pilate sentenced Jesus to death.

[Pilate sentences Jesus to death in Matthew 27:19–26.]

Tribes of Israel (TRIBES of IZ-ray-el)

were the groups that made up all the Hebrews. There were twelve tribes of Israel. Each tribe started with one of the sons of Jacob. The Twelve

Pilate held two trials for Jesus.

Tribulations are trials and troubles.

Jesus made a triumphal entry into Jerusalem.

Jesus is the True Vine.

Tribes of Israel are (1) Reuben, (2) Simeon, (3) Levi, (4) Judah, (5) Issachar, (6) Zebulun, (7) Joseph, (8) Benjamin, (9) Dan, (10) Naphtali, (11) Gad, and (12) Asher. The tribe of Joseph was made of the half tribes of Ephraim and Manasseh. Each tribe was given a portion of the Promised Land. The tribe of Levi did not receive land. They received a tithe from the other tribes.

[The Twelve Tribes of Israel are blessed by Jacob in Genesis 49:1–28.]

tribulation *(trib-you-LAY-shun)*

is the same as trials and troubles. Christians will have tribulation in the world. This is because the world does not like Jesus. The great tribulation is God's judgment in the last days.

[Jesus talks of the great tribulation in Matthew 24:21.]

Trinity *(TRIN-uh-tee)*

is the three persons of the one true God. The Trinity has God the Father, God the Son, and God the Holy Spirit. Each person of the Trinity is God. All three make only one God.

*[The Trinity is shown in II Corinthians 13:14. See **God the Father; God the Son; God the Holy Spirit.**]*

triumphal entry *(try-UHM-ful EN-tree)*

is when Jesus entered Jerusalem on the Sunday before He was crucified. Jesus rode on a young donkey as He entered the city. This was the way a new king entered a city. The people cried, "Hosanna!" and laid down palm leaves.

[Jesus made a triumphal entry into Jerusalem in John 12:12–16.]

True Vine, the *(TRUE VINE, the)*

is another name for Jesus. This shows that Jesus is the foundation of our faith. Christians are the branches of the True Vine.

[Jesus is the True Vine as shown in John 15:1.]

trumpet *(TRUM-put)*

is a type of horn. Trumpets were made of rams'

horns. Trumpets were used in war and in worship. God uses trumpets to announce judgments in the last days. The walls of Jericho fell because the people shouted and the priest blew trumpets. Trumpet judgments shows God's judgment is not hidden or secret.

[The priests blow seven trumpets in Joshua 6:20.]

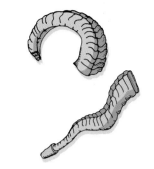

Some trumpets were made from rams' horns.

trust *(TRUST)*

is belief and hope. Trust means much the same thing as faith.

*[See **faith**.]*

truth *(TROOTH)*

is to be honest and factual. God is truth. Jesus is truth. Two of His names are the True Light and the True Vine.

[Jesus is truth as shown in John 14:6.]

twain *(TWAIN)*

means in two pieces. The veil separated the Holy of Holies from the rest of the Temple. The veil of the Temple was torn in twain by God. This happened when Jesus died on the cross. This showed that people could now come directly to God in the name of Jesus.

[The veil of the Temple was ripped in twain in Matthew 27:51.]

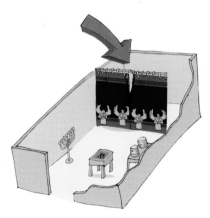

The veil of the Temple was torn in twain.

Twelve Disciples *(TWELVE di-SIPE-uls)*

are the twelve men chosen by Jesus. These were:
1. Simon (Peter),
2. Andrew (Peter's brother),
3. James (son of Zebedee),
4. John (son of Zebedee, brother of James),
5. Philip,
6. Bartholomew,
7. Thomas,
8. Matthew (the Publican),
9. James (son of Alphaeus),
10. Lebbaeus Thaddeus (Judas, brother of James),

Jesus selected the Twelve Disciples.

Twelve Tribes of Israel

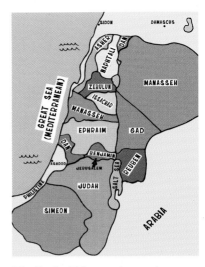

The Twelve Tribes make up the nation of Israel.

11. Simon (Zelotes, the Canaanite), and
12. Judas Iscariot.
Matthias was selected to replace Judas Iscariot. The apostles were with Jesus during His three years of ministry.

[The list of apostles is found in Acts 1:13.]

Twelve Tribes of Israel *(TWELVE TRIBES of IZ-ray-el)*

are the groups of Hebrews. They make up the entire nation of Israel.

[See **Tribes of Israel.***]*

Gentiles are also called the uncircumcised.

uncircumcised *(uhn-SIR-cum-sized)*

is to not be circumcised. Circumcision was a sign of the covenant between God and Abraham. The uncircumcised means the same as gentiles. The uncircumcised were considered heathen and unclean. Jews were not to eat with the uncircumcised. Jesus ate with the gentiles.

*[Jesus ate with sinners in Matthew 9:10–13. See **circumcision**.]*

unclean *(uhn-CLEEN)*

refers to those animals, foods, and things that were not allowed for the Israelites. These are unclean things with regard to worshipping and obeying God. Touching the unclean would make the Jew unclean. Jews were not allowed to enter the Temple or join in the feast until they were clean. This is why the Pharisees did not go in to see Pilate. They wanted to join in on the Passover feast.

[The Pharisees do not enter Pilate's hall in John 18:28.]

Israelites were not to eat unclean animals.

undefiled *(uhn-duh-FILED)*

is to be spiritually clean.

*[See **clean**.]*

understand *(uhn-der-STAND)*

is to know the meaning of something. God gives believers understanding of His Word. Jesus spoke in parables. This was to let only believers understand His teaching.

[Jesus talks of understanding in Matthew 13:10–17.]

unforgivable sin *(uhn-for-GIVE-uh-bul SIN)*

is a sin that God cannot forgive. The shed blood of Jesus has the power to forgive all sin. Sin must be forgiven by God in order for one to go to heaven.

BIRDS OF THE AIR HAVE NESTS, BUT THE SON OF MAN HATH NOT WHERE TO LAY HIS HEAD

Christians can understand the teachings of Jesus.

Worshipping idols is ungodly.

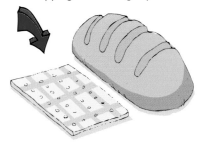

Unleavened bread does not have yeast.

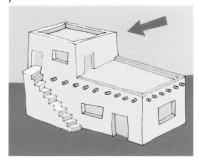

The upper room was a place for eating.

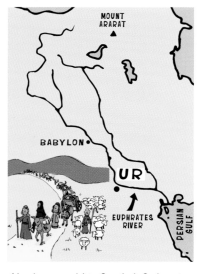

Abraham and his family left the city of Ur.

God does not make us worship Him. People are given the freedom to make that choice. Because forgiveness is a gift from God, a sinner has to ask for forgiveness. The sinner who has hardened his heart toward God does not ask for this gift. The Holy Spirit is then not able to convict their heart of sin. This is the blasphemy of the Holy Spirit. Their sin becomes an unforgivable sin.

[Jesus talks of the unforgivable sin in Matthew 12:22–32.]

ungodly *(uhn-GOD-lee)*

is anyone who does not obey God. The ungodly shall not go to heaven. Jesus died for the ungodly. The ungodly can have eternal life by following Jesus.

[Jesus died for the ungodly as shown in Romans 5:1–8.]

unleavened bread *(uhn-LEV-und BRED)*

is bread baked without using leaven or yeast. Unleavened bread was eaten during the Passover feast. This celebrated God's deliverance of Israel from Egypt. Because they did not have time for their bread to rise, they ate unleavened bread.

[The Hebrews ate unleavened bread in Exodus 12:8.]

upper room *(UP-er ROOM)*

was the name of an upstairs room. One upper room was chosen by Jesus. This was where the Last Supper was eaten. One hundred twenty disciples gathered in another upper room. This was where the early Christians met to hear the Gospel.

[Two disciples prepare the upper room for the feast of unleavened bread in Mark 14:12–16.]

Ur *(OOR)*

was a city in Mesopotamia. Abraham was born in Ur. The Lord brought Abraham out of Ur.

[Abraham followed God out of Ur in Genesis 15:7.]

Uriah (yuh-RYE-uh)

was a soldier and a Hittite. Bathsheba was the wife of Uriah. King David wanted Uriah's wife. Bathsheba carried a son by King David. King David had Uriah killed and married Bathsheba. He thought this would hide his sin. God sent Nathan to judge King David.

[Uriah is killed in II Samuel 11:14–17.]

Uriah was killed in battle when others backed away.

Urim and Thummim (OOR-im and THUMB-im)

are objects of the High Priest. He wore them over his heart. The Urim and Thummim were kept in the breastplate of judgment. The High Priest used the Urim and Thummin to make decisions.

[The Urim and Thummim are worn next to the High Priests heart as shown in Exodus 28:30.]

The Urim and Thummin were small stones.

Uzzah (UH-zuh)

was the son of Abinadab. The Philistines had given the Ark of God to Abinadab. King David wanted the Ark of God taken to Jerusalem. Uzzah and his brother drove the ox cart carrying the ark. God said no one was to ever touch the ark. The ox stumbled, and Uzzah reached to keep it from falling over. God struck Uzzah dead when he touched the ark.

[Uzzah dies in II Samuel 6:1–7.]

Uzzah took the Ark of God to Jerusalem.

God gave Cain a mark of a vagabond.

King Ahasuerus wanted Vashti to show her beauty.

Moses wore a veil to hide his face.

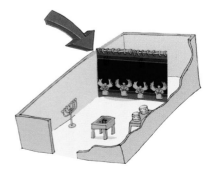

The Veil of the Temple guarded the Holy of Holies.

vagabond *(VAG-uh-bond)*

is a wanderer. This was a curse given to Cain. Cain had killed his brother. God gave Cain a mark so that people he met would know who he was. Cain was to be a vagabond for the rest of his days.

[Cain becomes a vagabond in Genesis 4:9–15.]

vail *(VAIL)*

is the same as veil.

*[See **veil**.]*

Vashti *(VASH-tee)*

was the Queen of Persia. King Ahasuerus wanted her to show off her beauty, but she refused. The King selected a new queen. He selected Esther.

[Vashti refuses to show her beauty in Esther 1:9–12.]

veil *(VAIL)*

is a cloth covering. Veils were sometimes used to cover the face. Rebekah wore a veil when she met Isaac. Tamar wore a veil when she met Judah. Moses talked to God on Mount Sinai. His face shone brightly with the glory of God. The people of Israel were afraid. Moses wore a veil to hide his face when he talked to the people.

[Moses wears a veil in Exodus 34:29–35.]

Veil of the Temple *(VAIL of the TEM-pul)*

was a curtain that separated the Holy of Holies from the Holy Place. The veil was about four inches thick and made of fine linen. The veil was blue, purple, and scarlet. There was a pattern of cherubim in the cloth. The veil kept men out of the presence of God. The High Priest could enter the Holy of Holies only once a year. The veil was torn from top to bottom when Jesus died on the cross. This shows that Jesus is our High Priest. We can now come boldly to the presence of God through Jesus.

[The veil is torn in Matthew 27:50–51.]

Vial is a small cup or bowl.

vengeance (VEN-junse)

is punishment given to one who has done an evil deed. The Lord says, "Vengeance is mine." This means that vengeance belongs only to God. Vengeance is God's punishment to the ungodly.

[Vengeance belongs only to God as shown in Hebrews 10:30.]

vial (VYE-ul)

is a shallow cup or bowl. Vials held oils for anointing. Some of God's judgments at the Second Coming of Christ will be vial judgments. This type of judgment shows how His wrath will be poured out on the wicked.

[The vial judgments begin in Revelation 16:1–2.]

Villages had no walls.

vile (VILE)

is to be evil or wicked.

*[See **evil**.]*

village (VILL-uhj)

is a place where people live. A village was small. It had no walls. Farming and fishing were the main jobs at most villages.

[Jesus visited many villages as recorded in Matthew 9:35.]

A vine is the stem of a climbing plant.

vine (VINE)

is the long stem of a climbing plant. Vine usually means a grapevine. The vine gives life to the branches and leaves of the plant. Jesus is the True Vine. He gives eternal life to believers.

[Jesus is the True Vine as shown in John 15:1–5.]

vinegar (VIN-ug-er)

was a sour wine. Vinegar and wine were forbid-

Jesus was given vinegar when He was crucified.

241

Grapevines grow in a vineyard.

A viper is a poisonous snake.

Gabriel told the virgin Mary that she would bear the Messiah.

The Virgin Birth of Jesus occurred in a stable.

den to Nazarites. Jesus was thirsty on the cross. Vinegar was put on a sponge and offered to Jesus.

[Jesus only drank the vinegar when his work on the cross was done as recorded in John 19:28–30.]

vineyard (VIN-yerd)

is a place where grapevines grow. Vineyards had hedges, walls, or trees around them. A vineyard had a winepress located in the middle. Queen Jezebel killed Naboth so the king could take his vineyard.

[The queen takes a vineyard in I Kings 21:1–14.]

viper (VYE-per)

is a poisonous snake. Jesus called the Pharisees vipers because of their sharp talk. Paul was bitten by a viper. Paul just shook the snake off. The viper did not harm Paul.

[Paul gets bit by a viper in Acts 28:3.]

virgin (VER-jun)

is a person who has not known another person intimately. Mary was a virgin. She became pregnant with Jesus. Joseph was supposed to marry her. He was confused when Mary became pregnant and wanted to stop the wedding. But an angel explained to him that a virgin was needed to bring the Messiah into the world. Joseph took Mary as his wife.

[An angel tells Joseph that Mary was still a virgin in Matthew 1:18–23.]

Virgin Birth (VER-jun BIRTH)

was the birth of Jesus in the flesh. Mary was a virgin. Mary was not married but was promised to Joseph. God gave her a child. That child was the Messiah. Isaiah said that the Messiah would be born to a virgin.

[Jesus has a virgin birth in Matthew 1:18–25.]

vision (VIZ-yun)

is a special sight given by God. A vision was one way that God used to give special messages. Amos, Hosea, Isaiah, and Ezekiel are some of the prophets who had visions. Daniel understood all visions. Kings came to Daniel to find the meanings of their visions. Stephen had a vision of heaven when he was being stoned to death.

[God gave Daniel a vision to explain the king's dream in Daniel 2:19–23.]

The apostle John had a vision of the last days.

vow (VOW—rhymes with cow)

is a promise made in return for something. A vow can be a one-time thing. A vow could be for a lifetime. Some Nazarite vows are life-long vows. A Nazarite vow was to dedicate someone solely to God.

[Samson was vowed to the Lord before his birth as recorded in Judges 13:3.]

A vow is a type of promise.

A wage is money paid for work done.

Babies can wail when they cry.

Walls protected a city.

The Israelites wandered in the wilderness.

wages (WAY-juz)

is the pay for the work done. Jacob's wages were a portion of the flock. God gives wages to those who follow His commandments. Sin demands a wage that everyone must pay. Christ paid the wages for those who trust Him.

[The wages for sin have been paid for by Jesus in Romans 6:23.]

wailing (WAIL-ing)

is to cry very loudly. Wailing was done to show pain or grief. Wailing and gnashing of teeth is used to describe a response to a very bad punishment. The ungodly will wail and gnash their teeth when they are separated from God.

[Jesus talks of the wailing and gnashing of teeth in Matthew 13:36–43.]

walls (WALLS)

are the outside structures of houses and cities. Walls are built for protection. They were made of stone or brick. The walls of a city were very thick. Rahab built her house on top of the wall of Jericho. The city walls of Babylon were wide enough for six chariots to ride side by side.

[Rahab lived on the wall of Jericho as recorded in Joshua 2:12–17.]

wander (WAHN-der)

is to travel without direction or purpose. The entire nation of Israel left Egypt and went toward Canaan. God guided them with a pillar of cloud in the daytime. God fed the Israelites with manna and quail. They wandered from Egypt to the land God promised to Abraham. Moses received the Ten Commandments during this time. Israel did not enter into the Promised Land the first time. They were afraid and did not trust God. God made them wander for forty years.

[Israel is to wander for forty years in Numbers 32:10–13.]

want (WANT)

is another word for need. Psalm 23 states that "the Lord is my shepherd, I shall not want." God provides all our needs.

[Our wants are met by God in Psalm 23.]

Priests used lavers to wash in.

wash (WASH)

is to clean with water. Priests were washed before they put on priestly robes. Animals were washed before they were sacrificed. The physical cleaning was an outward sign of the spiritual cleaning that was taking place. The blood of Christ washes us whiter than snow.

[The white-robed saints stand clean before God in Revelation 7:13–17.]

watches of the night (WAT-chuz of the NITE)

were different times of the night when soldiers were on duty. They were usually guarding or protecting something.

[We do not know during which watch of the night Jesus will return as shown in Luke 12:36–40.]

Watches of the night kept guard over cities.

water (WAT-er)

is a clear liquid required to support all life. Jesus offered the woman of Samaria living water. He said she would never thirst again. Jesus is the living water.

[Jesus offers a well of living water in John 4:7–15.]

Water was usually found in wells.

waterpots (WAT-er-pots)

are containers of stone or clay made for holding water. Large waterpots were kept indoors and filled with smaller pots. These larger waterpots contained the water for Jesus' first miracle. He turned the water into wine.

[Jesus has six waterpots filled with water in John 2:6–11.]

Waterpots were used to store water.

245

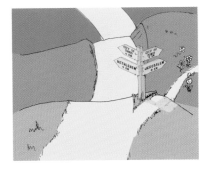

A way is a path or road.

wax *(WAX)*

is to grow in strength or numbers. John the Baptist and Jesus waxed strong in spirit as they grew up.

[Paul and Barnabas waxed bold in Acts 13:46–48.]

way *(WAY)*

is a path or a road. Broad is the way of destruction. Jesus is the way to come to God the Father. This way is narrow.

[The two paths of life are listed in Matthew 7:13–14.]

wealth *(WELTH)*

is the amount of gold, land, cattle, or servants a person has. Wealth is a blessing from God. God owns the cattle on a thousand hills. But the love of money is the root of all evil. Followers of Christ have riches untold.

[Riches can keep a person from God as shown in Luke 18:18–27.]

Wealth is the amount of riches a person has.

weary *(WEER-ee)*

is to become tired. God does not get weary. Those people who trust and obey God will not be weary. The Lord will renew their strength.

[The promise to not be weary is made in Isaiah 40:28–31.]

weep *(WEEP)*

is to cry in sorrow or grief.

*[See **grieve**.]*

well *(WELL)*

is a hole dug in the ground to find water. Wells were the main supply of water for the Israelites. Cities were built near wells or rivers.

[Jesus met the woman of Samaria at Jacob's well in John 4:6–10.]

whence *(WENTS)*

means from where. Many did not know whence Jesus came.

[Jesus asked whence came the baptism of John in Matthew 21:23–27.]

Weary is to be very tired.

whirlwind (WERL-WIND)

is a strong wind that travels in a circle. A tornado is one kind of whirlwind. God talked to Job from a whirlwind. Elijah was taken up to heaven in a whirlwind.

[Elijah's trip to heaven began in a whirlwind in II Kings 2:1–11.]

whither (WI-ther)

means which place or where. Abraham went where God said. He did not know whither he went. The Israelites went whither the Lord led. God let His nation wander in the wilderness for forty years.

[The Promised Land was whither God was to bring the Israelites, as shown in Leviticus 20:22–24.]

widow (WI-doh)

is a wife after her husband has died. Widows were to be taken care of. Elijah met a widow of Zarephath during a famine. She was going to make a small cake with her last handful of meal and the last of her oil. Elijah told her to make a cake for him first. The widow obeyed the prophet, and the Lord blessed her. Her barrel of meal and bottle of oil was always full until the famine was over.

[The story of the widow and the cakes is found in I Kings 17:8–16.]

wife (WIFE)

is the woman in a marriage. A godly wife is a crown to her husband. King Solomon said her value is more than rubies and pearls. Wives are to submit to their husbands. This was to show that a wife obeyed God.

[Peter asks wives to submit to their husbands in I Peter 3:1.]

wilderness (WILL-der-ness)

is the same as a desert. There is little rain and few people in a wilderness. Israel wandered forty years in the wilderness.

[The Israelites complain about the wilderness in Numbers 21:4–5.]

Water was obtained from wells.

Elijah was taken to heaven in a whirlwind.

The widow made small cakes for Elijah.

Wiles are tricks played on another person.

A winepress squeezes juice from grapes.

Winnowing is tossing grain into the air.

wiles *(WILES)*

are tricks. Christians are to wear the armour of God. This will protect them from the wiles of the devil.

[The wiles of the devil are shown in Ephesians 6:11–18.]

will of God *(WILL of GOD)*

is the same as God's will.

*[See **God's will.**]*

wine offering *(WINE OFF-er-ing)*

is wine offered to God. It is also called a drink offering. A wine offering was part of the sin and peace offerings.

[Jacob made a wine offering at Bethel in Genesis 35:10–14.]

winepress *(WINE-PRESS)*

is a place where grapes were squeezed to make wine. The grapes were squeezed by walking on them. The juice ran into a big tub. The juice fermented and was put into clay jars or wineskins.

[God's judgment at Armageddon is like a winepress in Revelation 14:15–20.]

winnowing *(WIN-owe-ing)*

is to toss the harvested grain into the air. The wind carries the chaff away, and the grain falls back to the ground. This was done until only grain was left on the harvest floor.

[Naomi tells Ruth to visit Boaz while he was winnowing barley in Ruth 3:1–5.]

wisdom *(WIZ-dum)*

is being able to use knowledge correctly. Wisdom comes from fearing God. God asked King Solomon what he desired. King Solomon asked for wisdom. God gave wisdom to King Solomon. People all over the world heard about the wisdom of King Solomon. The Queen of Sheba came to see if King Solomon was as wise as she had heard.

[God gives Solomon wisdom in I Kings 3:5–14.]

wise *(WIZE)*

is to have knowledge and good judgment. King Solomon was the wisest man who ever lived. The wise men from the east were looking for the King of the Jews. The wise men brought three types of gifts.

[The wise men go to see Jesus in Matthew 2:1–12.]

The wise men visited baby Jesus.

witch *(WITCH)*

is a female who does magic and talks to demons. King Saul went to the witch of Endor. King Saul wanted to talk to the prophet Samuel. But Samuel was dead. It was a sin to go to a witch. The witch of Endor brought up an image of Samuel.

[King Saul visited a witch in I Samuel 28:3–20.]

wither *(WI-ther)*

is to become smaller and weaker. God sent a worm to wither a gourd plant. This plant was giving shade to the prophet Jonah. Jesus cursed a fig tree because it did not have fruit. It withered and died. This was a lesson for His disciples. They were to be useful and produce good works.

[Jesus cursed the fig tree in Matthew 21:18–22.]

Jonah saw a gourd plant wither in one day.

withhold *(with-HOLD)*

is to hold back or keep. God will not withhold any good thing from the godly.

[God promises not to withhold good things in Psalm 84:9–12.]

witness *(WIT-nus)*

is to see something that has happened. A witness is needed to made a contract. Boaz called on the elders of the city to be witnesses to his redeeming of Ruth and Naomi. There were false witnesses at the trial of Jesus. They lied about the things Jesus had said and did. Christ told His followers to be witnesses to the world.

[Jesus tells believers to be witnesses in Acts 1:8.]

False witnesses accused Jesus.

249

A woman is an adult female.

Scripture is also called the Word of God.

WORD (ENGLISH)
דבר (HEBREW)
λογοσ (GREEK)

A word is a part of a language.

Wormwood is the name of a comet that will strike the earth.

woman *(WO-mun)*

is a grown female. The first woman was created from the rib of Adam. She was to be a good helper for him. A woman was not to be the master or the slave in a marriage. God said His creation was good. This included the creation of both man and woman.

[The first woman was created in Genesis 2:21–24.]

word *(WORD)*

is a saying or writing. Jesus is the Word. The Word has always existed. The Word became flesh and dwelt among us. This means that Jesus was human and lived among the Jews.

[The Word became flesh in John 1:1–14.]

Word of God *(WORD of GOD)*

means the Bible. God spoke to many different men. These men recorded the Word of God. The Word of God is also called Scripture. The Word of God is powerful and like a sword.

[The purpose of the Word of God is found in II Timothy 3:16–17.]

works *(WORKS)*

are the actions or things made by people. Jesus Christ came to do the work of God. Sinners cannot save themselves. They must rely on the grace of God. Salvation is the work of God. Christians are to have good works. Faith without works is dead.

[Salvation is by grace and not works as shown in Ephesians 2:4–10.]

wormwood *(WORM-WOOD)*

is a bitter plant. Wormwood is used to speak of bitterness and sorrow. John calls a blazing star Wormwood. This star destroys one third of the water. It is part of God's final judgment.

[The wormwood star hits the earth in Revelation 8:10–11.]

worship *(WER-shup)*

is to give respect, praise, and honor. Idols are not to be worshipped. This is one of the Ten Commandments. God is worthy to be worshipped. Worship may include praying, kneeling, or singing praises to God. We can worship God in private. Jesus worshipped God the Father in the Garden of Gethsemane. Many can come together and worship in a church. The early Christians worshipped God on the first day of the week.

[The Israelites were told who to worship in Exodus 34:13–17.]

wound *(WOOND)*

is a cut or a sore. Jesus was wounded for our sins. He died on the cross as the Lamb of God. He was the perfect sin offering. Jesus was wounded for our sin.

[Jesus heals our wounds in Isaiah 53:4–5.]

Wound is a cut or a sore.

wrath *(RATH)*

is an old word for anger. We are not to be angry with others. Paul says that the sun should not go down on our wrath. This means we are to settle our wrath in the same day it occurs.

[Paul tells us how to deal with wrath in Ephesians 4:26.]

Wrath of God *(RATH of GOD)*

is the action God takes against those who do not obey Him. God is holy and must judge sin. God's wrath destroyed the wickedness of the earth with a great Flood. God poured out His wrath on Sodom and Gomorrah for their sin. God's wrath is coming to the wicked people of the earth in the future. This is called Judgment Day. God does not want anyone to perish. That is why God sent His only Son to the earth.

[The Wrath of God during the last days begins in Revelation 6:16–17.]

Wrath is to be very angry.

wroth *(RAWTH)*

is to be very angry.

*[See **wrath**.]*

The Flood and the destruction of Sodom show the Wrath of God.

Xerxes I

Xerxes was the Persian king.

Xerxes I (*ZERK-zeez 1*)

was a Persian king. Xerxes was called Ahasuerus in the Bible. King Ahasuerus chose Esther to be his queen. Haman had King Ahasuerus make a decree. This decree would kill all the Jews. Queen Esther told King Ahasuerus of the plot of Haman. The king saved the Jews and hanged Haman.

[King Ahasuerus makes a decree in Esther 3:8–15.]

Yahweh *(YAH-weh)*

is the name of God. The four letters in Hebrew spell YHWH. No one knows how to pronounce this word. Scholars added vowels in order to spell Yahweh. The name Jehovah comes from this same word. All these names for God are shown just as the word *God* in the King James Version of the Bible.

[Yahweh or God is shown to be the God of Israel in Deuteronomy 26:16–19.]

A vow of a Christian should only be "Yea" or "Nay."

yea *(YAY)*

means yes. Christians are to be careful in swearing and making oaths. Jesus said we should only say yea or nay when we make a promise. James says our yea is to be a yea. Jesus and James are saying that our promises are to be trustworthy.

[James talks of our yeas in James 5:12.]

yield *(YEELD)*

means to give in to something. Israel was to yield itself to God. Christians are also to yield themselves to God. Christians that yield themselves to God become servants of righteousness.

[Paul tells us that we are servants to those things we yield ourselves unto in Romans 6:13–18.]

Christians are to yield to God.

yoke *(YOKE)*

is a wooden frame placed on the necks of oxen. This allows two or more animals to pull together as a team. Jesus tells us that His yoke is easy and His burden is light.

[Jesus wants to be yoked with you in Matthew 11:28–30.]

A yoke binds two oxen together.

Zacchaeus was a little man who hid in a sycomore tree.

Zacchaeus (zuh-KEE-us)

was a Publican or tax collector. He was also a little man. Zacchaeus climbed a sycomore tree in order to see Jesus. Jesus saw him and went to Zacchaeus' house. Zacchaeus became a follower of Jesus.

[Zacchaeus climbs a tree in Luke 19:1–10.]

Zachariah (zack-uh-RYE-uh)

was the son of Jeroboam. He became the king of Judah. Zachariah was an evil king. Shallum killed Zachariah.

[Zachariah was an evil king as recorded in II Kings 15:8–12.]

Zadok (ZAD-dok)

was a priest. David asked Zadok to carry the Ark of God to Jerusalem. Zadok anointed Solomon as King of Israel.

[Zadok anointed Solomon in I Kings 1:32–40.]

King David asked Zadok to take the Ark of God to Jerusalem.

zeal (ZEEL)

is being eager to do things. The Corinthians had a zeal to help the needy. Christians are to have a zeal for God through Jesus.

[A zeal for God through Jesus is shown in Romans 10:1–4.]

Zebulun (ZEB-yuh-lun)

was a son of Jacob and Leah. Zebulun was the father of one of the Twelve Tribes of Israel.

[Zebulun was born in Genesis 30:20.]

Zechariah (zek-uh-RYE-uh)

was a prophet of God. He lived at the same time as the prophet Haggai. Zechariah helped the Jews rebuild the Temple.

[The word of the Lord came to Zechariah in Zechariah 1:1.]

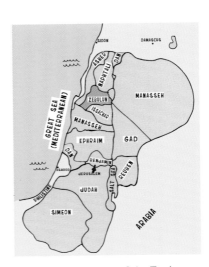

Zebulun began one of the Twelve Tribes of Israel.

Zechariah, Book of (zek-uh-RYE-uh, Book of)

is an Old Testament book written to the Jews in exile. Zechariah wanted them to finish building the Temple. Zechariah records eight visions. These visions show God's love for His people. Zechariah also shows the coming of the Messiah.

[The Messiah was to be crucified as shown in Zechariah 12:10.]

Zecharias (zek-uh-RYE-us)

was a priest. He was burning incense in the Temple. An angel told him that John the Baptist would be born to his wife Elisabeth. Zecharias did not believe the angel. The angel took away his speech until John was born.

[An angel visits Zecharias in Luke 1:5–25.]

Zedekiah (zed-uh-KYE-uh)

was a false prophet. Zedekiah lied to Israel. He claimed to give them the Word of God.

[Zedekiah is shown to be a false prophet in Jeremiah 29:22–23.]

zelotes (ZEL-otes)

is the Greek word for zealot. Zealots were Jews who did not want to obey Rome. They wanted Israel to be free. Simon the Canaanite was called Zelotes. He was one of the Twelve Disciples.

[Simon Zelotes was in the upper room in Acts 1:13.]

Zephaniah (zef-uh-NYE-uh)

was a prophet of God. Zephaniah lived at the same time as Huldah and Jeremiah.

[The word of the Lord came to Zephaniah in Zephaniah 1:1.]

Zephaniah, Book of (zef-uh-NYE-uh, Book of)

is an Old Testament book written to the Kingdom of Judah. Zephaniah calls Judah to repent. He tells them of God's coming judgment. Zephaniah ends with God's promise to restore Judah.

[Israel will be able to sing praises to God as shown in Zephaniah 3:14–20.]

Zechariah helped rebuild the Temple.

Zecharias could not speak until John the Baptist was born.

Zelotes wanted the Romans to leave Jerusalem.

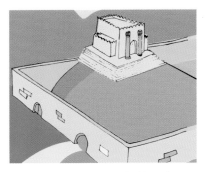

Zion is the hill where the Temple was built.

Zion (ZYE-un)

is one of the hills of Jerusalem. Zion became sacred when King David moved the Ark of God there. King Solomon moved the Ark of God into the Temple. The Temple stood on Mount Moriah. Zion came to include Mount Moriah. Zion can also mean Israel.

[King Solomon moves the Ark of God from Zion in II Chronicles 5:2–10.]

Zipporah (ZIP-er-uh)

was the daughter of Jethro. Moses saw Zipporah watering her father's sheep. Zipporah married Moses.

[Moses met Zipporah in Exodus 2:15–22.]

Moses saw Zipporah while she watered the sheep.